THE GODS
OF PREHISTORIC MAN

THE GODS OF PREHISTORIC MAN

by JOHANNES MARINGER

Edited and translated from the German by

MARY ILFORD

NEW YORK: ALFRED · A · KNOPF 1960

L. C. catalog card number: 60-11423

THIS IS A BORZOI BOOK,
PUBLISHED BY ALFRED A. KNOPF, INC.

 Manufactured in the United States of America. Published simultaneously in Canada by McClelland & Stewart, Ltd.

FIRST AMERICAN EDITION

Originally published in Dutch as *De Godsdienst Der Praehistorie* by J. J. Romen & Zonen in 1952. Enlarged and revised edition published in German as *Vorgeschichtliche Religion* by Benziger & Co. AG., Einsiedeln

TO THE MEMORY OF

my teachers

HUGO OBERMAIER (1877–1946)

WILHELM SCHMIDT (1868–1954)

FOREWORD

Prehistory, by definition, is the era prior to recorded history. Yet, like history, it has its records. Not records inscribed, with slate or pen, upon stone, metal, papyrus, or parchment, but extracted by pick and shovel from the immense "archives" of the earth—weapons and tools of stone, bone, or metal; urns and other ceramics; graves, settlements, fortifications; in brief, all the relics of the human past which the earth has preserved from the corroding action of the elements.

Necessarily, these relics are all of a material nature; but what they tell us relates to much more than the purely material aspects of prehistoric men's lives. From graves and burial forms we learn something of these men's beliefs concerning death; from fortifications we learn of troubled, war-plagued times, and modes of political organization; from ceramics and their ornamentation we learn of usages and tastes, varying according to time, place, and people.

Religion seldom remains without some material expression—in the form of ritual vessels, sanctuaries, pictures, sacrificial or votive gifts. Art has always been used in the service of religion. And almost every people has expressed an important part of its religious beliefs in its burial customs—the position in which the body is interred, the way tombs are built, the objects placed in a grave. In these and many other ways prehistoric men bore witness to their beliefs, with the result that those beliefs can be intelligible to us so many millennia later.

The specific tasks that face the research scholar are: to define the religious forms of the individual prehistoric periods; to trace the various processes of development; and to arrive at a picture of prehistoric religious manifestations as a whole.

In the chapters that follow, I have attempted to arrive at a general view of prehistoric religion as derived from the results of excavation. The point of departure is the prehistoric find as such. The finds are described and considered in the light of the cultural environment; and some attempt at interpretation is made by evaluating each find in the context of the site, stratum, and other pertinent factors, and by comparing it with similar or related finds.

Finally, as to the meaning of a find, I have had recourse to ethnological analogies, always taking care to remain within the same period of cultural history. I have avoided the practice of citing all the analogous data given by ethnological research, for this would contribute little to the actual clarification of the finds concerned.

I have been careful, also, when considering the prehistoric material, not to assume too narrow a concept of religion. Opinions concerning the nature of religion differ vastly. For my part, I have followed Wilhelm Schmidt's definition,* according to which religion is the knowledge

* *Handbuch der vergleichenden Religionsgeschichte* (Münster, 1930).

and sentiment of one's dependence upon one or several supernatural powers—God, gods, demons, ancestors, spirits of the dead, or other beings, with whom man enters into a mutual relationship—as well as the totality of the actions by which this knowledge and this sentiment are expressed—sacrifice, prayer, asceticism, dedication, processions, rites, ritual painting, sanctuary building.

Excavation for purposes of prehistoric research has been most actively conducted, thus far, on the European continent. What emerges from this study is therefore in the main a picture of the prehistoric religions of Europe. Still, I have attempted to show how far it is possible today to proceed, from an analysis of isolated religious practices, to an understanding of both the broad religious forms (to which these practices belong) and their development—and finally to arrive at a general picture of religion in prehistory.

J. M.

CONTENTS

IV. THE NEOLITHIC PERIOD

V. THE RELIGIONS OF PREHISTORY

LIST OF PLATES

LINE DRAWINGS

IN THE TEXT

Part I

THE EARLY PALEOLITHIC PERIOD

I

PRIMITIVE HUMANITY

THE SKELETAL REMAINS thus far unearthed give valuable information about the physical appearance of primitive man.* The greater part of these finds and the most complete ones belong to the first half of the last (Würm) ice age, which corresponds to the last part of the early paleolithic period.

Primitive man of that time is represented to us by Neanderthal man, named for bones dug up, in 1856, in the Neander valley near Düsseldorf. By modern standards, there was something very alien, not to say brutish, about this race of men, who inhabited mainly the region we now call western Europe. Neanderthal man was of medium height and stocky build, with a massive skull. His face, lacking what we call a forehead and a chin, was something of a snoutlike protuberance: broad nose and large, round eye sockets set deep under a prominent eyebrow ridge. We know nothing of the modeling of his features, which may have softened the simian character of the bone structure; neither do we know to what extent he was covered with

* I use the terms "primitive" man and "primitive" humanity here in a fairly loose sense, as applying to early paleolithic man generally.

hair. The popular picture of Neanderthal man as an exceedingly hirsute and stooping, animal-like creature has very little scientific foundation.

Neanderthal man was once thought to be the sole representative of primitive humanity. According to early theory, his simian traits argued an animal-like mode of existence, without any rudiments of spiritual culture. We shall see later how unjust was such a verdict. In any case, the physical differences between primitive and modern man are far less marked than those that separate Neanderthal man from the Pongidae, or manlike apes of our own time.

An increasing number of well-authenticated hominoid skeletal finds, suggesting forms much earlier than the Neanderthal, have been made in Europe, Asia, and Africa. One group apparently possessed Neanderthaler's primitive traits, perhaps to an even greater degree, while other types seem to have been closer to Homo sapiens. It becomes increasingly evident that the earliest development of man, like his origin, was far more complex than is usually imagined, even in scientific circles.

Primitive humanity lived through profound and far-reaching changes in the earth's history. Twice, at least, great parts of Europe—all Scandinavia, most of England and Holland, almost the whole of northern Germany, and considerable portions of Poland and Russia—were overrun by huge ice masses, glaciers that had descended from the Alps and other high mountain ranges. Everywhere, under the influence of an arctic climate, the flora and fauna changed completely. And twice, similarly, during the interglacial periods, this process was repeated in reverse: a climate even warmer than the European climate of today set in, and the natural environment changed accordingly. Related events occurred in Asia and in Africa, where, in the period known as the Pluvial Age, they took the form of extraordinarily heavy rainfalls.

Whatever the differences of opinion concerning the figures suggested by geologists and astronomers, there can be no doubt that all these events were spread out over an immense span of time. They must have taken place, moreover, so gradually that the individual could never have been aware of them, nor could they have become a part of the "collective memory" of peoples. Humanity as a whole is without any recollection of its ice-age past. The position would undoubtedly be far otherwise had the transition to glacial cold periods or interglacial warm periods taken place with catastrophic suddenness, or had the processes themselves extended over considerably shorter periods.

For reasons not yet fully apparent, primitive man seems to have inhabited the European continent only during the warm interglacial times. To attribute this to his alleged unfamiliarity with fire is fallacious. A far weightier reason would be that the caves that were to serve late paleolithic man as dwellings did not yet exist. These caves or fissures, formed for the most part by the action of water on rock in mountainous regions, seem to have come into being only in the last ice age but one, the Riss. That primitive man, too, inhabited caves when he could find them, and that he was familiar with fire, are evidenced by the remains of Peking man found in the Choukoutien caves in China.

Great parts of the Europe through which primitive men roamed were covered, at different times, by tropical forest; other parts consisted of grassland, and at the height of the warm interglacials there may even have been hot, dry desert belts. The fauna was quite unlike what we know today. The southern elephant appeared during the first interglacial, followed later by the forest elephant. Close upon the elephant, to judge by the record of fossil bones, came the rhinoceros. The hippopotamus, third of the great pachyderms, made its home along the reedy water courses. Bison, deer, and wild horses ranged the huge grassland. During the last interglacial the cave bear—a ferocious beast one-third larger than the brown bear—multiplied in the Alpine regions. Other carnivores proliferated as well: the panther, the wolf, the hyena, and also that most dreaded of beasts, the saber-toothed tiger, with its immensely developed upper canine teeth, admirable weapons against the great pachyderms. We know that the saber-toothed tiger was contemporaneous with early primitive man; the species later became extinct, and its place in the animal hierarchy was taken by the lion.

With the return of the ice, dry and freezing winds swept over the northern hemisphere, wasting the forests and turning eastern, central, and northwestern Europe into tundralike steppes. However, in the southern and southwestern parts of Europe, which escaped glaciation, the climate was much more temperate. And what is now desert in Africa enjoyed at that time a temperate climate with abundant rainfall, which made it an ideal refuge for the warm-blooded animals retreating before the advance of the ice. The areas they abandoned, when not actually covered by the Scandinavian and Alpine glaciers, were soon occupied by other warm-blooded animals more adapted to withstanding extremes of cold—notably the hairy mammoth and the woolly rhinoceros, which moved in from Asia. The steppes teemed with wild horse, wild ass, and bison, while the tundra bordering the ice cap was populated, during the short arctic summers, by enormous herds of reindeer, which migrated back to the shelter of southwestern Europe at the approach of winter.

This, roughly, was the world of primitive man. At each advance of the polar ice cap and the Alpine glaciers he left Europe, along with those animals that could not tolerate extreme cold. During the milder interglacials he could survive quite well in the open. He probably shielded himself from rain, wind, and sun by means of windbreaks made of boughs and saplings, covered with bark, skin, or heavy grasses. Fire was known, apparently, to all human species thus far discovered by archaeological research; and with fire primitive man could warm himself, cook his meat, and keep wild beasts at bay. Obviously nothing remains of these open-air encampments beyond bone heaps and stone tools.

These early settlements appear to have been made principally along river banks and at the seashore. Both sites would have offered a variety of stones, sea-polished or glacier-smoothed, suitable for the manufacture of hand axes and other stone-age implements. Wood and animal bone were used as well, and here again the water courses and seashores were good hunting spots, where primitive man could fish and prey upon land animals coming to drink. Immense deposits of bone indicate that choice sites were occupied generation after generation.

It is tantalizing to speculate on how the earliest men hunted the large beasts. Pitfalls and snares along the well-beaten tracks to water holes were doubtless among early methods. When we see in our own time the African pygmy, with the most meager equipment, giving chase to the great elephant and bringing him down at dangerously close quarters, we can the more readily credit the earliest primitive men with at least similar skill. The men of the later paleolithic, of course, developed astonishing ingenuity in hunting techniques, as any visitor to a modern museum can see from the collections of stone-age axes, spears, harpoons, javelins, fish hooks, and other weapons.

One last advantage for a hunting community was to be found along water courses: here the women and children could gather a variety of fruits, berries, roots, and herbs with which to supplement and diversify their staple meat diet.

Primitive man was a hunter, and therefore a nomad. He had to follow the game or starve. And while natural barriers might have limited the extent of the wanderings of any given human group, man as a species wandered far and wide. Excavation has revealed an astonishing diffusion of similar tools over vast territories.

The stone tools of primitive man fall into two well-defined classes: the flake and the core. The flake, as its name suggests, is a piece fractured from a block of stone, and sharpened only on one face. The core, which remained after a suitable number of flakes had been struck off from both sides of a block of stone, and after bifacial retouching, is known as the core biface, and characterizes the famous lower paleolithic "hand axes" of the Abbevillian and Acheulean industries. The hand ax is believed to have been a generalized tool, not a real ax. In Europe, core and flake tools appear separately, while African industries often show them used simultaneously.

The hand-ax cultures known as the Abbevillian and Acheulean were clearly at home in western and southern Europe, in Africa, in India, and in southern Asia. During the interglacials, when the hot, dry zones of Africa expanded, the bearers of the hand-ax culture, following in the tracks of the southern fauna, moved deep into the heart of Europe, where the climate was more clement. In so doing, they apparently drove the flake-culture peoples (Clactonian, Levalloisian, and Mousterian) before them, while at the close of the warm period they were themselves driven back south by the peoples they had displaced.

These movements of populations were not in any sense mass migrations, but simply the advance or withdrawal of small groups, bands of hunters, living together. During the second interglacial the groups were already larger, and they became larger still, apparently, during the last interglacial.

An appreciable advance took place from the time of the first-known primitive men to the close of the paleolithic period, although it certainly did not take place without interruption. This advance must have been accompanied by a marked improvement in living conditions and culture generally. The findings of modern research support the view that the evolution of primitive man and his culture should be regarded as a unity. Yet this "unity" is exceedingly complex, and future research will doubtless enable us to make finer distinctions between the periods and peoples that composed it.

The size and formation of fossil man's cranium has often been taken as an indication of his intellectual and spiritual capacity and, especially, incapacity. It is therefore significant that the late Franz Weidenreich, one of the leading modern anthropologists and a firm partisan of the theory of evolution, should have asserted, in a posthumously published study, that neither the size of the brain cavity nor the number or intricacy of the convolutions of the brain have any bearing on the intelligence of the individual, and that certain advances in brain surgery made it also necessary to revise our views concerning the localization of particular faculties in the brain. Only by their culture—or what they created—can we judge of primitive man's intellectual capacities.

Again, Lucien Lévy-Bruhl's doctrine of the "prelogical" soul of primitives has often been cited in support of the theory of the evolution of the human spirit from animal origins. But Lévy-Bruhl himself finally yielded to the evidence and the arguments of responsible scholars, and announced, shortly before his death, his conviction that all men, at all levels of culture, were equal in respect to their mental and spiritual potentialities.

Georg Kraft thoroughly establishes the unmistakably human character of primitive man's mentality.* An impassable gulf, he maintains, separates man from beast. For proof, we need only consider the artefacts of primitive man. However crude and unimpressive they may appear, they attest to something specifically human and rational, which is altogether lacking in the beast. They are not merely objects used as tools—experiments have shown that apes too are able to use tools—but deliberately fashioned instruments that in their turn could be used to fashion others. To quote K. J. Narr, these tools were not merely fashioned and used occasionally, but repeatedly; they did not serve as temporary means for dealing with the particular problem of a single individual, but were the product, rather, of planning and consistent action by methods handed down from generation to generation. On the other hand, the much cited ability of apes to handle tools—as Georg Kraft demonstrates—does not go beyond the utilization of objects for the purpose of achieving some goal directly related to a particular situation.

Primitive man's tools were neither a mere extension of the body and its organs nor their unconscious reproduction, as was long and widely believed. To quote Kraft again, even the most ancient tools of man are genuine, valid fruits of his creative spirit. Boucher de Perthes, one

* *Der Urmensch als Schöpfer: Die geistige Welt des Eiszeitmenschen* (Berlin, 1942).

of the earliest champions of this view, wrote that the man who first struck one flint against the other was also, so to speak, the first to chisel the marble of the Parthenon. In the same vein, Kraft declared of certain crudely fashioned stones he was examining that with all their imperfection, they offered as effective testimony to man's existence as the Louvre.

The tending and use of fire may with good reason be regarded as one of the oldest indications of a culture. Man and beast alike encountered this natural element, but only man was able to grasp its significance and thus to use it as he chose. Man overcame the deep-seated fear all animals have of fire. He made fire his servant, using it for warmth, for cooking, and for many other purposes; he even exploited the animals' fear of fire to protect himself from their marauding. This utilization of fire shows primitive man to have possessed the faculties proper to a rational being: he was capable of deliberate choice; he could use his imagination constructively; he could plan ahead; in a word, he was capable of autonomous action.

Speech, too, must be as old as tools. As early as the first interglacial, from which the first stone tools we can reliably define as such derive, primitive man hunted the great beasts in common with his fellows. And in this connection we may say, with Kraft, that, barring future evidence to the contrary, as soon as man comes into our view, he is working in collaboration with his fellows, and that for this he needs speech. If co-operative ventures are to afford any hope of success, they require at the very least a "basic" language consisting of verbs and certain key words denot-

Skull (minus lower jaw) of three-year-old cave bear, with the femur of a younger animal thrust through the arch of the cheek-bone. Two long bones from yet another cave bear form the foundation. Drachenloch, Switzerland.

PLATE I

Entrance to the Mas d'Azil cave (Ariège), France.

PLATE II

Domed ceiling of "bull chamber." Lascaux (Dordogne), France.

PLATE III

Bull frieze, Lascaux (Dordogne), France.

PLATE IV

ing place and time. On analogous grounds, Weidenreich, after studying the Choukoutien finds from an anthropological point of view, concluded that Peking man, though apparently lacking a chin, possessed a language.

Thus, by his tools, his use of fire, his co-operative action, and his speech, earliest primitive man is revealed as a being endowed with mind. And I agree with Kraft that earliest primitive man, because of his creative accomplishments, which may truly be regarded as pioneering works, was superior to the modern primitive. Finally, let us recall Wilhelm Koppers's dictum that if there is one absolutely certain conclusion of recent anthropological research, it is that the primitive of our own day, whatever his physical or racial characteristics, is mentally a complete human being.

It would be mistaken to conclude from the paucity of primitive man's material possessions that his spiritual capacities were correspondingly low, so that in his almost animal-like existence he could hardly have felt any stirrings to higher things, least of all to religion. This conclusion is justified only in connection with particular manifestations of the spiritual and religious life.

As earliest primitive man possessed the same psychological qualities and faculties as modern man, nothing that is specifically human could have been alien to him. It follows that he must have sought to satisfy his religious needs in one form or another.

II

PRIMITIVE MAN AND HIS DEAD

If we ask ourselves which type of early find best clarifies primitive man's religious thought and feeling, we shall see that the human skeletal remains alone provide the answer. For the stone tools and animal bones that have been found cannot tell us much more than what pertains to the economic and the culinary. However, human skeletal remains from before the beginning of the last interglacial are very few and fragmentary. In a number of cases the dating is still in dispute, either because the stratigraphical data have not been clarified, or because the somewhat recent appearance of the find tends to cast doubt on earlier assumptions concerning the stratigraphy of the site.

In Europe the few reliable finds come from sites in southern Germany and southern England: a lower jaw was found at Mauer, near Heidelberg, a skull at Steinheim, and two fragments of skulls at Swanscombe, not far from London. The Mauer find dates back to the second (Mindel) glacial, the Swanscombe and Steinheim finds date back to the second (Mindel-Riss) interglacial. To these older finds should be added a twofold find made in France in 1947—a cranium and a frontal bone discovered in a late Acheulean (Tayacian) layer near Fontéchevade (Charente). The fragments belonged to two different individuals, and the fluorine test places them in the last (Riss-Würm) interglacial. Like the Swanscombe and Steinheim men, the Fontéchevade man must have possessed a skull formation very similar to that of modern man, which would indicate that in Europe, even before the Neanderthalers and perhaps contemporaneously with them, there lived a more highly developed race of men.

Primitive man's reaction to the experience of death is reflected in his treatment of the corpse—to a considerable extent in what we call burial.

The finds just referred to offer no proof of any deliberate burial. Indeed, the scanty hominoid remains found in Europe cannot throw very much light on our present problem. Two circumstances, however, should be noted. First, it is always the skull and lower jaw that have been found. Yet the sites have been combed, sometimes over a period of decades, in the hope of discovering other human remains. The skull and lower jaw are, of course, very strong bones, but it is doubtful that they are so much stronger than any others that they alone should have been preserved. Secondly, the sites of the finds appear to have been ancient settlements. The Swanscombe site was an old river terrace that, to judge by the stone tools discovered near the skull fragments, must have been either a settlement or an area closely adjoining a settlement; and the Fontéchevade site was a cave that must have been in constant use as a dwelling place of ice-age man, as successive culture layers had been built up from the floor to the Magdalenian phase. The bones found in Germany, on the other hand, were lying in alluvial deposits and had clearly been displaced by the movement of water; but if we recall that primitive man settled by preference on the banks of rivers, then it is at least possible that these bones had been swept away from some ancient settlement on the swollen waters of a river and deposited on the sites where they were discovered in modern times.

All this would seem to indicate that some special, perhaps ritual, significance attached to the presence of the skull and lower jaw of the dead in the dwellings of the living.

This hypothesis is supported by the extensive finds made in the Choukoutien caves in China. The caves were discovered in 1921, and the interest of the scientific world was aroused two years later when a fossil human tooth was found there. Between 1927 and 1937 regular excavations took place, and they were resumed after World War II. A considerable number of skeletal remains of Peking man were found, though at first only in the form of skull fragments, lower jaws, and isolated teeth. Only during the more recent excavations were some long bones discovered. It has been possible, so far, to determine the remains of forty individuals, fifteen of them children. A number of hearths have also been identified. In addition, quantities of animal bones have been found, indicating that Peking man cooked and ate selected parts of the rhinoceros, wild horse, bison, and other game. The discovery, during the most recent excavations, of heaps of cherry pits reveals the food-gathering role of the women and children.

The caves—typical rock fissures—were first inhabited, according to the geologists, during the period corresponding to the second European (Mindel-Riss) interglacial. In appearance, Peking man must have been in many respects even more primitive than the Neanderthaler.

As for the skeletal remains, several circumstances are worth noting. First, the bones found at Choukoutien consist preponderantly, though not exclusively, of skull fragments. Secondly, these bones appear to have been scattered about indiscriminately, just like the animal bones. And thirdly, the human bones, like those of numbers of animals, had been split. These facts have led many scholars to conclude that Peking man must have been addicted to cannibalism, regarding the human brain and marrow as particular delicacies. But as, with the teeming animal world around him, he could not have suffered from any shortage of food supplies, it has been assumed that his cannibalism was of a ritual character, connected with some belief in the magical properties of the human brain and marrow.

For a considerable time, too, Peking man was believed to have been the first head-hunter. This theory, however, was exploded by the discovery of bones other than skull and lower jaw. But neither could this theory be upheld in view of the absence of the first two cervical vertebrae, which remain attached to the skull when the head is severed from the body. On the other hand, had Peking man been a mere cannibal, many more bones from different parts of the human body should have been discovered.

We are therefore left with the theory of a ritual cannibalism, centering around the brain and marrow. But the enlarging of the *foramen magnum* in some of the skulls, which is believed to have been effected by human agency, does not necessarily point to cannibalistic practices. The same operation occurs in connection with practices related to the two-stage burials familiar to ethnologists.

The general evidence of excavation points unmistakably to the fact that the skull, the lower jaw, and certain other bones were assigned some special role in the dwelling places of primitive man. But what that role was cannot be established with any degree of certainty from the finds themselves. The aforementioned theories about cannibalism and head-hunting are obviously based, by analogy, on well-known ethnological data. But both head-hunting and cannibalism are fairly recent developments among modern primitive peoples, and the magical and animistic beliefs bound up with such practices cannot easily be attributed to the primitive hunters and food-gatherers of prehistory.

Abbé Breuil was the first to draw attention to a practice current among Australian and other primitive tribes: they reclaim the skulls of their dead after decay of the soft tissues and treat the skulls as family relics. The late Wilhelm Schmidt developed this ethnological analogy by showing that the practice is common precisely among the least developed of modern primitive peoples.

The Andaman Islanders, the Negritos, and the Tasmanians, all extremely primitive tribes, carry the skulls of their dead around with them as amulets. The Kurnai, the oldest tribe of southeastern Australia, follow the same practice, preserving the lower jawbone as well as the skull. Two research scholars, E. H. Man and A. R. Radcliffe-Brown, give us the following account of the rites observed in this connection by the Andaman Islanders. After due burial of the deceased, a period of mourning is observed, during which the members of the family abstain from all pleasures and from certain foods. This period lasts for several months, until such time as the soft tissues of the deceased fall away. Then the men dig up the corpse. The bones are assembled and cleaned in the sea or in a stream, and brought back to the settlement, where they are received by the women with lamenting. The skull and lower jaw are dyed with red and white loam pigment, and each piece is secured with a plaited cord, on which it then is worn on breast or back. Parents, for instance, make a point of carrying upon their persons the skulls of their children; women often carry the skulls of their husbands and children, and often those of their brothers and sisters. As these people readily and joyfully give away or lend any of their possessions, they also lend and exchange these souvenirs. It may therefore happen that the owner of a skull no longer knows whose it was. Other bones too are preserved as souvenirs, but not carried about; they may be broken up into small pieces, and are not treated with similar reverence; frequently they are lost. While one can be certain of finding a number of skulls and lower jaws in every settlement, long bones are rarely found.

The parallel with Choukoutien is truly striking. If we consider, in addition, that Peking man and the Andaman Islanders seem to have been at the same stage of cultural development, it would be by no means far-fetched to explain the Choukoutien finds in terms of the Andaman customs. To be sure, it has been argued that the Andaman Islanders must have been influenced by practices deriving from a farming culture of much more recent date—in which case cannibalism would remain the simplest explanation of the Choukoutien finds; but if this assumption is correct, that cannibalism would have had to be very different from the ritual anthropophagy of more advanced primitive peoples. That more recent influences have been operative among the Andaman Islanders, the Negritos, and other primitive peoples remains to be proven. And until such proof is forthcoming, we may regard it as highly probable that the practice of venerating the bones of the dead originated in the most remote prehistoric times.

Such a practice is evidence of a strong sense of attachment, and we therefore have to credit primitive man with a genuinely human sensibility. He was devoted to his dead. Fear of the dead, that sinister force that has played no small part in the history of religion, seems to have been altogether foreign to him. The indestructible physical relics of the dead—in particular the skull—bound him to their erstwhile possessors in what seems to have been a positively familiar relationship. Through the skull and, to a lesser extent, through other parts of the skeleton the dead were apparently believed to be still present among the living.

It is possible, too, that primitive man of prehistory, like modern primitives, carried about with him the skulls of dead persons who had been very close to him during their lifetime. Eventually, these relics would have suffered the fate of all things: they were damaged, or forgotten, or left lying somewhere, or even thrown into the water. But in itself the practice was an expression of attachment, fidelity, and pious remembrance. It is also possible that the dead were regarded as benevolent tutelary spirits and unseen helpers in all big hunting expeditions.

It would be going too far to posit this practice of the whole of primitive humanity on the strength of the evidence we have adduced. On the other hand, the finds suggest no other practices, nor has it been possible, thus far, to determine what burial customs earliest primitive man observed, or the beliefs associated with such customs.

WITH the transition to the last interglacial, and to what was essentially the Mousterian culture, the finds present us with a far more complex picture. Now, for the first time, we come upon what were indubitably burials, all of them located in caves or under rock shelters. That they were so located is certainly of decisive importance for their preservation during the millennia, but is no argument against the practice of burial rites by earlier primitive man. If he did bury his dead, but only in the open country, then the prospects of unearthing any evidence to this effect are extremely slender.

The most ancient true burials known to us are those discovered in the Kiik-Koba cave on the Crimean peninsula in 1925; in the et-Tabun and es-Sukhul caves on Mount Carmel, in Palestine, between 1930 and 1932; and in the Teshik-Tash cave in southeastern Uzbekistan, in Central Asia, in 1938.

The Crimean cave contained the graves of a man and a one-year-old child. The man had been laid in a trench dug in the cave floor; and it is interesting to observe that the portions of the trench at the level of the head and pelvis had been slightly widened. The skeleton lay on its right side, its legs a little drawn up. The infant, whose grave was some three feet away from the other, had been laid on his left side, the legs likewise contracted, the left hand under the left knee. At a much later period the cave was inhabited by another group of people, obviously unrelated to the dead who lay buried there, for those new inmates placed their hearth directly above the grave, and, in digging the trench for their fire, almost destroyed the grave and its contents.

In the et-Tabun cave on Mount Carmel, the skeleton of a woman of about thirty was found lying on its back, and nearby, in the same deposits, the lower jaw of a man of about the same age.

As for the es-Sukhul cave, its antechamber appeared to have been a prehistoric cemetery. No fewer than ten burials could be traced. The skeletal remains are of five men between thirty and fifty, two women between thirty and forty, and three children between four and ten years of age. The positions of the dead and the directions in which they faced varied considerably, but in all cases the legs had been so tightly drawn up that the feet touched the buttocks. In several cases it could be established that graves had been dug for the interment.

The Teshik-Tash cave in Uzbekistan revealed a child's grave just below a Mousterian layer. The one-time inhabitants of the cave had placed a circle of ibex horns around the corpse. The cave had frequently served as a dwelling place for lower paleolithic man, as attested by the number of hearth places found there. The grave had been greatly damaged by a wild beast, probably a cave hyena, which had torn the little skeleton apart, while hardly displacing the circle of horns. There can be no doubt as to the deliberate and indeed careful burial of the child, accompanied by certain ceremonies, though the ideas and religious conceptions bound up with such ceremonies are not immediately discernible.

A greater number of burial places have been found in western Europe. They belong to a somewhat later period—the first half of the last ice age. This, of course, was both the region and the period of the Neanderthalers, and there is no doubt that this particular primitive man gave his dead due burial.

The very first find was at Le Moustier (Dordogne) in 1907—a youth between sixteen and eighteen, interred by his kinsmen with evident care. The skeleton was lying on its right side, the legs slightly bent, the head resting on the right arm as in sleep, the right hand close to the back of the head. The head itself was supported by a pillow of flint flakes. The left arm lay along the body; a fine hand ax and a flint scraper were lying near the hand. Other tools, as well as a considerable quantity of animal bones, were scattered around the corpse.

At about the same time the "old man" of La Chapelle-aux-Saints (Corrèze) was discovered. The general picture was very much the same. The skeleton of a man of about fifty was lying in a trench dug by human hand. A whole bison leg, several flint tools, and lumps of ocher were lying close to the right arm, which was bent upward. At the en-

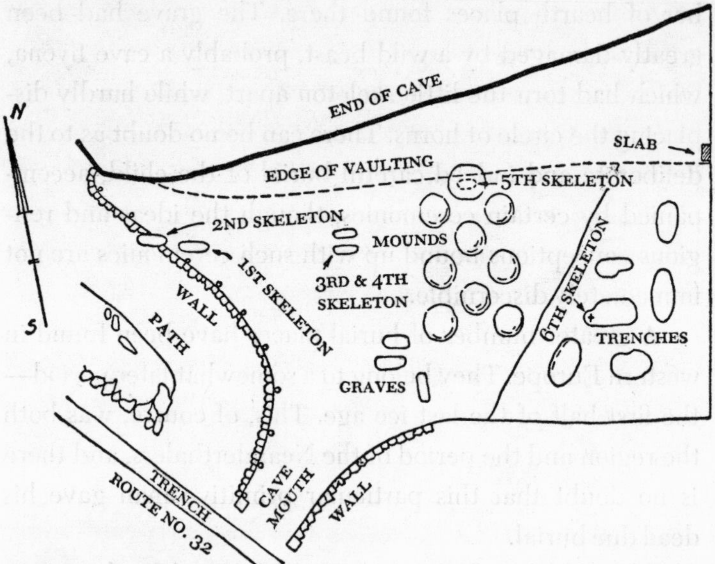

Fig. 1. EXCAVATIONS AT LA FERRASSIE (DORDOGNE), FRANCE. SCALE 1:200

trance to the cave, there was a hearth containing charrings and ashes of bones. Broken animal bones were strewn over and around the man.

In the course of excavations conducted between 1909 and 1921, a veritable family sepulcher was discovered near La Ferrassie (Dordogne) (fig. 1). It contained six skeletons in all, and presented a number of special features.

The first skeleton to be found was of a man lying prone

in a shallow depression, the head turned slightly to the left, the left arm extended, the right arm and leg drawn up close to the body. Stone slabs had been set in the earth near the head and shoulders, forming a kind of protective wall.

A little to the east the excavators came upon the skeleton of an elderly woman lying on its right side. A striking feature of this burial was the tightly flexed position of the body: the knees were sharply bent and the legs thus folded against the body; the right arm was bent and pressed against the breast. Near the corpse were quantities of animal bones, as well as flint tools and fiber threads—more, in fact, than in any other part of the site.

A little farther to the east two more graves were found, each containing the skeleton of a child. Three similar trenches contained only tools and animal bones. Still farther east the excavators came upon nine conical earth mounds, arranged in three rows of three, running north-south. Under one of them they found the remains of a foetus or very young infant; they found nothing under any of the others.

Finally another grave was discovered on the eastern edge of the same stratum, containing the tightly flexed skeleton of a child between five and six years old. Curiously enough, the skull was missing, but it was discovered about three feet away under a limestone slab (fig. 2). The underside of the slab was marked with cup-shaped depressions, arranged in pairs; D. Peyrony, who first noticed them, believed that they had been hollowed out deliberately.

All the bodies at La Ferrassie were orientated from east to west, with the exception of the woman, who faced the other way.

Many prehistoric graves have been found severely damaged, and it was probably in one such grave that the

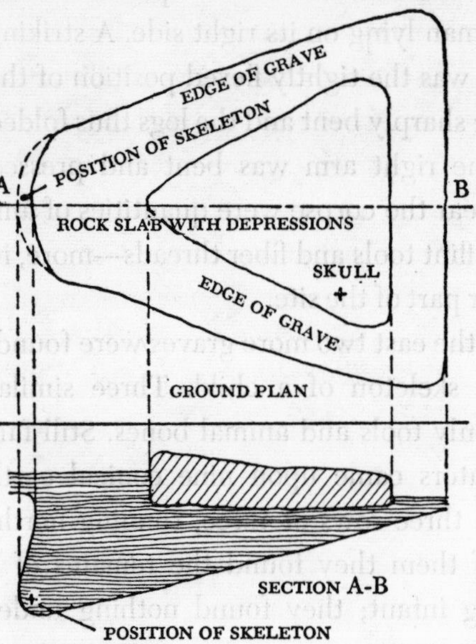

Fig. 2. LA FERRASSIE. PLAN AND SECTION OF TRENCH CONTAINING SKELETON NO. 6. SCALE 1:24

man whose remains were found in the Neander valley in 1856 had originally been laid. As for the two Neanderthal skeletons found in the Spy cave in Belgium in 1886, they had certainly been buried. A thin layer of charcoal covered the graves, showing that fires had been lit over them.

The various finds I have mentioned show very clearly that the Neanderthalers of the last interglacial and the beginning of the last ice age—that is, the Mousterian—concerned themselves closely and in a variety of ways with their dead, treating them with solicitude.

What were the beliefs underlying this attitude?

Primitive man must assuredly have believed in an afterlife. The position in which he often buried his dead—namely, that of sleep—would seem to indicate that he conceived of death as a form of sleep. This inference is strengthened by the curious "pillow" under the head of the youth at Le Moustier. Whether this sleep was regarded as a transitional stage prior to an awakening in another world it is hard to say. Only at La Ferrassie do we find a certain orientation of the dead in the direction of the setting sun. Possibly the west was believed to be the land of the dead.

Grave goods in the form of tools, food, and ocher for the painting of the body are neither as certain nor, above all, as abundant in the Mousterian period as in the upper paleolithic. If these objects were really grave goods and not things that simply happened to be lying near the dead and in the same stratum, then we may assume that they were intended as equipment for the dead and provisions for their journey. If this assumption is correct, life in the world beyond was conceived of as virtually identical with life on earth.

The finds provide us with absolutely no clue as to whether this belief in an afterlife was in any way connected with the idea of a divine being, of judgment, or of rewards for good and sanctions for evil. What they do tell us is that the fact of death does not seem to have been really grasped by the living. The otherness of death was, of course, very apparent: a living being had become stiff, cold, pale, already in process of decomposition. Yet somehow, in this corpse, the living person continued. In a sense, the "living corpse" existed in a state of helplessness in which the responsibility for his care devolved upon his kinsmen and friends. Care of the dead constituted a social and moral obligation. Thus the finds wrested from the earth give us valuable insights into the social life of primitive man, into the whole realm of mutual responsibilities and sentiments.

At the same time, primitive man must have believed that the dead had a certain capacity for action. In the tightly flexed skeletons on Carmel and at La Ferrassie we can hardly help seeing an attempt to shackle the dead. Possibly the survivors had some special fear of these particular dead, and were trying to prevent them from returning from the grave and drawing the living in their train. At La Ferrassie the head had been severed from the trunk, perhaps in order to make sure the corpse would stay dead. Yet why should the living have feared a five- or six-year-old child? At Spy, fires were lit over the dead. The resulting layer of ashes may have been regarded as a covering that no corpse could pierce, and that would thus confine it to its grave. However, the layer may have been intended to warm and comfort the frozen body; this feature of funerary practice is well evidenced in finds made in upper paleolithic deposits.

It is impossible, on the basis of the existing finds, to say whether the Mousterians placed votive offerings at the graves of ancestors or other dead in order to solicit their protection, good fortune in the hunt, or other favors.

One of the excavators of the La Chapelle-aux-Saints site, A. Bouyssonie, points out that as the roof of this cave is very low, the cave could hardly have served as a dwelling place. It must therefore be assumed that the vast numbers of broken animal bones that littered the grave and the surrounding floor were the refuse of funerary feasts held in the cave. No fewer than twenty-two reindeer, twelve bison, two or three wild horses, and one ibex had been completely or partially consumed at these meals. Either the participants were very numerous, which would seem improbable given the small dimensions of the cave, or many funerary feasts must have been held. In the latter case, which appears by far the more probable, the feasts may well have been in the nature of memorial, or sacrificial, meals.

We thus possess indications that primitive man believed the dead to be capable of some action, both for weal and for woe. He ascribed to them higher powers than those proper to the living. We may therefore assume that primitive man practiced a definite cult of the dead, which included rites intended both to safeguard the living from the power of the dead and to obtain from the dead protection, favor, and help for the tribe, particularly in connection with its quest for food.

Skulls and lower jaws continue to occur in deposits dating from the last interglacial and right into the last ice age; indeed, they become considerably more frequent in this latter period of primitive humanity. The substantially unaltered character of the finds supports the theory that these relics of the dead were assigned a special role in the dwellings of the living.

In 1926 D. Garrod dug up the skull of a child between five and six years old in the Devil's Tower cave on the northern edge of the Rock of Gibraltar, together with a number of flint tools. The skull bones had been separated and scattered by the waters of a spring flowing in the cave, which had later deposited the layer of limestone the bones had been preserved in. The absence of any other skeletal remains in the same stratum makes it quite certain that only the skull had been placed in the cave. Garrod believed the skull to have been either a trophy or a relic.

In 1939 A. C. Blanc found a skull in the Guattari cave on Monte Circeo, on the north side of the Gulf of Gaeta. This cave had, demonstrably, emerged from the sea only during the last advance of the ice cap. Later a mountain slide blocked and hermetically sealed the cave, right up to our own day. The ancient entrance was discovered during some quarrying operations.

The cave consists of several chambers. Large quantities of flint tools, traces of charring, and broken animal bones prove that the anterior chamber was repeatedly a dwelling place of primitive man. At other times the cave hyena took possession, as we see from the numbers of bones bearing its tooth marks. In one of the rear chambers, which could be reached only by crawling on hands and knees, a single skull was found on an elevation formed by several layers of earth and stone. It had no lower jaw, and lay on its left side. A circle of stones could clearly be distinguished around the skull. The lower jaw of another human being was found elsewhere in the same chamber. As the skull showed no trace of animal tooth marks, it must have been placed on its dais at a time when the cave was inhabited by men and the entrance protected from marauding beasts. (The period must have been shortly before the mountain slide; this is further attested by the nature of the topmost deposits of the elevation.) Strewn haphazard near the skull and over the entire cave floor are bones of wild horse, buffalo, and deer. Some of these were also found near the entrance, to the left, under three big stone slabs set against the wall.

A closer examination of the skull revealed an old wound in the right temple. S. Sergi, the anthropologist who examined the skull, found that it had belonged to a man forty or fifty years old, who had been killed by a blow with a pointed object. He also established the presence of injuries at the base of the skull, which he attributed to an artificial enlarging of the *foramen magnum.* He thought this operation had been undertaken by primitive man for the purpose of extracting the prized brain. Primitive man, in Sergi's view, had been a cannibal.

The question now arises of whether these two finds, and particularly the rather unusual one in the Guattari cave, can illuminate the earlier finds of isolated skulls and lower jaws.

The Guattari finds tell plainly of a cult centering around the skull. Originally the skull had probably been set up on a stick. Eventually the stick had rotted away and the skull fallen. The ring of stones suggests a magic circle.

This whole section of the cave apparently served the occupants of the outer chambers as a sanctuary, for it was difficult of access even originally. It may be assumed that the quantities of animal bones—no human bones were found among them—derived from ritual meals. The bones found under the protective stone slabs may well have been votive gifts.

A. C. BLANC, following Sergi, thought that the primitive inhabitants of the Guattari cave had been man-eaters. The finds, he maintained, certainly proved their intent to propitiate the victim whose brain they had eaten by paying due honor to his skull. Blanc supported this theory by reference to two Melanesian skulls from the anthropological collection of Rome University. These skulls also had had their basal openings enlarged, presumably by modern cannibals who wanted to extract the brain. And Blanc drew attention to the fact that the Steinheim skull showed similar changes, and that its discoverer had not ruled out the possibility that these had been effected by human agency. No other find, Blanc felt, was so clear or so convincing; the cannibalism of primitive man could no longer be questioned.

During excavations undertaken at Ehringsdorf, near Weimar, in 1914, 1916, and 1925, the lower jaw of an adult, the partial remains of a ten-year-old child, and the cranium of a woman were discovered in a limestone quarry dating back to the last interglacial. According to Weidenreich, the woman's skull bore traces of repeated blows on the frontal bone. These blows must have been inflicted by both pointed and blunt instruments when the skull was still covered with flesh. Although Weidenreich did not at first exclude the possibility that these injuries had occurred after the woman's death, he finally concluded, from the circumstances of the find, that she had been killed. The head had then been severed from the trunk and the base of the skull removed, apparently so that the brain might be extracted.

The geology of the Ehringsdorf limestone has an important bearing on the interpretation of the finds. The limestone was not deposited by running water but by spring-fed pools: hence the skeletal remains could not have been washed in. During the summer months the pools dried up, leaving their limestone beds exposed. The Ehringsdorf people settled around these pools, on their banks, and, in the dry season, even on their beds. Two layers of finds could be made out. One had been darkened by charcoal and ash, and contained broken and charred animal bones, as well as artefacts and flint flakes; this was the layer of the one-time dwelling places and hearths. The other consisted of fairly loose travertine, rich in fossil plants. This layer also contained broken animal bones, not in stratified sequence but haphazard throughout the mass of stones, where they had evidently fallen while it was still loose rubble. Here were obviously the beds of pools and ponds near which primitive man had settled and into which he had thrown his refuse.

The human remains were all from these layers of refuse. That they were mixed with general food refuse certainly gives grounds for suspecting the Ehringsdorf people of cannibalism.

But it is finds made in the Krapina cave in Croatia (now part of Yugoslavia) between 1899 and 1905 which are most often cited as evidence of primitive man's cannibalism. Here the remains of no fewer than twenty-one men and women of different ages, though mostly of women and young people, were discovered strewn at random among animal bones. They were greatly damaged and partially burned. Two of the skull fragments showed definite signs of violent handling.

And now let us consider a few objections to the "mere cannibalism" theory. J. Tomschik, for instance, has established that the human bones at Krapina had none of the marks to be expected had they been split when still fresh. Weidenreich maintains that neither of the two presumed skull injuries had been inflicted before death. And O. Menghin points out that the bones would have presented a very similar picture if they had been disturbed by animals or men after burial.

That such disturbances actually did take place is well known from the Kiik-Koba site, from the Carmel sites, and from many sites in France. Primitive man did not generally inter his dead deep in the earth. Carnivores like the cave hyena could make their way into caves after men had abandoned them, dig up the graves, and tear the skeletons apart. And men, too, settling later in such caves, might easily have destroyed old burial places by placing hearths over them, thereby scorching the interred bodies. The constant activity within the cave would have tumbled the human bones with other refuse, and the destruction of the original graves would be completed.

It is quite possible that Krapina was an ancient burial place that had been subjected to repeated disturbances, and that its finds do not at all support the assumption of cannibalism.

Then too, it is a striking fact that at sites such as Ehringsdorf and Guattari where the human skulls are believed to be relics of cannibal feasts, no other human bones have been found in the same deposits. Mere cannibals would most likely have eaten the fleshy muscles and all the viscera, as well as the brain, which they would have treated at most as the "*bonne bouche*."

Such finds, therefore, would favor the idea of a "brain cannibalism" only, in which case primitive man must have been a head-hunter. But how can this theory be reconciled with the circumstance that the first two cervical vertebrae are always missing in these cases of decapitation? The apparently artificial enlargement of the *foramen magnum* can tell us very little, as so far only one skull (Saccopastore I) has been found with its base intact. Even skulls interred with the rest of the body show the enlargement. In any case, it remains to be proven that the enlarging of the *foramen magnum* occurred while the bone was still fresh.

Thus we see that a good many serious objections can be adduced on the strength of the finds themselves. At the same time, there is much in the finds that argues strongly in favor of primitive cannibalism, and even more, in my own view, in favor of head-hunting.

Basically the theories favoring cannibalism or head-hunting in the preceding cases are drawn from anthropological analogies; and I should therefore point again to the relatively late ethnological period in which these practices occur. The old assumption that cannibalism was a general feature of the primitive state of mankind is wholly unsupported by the evidence. Ewald Volhard, for instance, in his book on cannibalism published in 1939, wrote as follows:

> It became patently clear, especially to many nineteenth-century scholars, that the man-eating peoples had not stood at the beginning of the road, but rather could look back over a long past. With evident surprise, different travellers in the most varied regions were obliged to conclude that the cultural level of the [modern] cannibalistic peoples was distinctly higher than that of the non-cannibalistic peoples. It must be regarded as one of the major achievements of nineteenth-century scholarship in the field of cultural history to have established this fact by objective scientific investigation, and thus to have exploded definitively the myth that primitive man was a cannibal.

Nonetheless, this myth, though a relic of a long outdated theory, still haunts many minds.

Blanc's interpretation of the Guattari finds as evidence of cannibalism was based in good part on an analogy with two Melanesian skulls. However, the Melanesians, relatively recent arrivals in the South Seas, belong culturally to the neolithic period. And this applies generally to peoples who practice cannibalism and head-hunting: they are never simple food-gathers, comparable to the primitive hunters of the lower paleolithic period or even of the last phase of that period.

Thus, despite a number of superficial indications to that effect in the finds, we have to dismiss the theory that cannibalism or head-hunting were means of mere food-getting among primitive men. The practice of mounting skulls can in all likelihood be regarded as a form of skull cult, by means of which the memory of the departed was cherished and their help and protection sought for the tribe. The artificial enlarging of the *foramen magnum,* which has been established in so many cases and is usually taken as proof of cannibalism, can be satisfactorily explained in terms of a practice connected with the two-stage burial rite familiar to anthropologists. After decomposition of the soft tissues in the earth, or by exposure of the corpse on a tree or trestle, it only remained, usually, to remove the brain, which decayed more slowly; and the simplest way to do this was to enlarge the opening at the base of the skull.

III

HUNTING RITES

FINDS OF HUMAN REMAINS afford us some insight into primitive man's higher sentiments and concepts related to the sphere of religion. But the animal remains are, of course, far more extensive on all the sites, and these give us a picture of the hunters' paradise in which primitive man dwelled. The broken and charred bones that constitute some of the refuse of primitive man's meals tell us about his menu. But in the deposits of the last interglacial are skeletal remains of game preserved with unmistakable devotion by primitive man. And this opens up a new avenue to the ritual and specifically religious sphere of primitive man's life.

In those times the cave bear—an enormous and immensely strong, shaggy beast—inhabited the well-wooded Alpine regions, and even the lowland approaches to the Alps, using as places of refuge the caves in which the area abounded. A famous cave of this type is the Drachenhöhle near Mixnitz in Styria, Austria. It has been estimated that some 30,000 to 50,000 cave bears must have died in that cave. After World War I, the cave soil, saturated with the bones of these beasts, was exploited for the extraction of phosphates for industrial purposes. If we assume, as there are grounds for assuming, that three to six families of bears at most occupied the big, multichambered cave at any one time, then the cave must have served as a regular bear dwelling place for close to 10,000 years.

Because of its size and strength, the cave bear had few serious rivals in the open hunting ground. And although the cave lion and the cave panther were still to be found in the same regions, the cave bear's main adversary was man. Primitive man followed that beast over 8,000 feet up into the mountains, contended with it for the possession of its lairs, and with extraordinary audacity challenged it and killed it. Of course he did not always succeed in getting his prey; this is apparent from bear skulls and other bones (found in another cave, the Drachenloch) marked with the scars of wounds that had clearly been inflicted by man-made weapons and had subsequently healed. Many a hunter must have lost his life during those hunting expeditions, although we have no evidence of this in the shape of skeletal remains of cave-bear hunters. However that may be, protection and success in the chase must have been among the most fervent aspirations of these people.

Not until the first decade of the twentieth century was it realized that primitive man had roamed the Alps and hunted the cave bear, and the discovery aroused no little astonishment. For it had previously been believed that the trackless and inhospitable Alps could have been inhabited by man only at some late date in the postglacial age, and not before. The astonishment was even greater when finds of an obviously ritual character were made inside most of the Alpine caves settled by primitive man.

The cave that has proved richest in finds and at the same time is highest in elevation (nearly 8,000 feet) is the Drachenloch, in the eastern part of the Swiss Alps. The mouth of the cave is in the east wall of the Drachenberg, nearly 5,000 feet above the present level of the valley formed by the waters of the Tamina which flow into the upper Rhine near Ragaz, Saint Gallen. The cave was excavated between 1917 and 1923 by Emil Bächler.

The cave had served repeatedly as a shelter or dwelling place for hunters of the last interglacial, whose principal quarry had been the cave bear. Only a very small proportion of the bones found there belonged to other animals, such as the chamois, the ibex, the stag, and the Alpine hare; as the finds prove, the primitive hunters had now and then also killed cave lions, cave panthers, common wolves, and Alpine wolves.

The Drachenloch is a tunnel cave about 230 feet long. The entrance leads into an antechamber 88½ feet long, 18 feet wide, and nearly 28 feet high. This is by far the most spacious part of the cave.

It is almost fully penetrated by daylight. Contrary to expectations, the floor yielded few finds; this chamber, therefore, could not have played any great part in the lives of the ancient occupants of the cave. At the farther end of the antechamber, on the left, a narrow passage leads to section II of the cave, a vaulted chamber 26 feet long, about 18 feet wide, and just over 11 feet high. This must have served as the living quarters proper, as is evidenced by the numerous finds made there—in particular, two fireplaces, one at the entrance, the other, in the shape of a carefully covered stone chest, in the narrow passage leading to section III. This last is 52½ feet long, and leads into three other much smaller cave chambers (fig. 3).

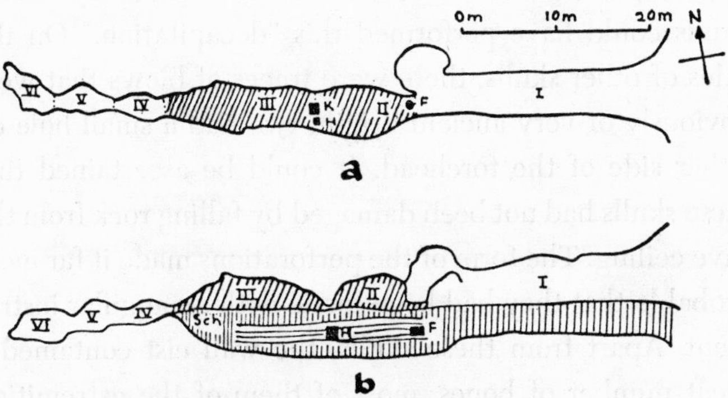

Fig. 3. DRACHENLOCH, SWITZERLAND.
A. GROUND PLAN B. VERTICAL SECTION

CAVE CHAMBERS II AND III PRINCIPALLY USED BY MAN

FILLING OF CAVE FLOOR

CULTURE LAYERS

F = OPEN FIREPLACE
H = CLOSED FIREPLACE
K = STONE CHEST
SCH = SKULL DEPOSITS

In the "living quarters," the excavators came upon a low wall formed of small limestone slabs 31½ inches high, standing between 15¾ and 23½ inches away from the left cave wall. In the cistlike space thus created, they found a veritable store of cave-bear bones. What was most striking was the great number of skulls, partly intact, partly broken, often arranged in groups, and, apparently, in the same orientation. In most cases the first two cervical vertebrae of the skull could also be distinguished. In one instance the entire posterior portion of the skull had been knocked away, and although a thorough search was made for the missing pieces, none was found. It follows that only human hands could have performed this "decapitation." On the sides of other skulls, there were traces of blows that were obviously of very ancient origin; two had a small hole on either side of the forehead. It could be ascertained that these skulls had not been damaged by falling rock from the cave ceiling. The form of the perforations made it far more probable that they had been made with an angular instrument. Apart from these skulls, the wall cist contained a great number of bones, most of them of the extremities, but of these only two or three belonged to the same skeleton, and this only in a few cases. Most of the marrow bones were intact, some obviously split by human agency.

Further surprises awaited the excavators as they proceeded from section II to section III of the cave. Close by the stone "chest" described above, they found a second one set in the floor, 3¼ feet in length, width, and height, closed with a limestone slab some 4½ inches thick. When the lid was removed, the chest was found to contain seven well-preserved cave-bear skulls and a number of long bones. All the skulls were orientated with the muzzles facing the cave exit (fig. 4). In two instances the higher cervical vertebrae were also found.

Section III brought still greater surprises. Again, the left wall had been given distinct preference. Six cave-bear skulls were discovered set in niches, some of them together with other bones. The skulls were all lying on stone slabs, bordered by other slabs, and covered with a protective

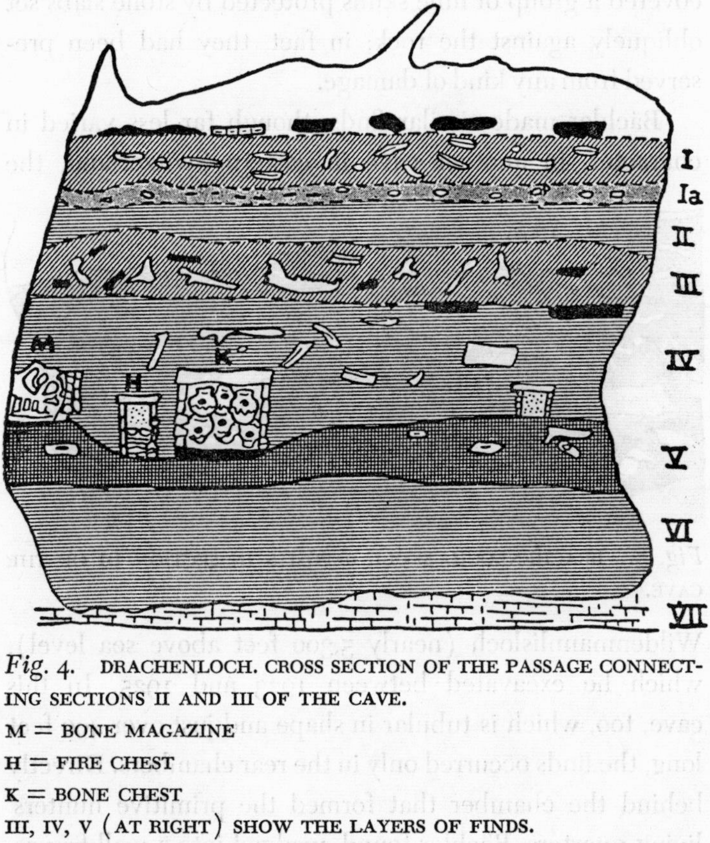

Fig. 4. DRACHENLOCH. CROSS SECTION OF THE PASSAGE CONNECTING SECTIONS II AND III OF THE CAVE.

M = BONE MAGAZINE

H = FIRE CHEST

K = BONE CHEST

III, IV, V (AT RIGHT) SHOW THE LAYERS OF FINDS.

slab (fig. 5). The most remarkable find was the very well-preserved skull of a three-year-old bear with the femur of a younger animal thrust through the arch of the cheekbone in such manner that it was very difficult to extract. Two long bones belonging to yet other cave bears formed the foundation. Here, then, primitive man had deliberately assembled parts of four different cave bears (plate I).

Finally, in the terminal wall of the cave, Bächler discovered a group of nine skulls protected by stone slabs set obliquely against the rock; in fact, they had been preserved from any kind of damage.

Bächler made similar finds, though far less varied in character, in another cave in eastern Switzerland, the

Fig. 5. DRACHENLOCH. SKULL DEPOSITS IN SECTION III OF THE CAVE.

Wildenmannlisloch (nearly 5,300 feet above sea level), which he excavated between 1923 and 1925. In this cave, too, which is tubular in shape and just over 490 feet long, the finds occurred only in the rear chambers. Directly behind the chamber that formed the primitive hunters' living quarters, Bächler found, wedged into a wall fissure, a bear's skull minus its lower jaw but associated with three long bones; this assemblage was covered with a protective limestone slab. Four hundred and twenty feet inside the cave, five skulls minus their lower jaws were found, each of them associated with several long bones.

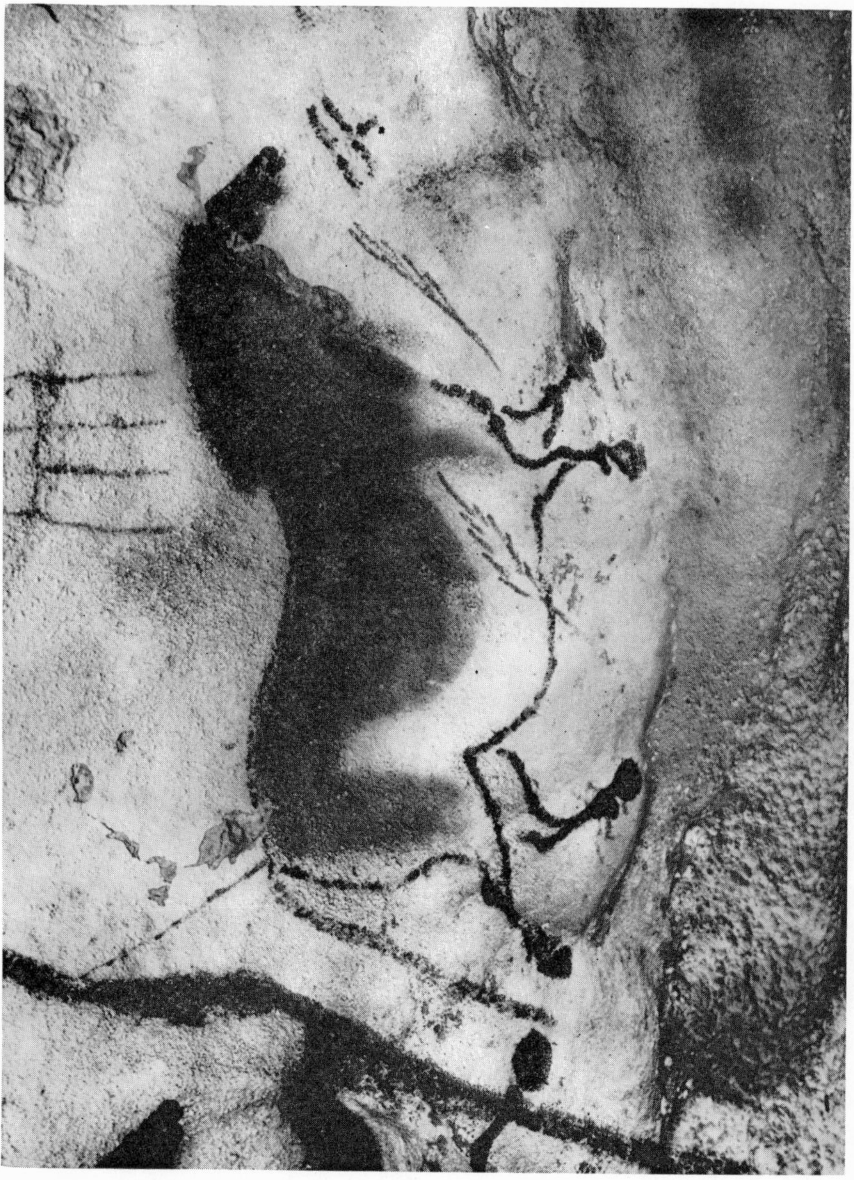

Horse painted on passage vaulting, Lascaux.

PLATE V

PLATE VI

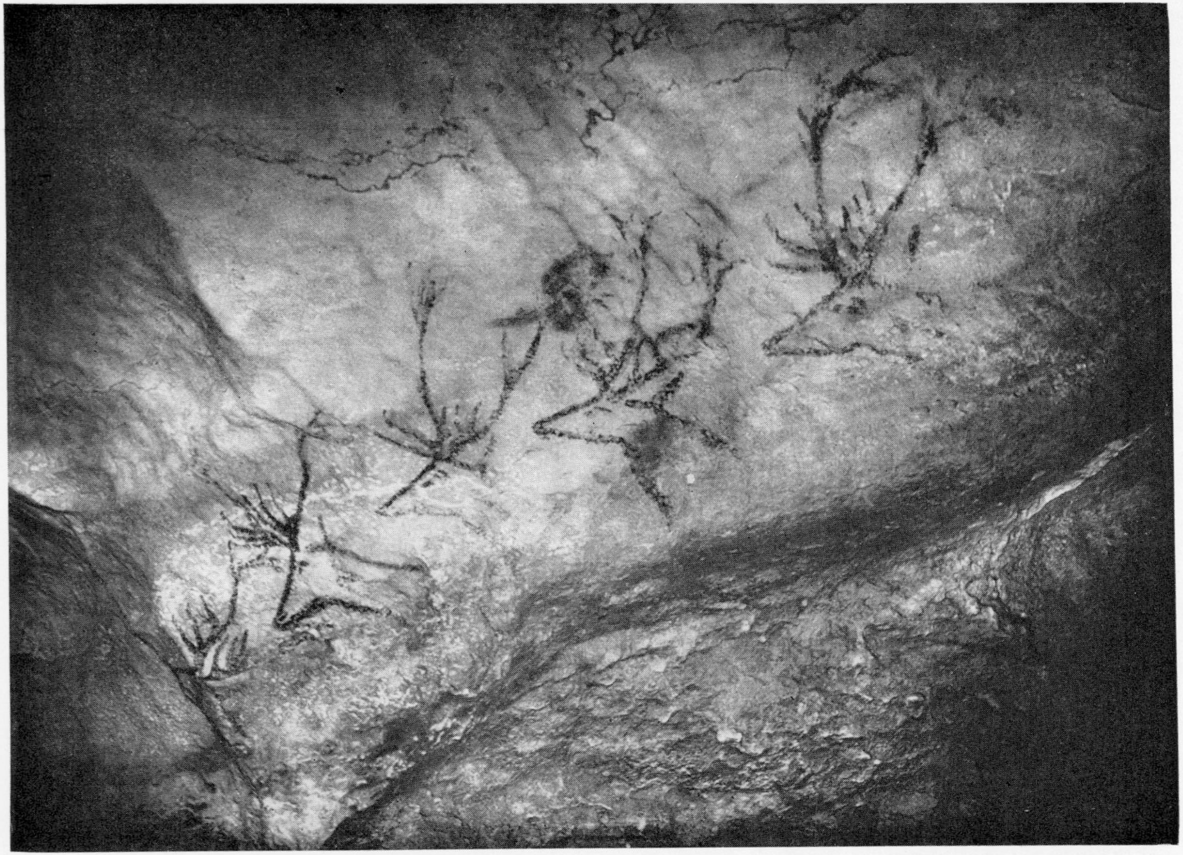

Herd of swimming deer, Lascaux (Dordogne), France.

Painting of horse and imprints of human hands. Pech-Merle (Lot), France.

PLATE VII

a. Ibexes and horses with rectangular signs. Lascaux (Dordogne), France.

b. Hunting scene: wounded bison, its head turned as though to look at the injury, charging a man; the bird perched on the pole represents perhaps a standard used in burial practices. Note the schematic treatment of the human figure, as opposed to the realism of the animal; the artist may have tried to represent the "deadness" of the hunter. Lascaux.

PLATE VIII

Remarkable finds like these are by no means confined to the Swiss Alpine region. Their wide diffusion is illustrated by the Mornova cave, in the sub-Alpine region of Slovenia, Yugoslavia. In a niche in the innermost part of this cave, which is over 160 feet long, and behind what were the living quarters of the primitive hunters, a cave-bear skull was discovered. Its lower jaw was missing, but it was otherwise unimpaired. Directly above it and across it there lay several limb bones that had not been split open.

Another site that has proved very rich in finds is the Petershöhle, near Velden, Franconia, in the foothills of the south-German Alps. This cave, excavated by K. Hörmann between 1914 and 1928, is divided into a number of principal and lateral chambers. In one of the lateral chambers Hörmann came upon tremendous collections of cave-bear bones, and skulls tucked away in almost every niche. At first it appeared as though an inrush of water might have washed the bones out of the cave floor and swept them into a corner. Then, however, came the discovery, in a neighboring chamber, of five cave-bear skulls set in a niche 3¾ feet above the floor, and covered with the dust that must have settled on them in the course of the millennia. Given that height, there could be no doubt that men's hands had placed the skulls in position.

Another niche, nearly four feet above the cave floor, contained two skulls, one on top of the other. A third skull was set on a high rock ledge, the muzzle and both canines protruding over the side. In the center of one of the bigger cave chambers no fewer than fourteen skulls had been deposited on a series of stone slabs. Ten of the skulls were wholly unimpaired. At three places along the terminal wall of the same chamber lay heaps of bones, among them skulls.

In a narrow passage Hörmann discovered an irregular arrangement of stone slabs supported by large limestone boulders; and under one of the slabs he found an enormous cave-bear skull, the muzzle pointing east. The frontal bone had a hole the size of a fist, surrounded by splinters of bone; the back of the skull had been split open. In front of the skull lay the femur of another bear. The whole area was thick with charcoal deposits, which had even penetrated the skull. However, the bones bore no marks of charring, and must therefore simply have been placed in the ashes (fig. 6).

More recent excavations support the evidence of these discoveries. One of the new sites lies at some distance from the Alps; this is the Furtins cave, between Mâcon and Cluny (Sâone-et-Loire), France. Here, in 1946, A. Leroi-Gourhan found seven cave-bear skulls, arranged in a distinctive concentric pattern, five feet from the mouth of the cave. Three of them, of young bears, occupied a stone slab, with the remaining four surrounding them. Probings in the anterior cave chamber revealed a Roman culture layer, below which was a middle Aurignacian level, and still deeper down, a layer filled chiefly with cave-bear bones and crudely fashioned tools reminiscent of the stone tools of the Alpine caves.

The finds made in the Salzofen cave, in the Totes Gebirge of the Austrian Alps, at 6,550 feet, deserve especial attention. The cave had been explored since 1924, but not until 1950 did it yield sure proof of habitation by cave-bear hunters of the ice age.

Like other caves in the central Alpine region, the Salzofen cave was accessible in the Quaternary only during interglacials or temporary thaws; at other times it was far removed from all living things, surrounded by a sea of ice.

Fig. 6. CAVE-BEAR SKULLS ENCLOSED BY STONES. PETERSHÖHLE, FRANCONIA, GERMANY.

STONES

CULTURE LAYER

COAL

Unlike most of the other caves, however, the plane of Salzofen is not horizontal, but slopes sharply to form a deep, narrow shaft.

In the summer of 1950 Kurt Ehrenberg undertook new excavations, and discovered three cave-bear skulls deposited in the same stratum in nichelike hollows in the cave wall. The skulls occupied three rocks, completely surrounded by others, and were covered with a film of charcoal. Near each skull lay some cave-bear bones. These can hardly have been anything else than supplementary offerings connected with the skulls. All three sets of bones were orientated from east to west; their orderly and undisturbed arrangement rules out the possibility that they might have been deposited by flooding or sedimentation. Another interesting feature of this find is the association of a penis-shaped bone and a claw phalanx with two of the skulls.

In these finds, there is obviously something more than mere refuse of meals. They contrast sharply with the spectacle that so often meets the excavator—broken animal bones strewn at random. We have here undoubtedly a selection of the most prized parts of the prey that was the hunters' main source of food. Frequently these bones—the cranium and long bones—are intact, a sign that the ancient hunters had not extracted the brain and the marrow, which, as mentioned before, were regarded as delicacies. Skulls and limb bones were displayed with unmistakably pious care, usually in the farthest and darkest parts of the cave. The men who had placed them there were obviously seeking to guard these objects from damage or desecration.

Interpretations of a purely secular character have not been wanting. The Drachenloch finds, for instance, have been described as evidence of an ancient supply depot, a kind of cellar where meat was stored. According to another theory, the finds point to the practice of storing brain and marrow either as delicacies or as possible tanning agents for the treatment of skins. Still another theory explains these finds as hunting trophies; but, as Emil Bächler has rightly pointed out, it seems unlikely that the men would have placed their trophies in precisely the darkest corners of their caves. As for the storage theory, brain and marrow would hardly have kept fresh for any length of time. Nor can these finds be evidence of a general practice of storing meat—which would have been exposed to marauding animals during the hunters' absence. Bächler, who examined the bones in the "wall cist"—which had no lid—could observe on them only a few marks of rodents' teeth. Finally, the bones had been piled up so closely as to preclude the possibility that they had been covered with flesh when first placed there by the hunters.

If we consider the different finds as a whole, and take into account all these arguments, we are left in no doubt as to their ritual character. Moreover, both Bächler and Hörmann independently favored the religious interpretation. Looking for similar practices among modern hunting peoples, they concluded that the ritual of the circumpolar peoples, centering about the head or skull and other bones of their prey, offered the most striking analogies. Hörmann maintains that the paleolithic finds must be explained partly in terms of an animal cult and of magic, partly in terms of sacrifice. Bächler concludes his study as follows: "Beyond any doubt, we are dealing here with the kind of deliberate storing of hunting trophies . . . which falls within the framework of the primitive hunting and sacrificial ritual." He was thinking especially of practices observed among Caucasian mountain peoples, whose environment is similar to that of the old cave-bear hunters. Among the Chevsur, each man, before setting out for the hunt, promises his hunting god a part of his kill. Circular walled sacrificial sites consecrated to the hunting god are to be found on heights dominating the entire hunting territory; they are filled with bear skulls, deer antlers, and ibex horns—the votive offerings of successful hunters.

In this lively controversy, two ritual forms known among arctic peoples have received special attention because they undoubtedly offer analogies to the prehistoric practices.

In circumpolar regions the practice exists of making sacrifice, either directly or indirectly, to a supreme being whose name signifies "universe" or "heaven," and whose attribute of "dispenser of hunting fortune" is often conceived of as an independent being. The matter of the sacrifice is the head, skull, and long bones of animals killed in the hunt, as well as of domestic reindeer. A. Gahs has made a thorough study of the peoples who pursue this practice, and of their religious ideas. The Samoyedes, for instance, who herd reindeer on the banks of the Pechora River, mount the head and long bones of a sacrificed reindeer on a rectangular board supported by a tall stake. Along the Siberian coast, between the Pechora Bay and Yanisei, many old sacrificial sites have been found where bones of bear, reindeer, and red deer are heaped in profusion. According to P. G. Pallas, as late as the eighteenth century the Samoyede Karagasses of the Sayan region sacrificed the heads of bear mounted on pieces of bark. Relics of such bear sacrifices have also been preserved among the Tungus and the Ainus.

The Yurak Samoyedes also direct sacrifice to a supreme

being, whom they call Num. The manner of sacrifice has been described by Venjamin as follows: Usually a white reindeer is sacrificed to Num on a hill. The animal is faced toward the east and strangled. As the rope is placed about its neck, the shaman takes hold of the left hind leg and says in a loud voice: "Num, we give you our reindeer, take it!" The meat is consumed raw, and the head and bones are placed on a raised board, facing east. All present turn to the east and bow several times, believing that Num will descend from heaven and accept their sacrifice.

The Ainus set the skulls of animals taken in the hunt along the east wall of their huts, the place of sacrifice consecrated to their highest god, the sun. The Tungus place the skulls of their game on trees, bowing meanwhile in the direction of the sun and uttering short, fervent prayers. The cis-Baikal Tungus sacrifice the first animal they take in the hunt to the "devil"; the flesh of the animal is consumed, but the bones are placed on a stand. The object is to prevent the "devil"—that is, the spirit of the forest and of the chase—from setting any obstacles in the way of further hunting.

A. Gahs, in his study of the central Eskimos of the North American continent, has clearly established the fact that these sacrifices do not turn primarily upon the bones. And K. Rasmussen writes of the Eskimos of King William's Land: "No marrow bones might be eaten, no gourmet might regale himself with fresh reindeer brain; instead, as soon as the flesh had fallen away from the heads, these had to be carefully submerged in a nearby river in which there was no fish. The people's future hunting fortunes were dependent upon the faithful observance of these prescriptions." Thus, the marrow and brain are not to be touched; the bones are important only as containers, as sacrificial vessels, so to speak.

Here we have a taboo practice associated with the belief in a female deity, the "mother of beasts." As Gahs shows by comparative studies, this figure with its accompanying myth must have been brought to the Eskimos from elsewhere. Yet its role corresponds to that of the supreme being worshipped by the most ancient Eskimos, who is also conceived of as the divine dispenser of hunting luck. The particular significance of the Eskimos' sacrifice lies in this, that it reveals the actual matter of the sacrifice —the brain and the marrow.

Gahs then points out the striking affinity between these contemporary sacrifices of head, skull, and long bones and the bones found in the Alpine caves. We may therefore conclude that the prehistoric cave-bear hunter also sacrificed to a superior power, whom he may even have conceived of as a supreme being, and whose attribute of "dispenser of hunting fortune" is strongly attested by the type of sacrifice.

Wilhelm Schmidt maintains that in the primitive arctic culture the preserving of the head, or skull, and long bones represents a sacrifice to the supreme being. He regards the objects found at the Drachenloch and other sites as proof positive that the cave-bear hunters of the last interglacial were already making such sacrifices, and that they must therefore have believed in a supreme being, or at least in a god of the forest and the chase. And he concludes that as this divinity of the chase was a later development—a derivative, as it were, of the supreme being—belief in a supreme being must have been current even among the predecessors of the cave-bear hunters.

Superficially, however, there are no less striking elements of comparison with another set of religious practices found among contemporary circumpolar peoples—namely, the bear cult with its ceremonials. According to Alfred J. Hallowell's excellent study,* this cult is a specific phenomenon in the history of culture. Even if it is not coextensive with the whole area where the bear is hunted, it is still amazingly widespread, reaching from Lapland and Finland in northern Europe, across northern Asia, deep into the northernmost parts of North America. The focus of this cult, Hallowell maintains, is to be sought in the Old World.

The bear enjoys particular veneration among the adherents of this cult. It must not be called by its animal name, but rather "grandfather," "old father," "fur father," or simply "he." Often the bear is regarded as a kind of intermediary between man and the spirit of the mountain or forest. The Paleo-Siberian tribes regard the bear as a mythical first man, and venerate it together with their ancestors.

An elaborate ritual has been developed to honor the slain bear. As soon as it is trapped, but especially after it has been killed, the hunters offer it their profound apologies. The Koryaks, for instance, welcome the dead bear

* "Bear Ceremonialism in the Northern Hemisphere." *American Anthropologist*, Vol. 28, 1926.

to their camp with dancing and by swinging torches. One of the women puts the bear's head on her own head, wraps herself in its skin, and dances in this attire, at the same time exhorting the bear not to be angry or sad. Afterward the skin, with head attached, is displayed in a place of honor. The bear is a guest at the feast where its own flesh is eaten. The banqueters shower it with fine phrases and offer it their choicest dishes. Among other tribes the practice is for the women to weep and lament over the dead bear as for a departed loved one; the bear, meanwhile, is festively adorned, placed upon a mat, and plied with food and drink. The hunters make offerings to it, address speeches to it, and became increasingly boisterous. Finally they carve the bear up, drink its blood, and share its flesh. But the high point is always the eating of the flesh of the head, which, as a rule, includes the brain.

The last act of the ceremony is the deposition of the skull in a hallowed place, or its solemn interment, usually along with the rest of the bones. Among the Tungu and Yakut tribes the banqueters may not break a single bone. All bones are wrapped in birch bark or similar material, and then placed on a tree.

In the Bear Songs of the Finnish epic, *Kalevala,* the bear is respectfully requested to give of itself piece by piece. After the bear has divested itself of all its beautiful and useful properties, its skull is invited to take up a secure abode, with a splendid view, in the topmost branches of a fir tree.

The Lapps prepare a grave for the bear, lining it with birch twigs. There they deposit all the bones in anatomic order: the spinal vertebrae are threaded on a rod; the nasal bones, the generative organs, and the tail are put into place; and the whole is then covered with twigs and earth.

This ceremonial treatment of the bear insures that the spirit of the forest will send the hunters another bear the following year, or else the bones of the dead bear will be covered afresh with flesh and fur, and the beast will again present itself as a quarry for the hunters.

Many authors, such as Carl C. Clemens, Bolke von Richthofen, Leonhard Franz, and Georg Kraft, have drawn parallels between the prehistoric finds and this contemporary bear cult. They suggest that in both cases we are dealing with hunters for whom the bear represents the principal prey. And they consider the special treatment of the bones and, in particular, of the skull a form of hunting magic intended to preserve the supply of game.

The hunters' concern to keep their hunting grounds well supplied is the evident motive behind the complex rites connected with skull and bones. In many cases these rites are magical in character; in others they are the product of animistic beliefs in reincarnation. The latter is true, for instance, of the Chugach Eskimos of Alaska. K. Birket-Smith reports that according to their beliefs, every animal and every man has a soul. After a man dies, his soul continues to live in a heavenly land that resembles the earth, with forests, mountains, and seas. The souls of animals are reborn in new animals provided that the hunters who have killed them observe the proper rites. The bear's soul is located in its head, and looks like a bear in miniature; therefore, when a bear has been killed, its skull must be left at the spot where it was slain, muzzle down; then the bear's soul will be reborn in another bear, for man's advantage. The souls of fish, on the other hand, are located in their entrails, and these should therefore be thrown back into the water; but if they are cast back on the shore, the fish soul dies.

K. Meuli, in his *Griechische Opferbräuche* (1945), points out that the ritual connected with the bear's skull and bones is only a part of a widespread practice of "animal interment." Other animals have often been treated in similar fashion. The objective is not merely to give careful burial to the remains, but also to restore whatever the animal requires for its resurrection. A Lapp, asked why he placed the head, feet, and wings of the mountain cock on a stone, replied: "New birds grow out of them, which I can catch." The Lapps also place the bones and scales of fish on a particular stone under the protection of the fish god; the fish, they believe, then begin to swim again. The Ten'a of Alaska believe that, like each of the big-game animals, all the fish have their guardian spirit who requires these attentions.

Meuli believes this practice of animal interment to be the oldest hunting ritual. Originally, he maintains, it was connected neither with magic nor with totemism, nor indeed with any belief in a divinity; the only protagonists were the hunter and the beast. Today, however, the practice is often cited as a matter of divine prescription.

Meuli also believes that the Alpine cave bones point to nothing more than animal interments. In addition, they would show that the original objective was not to preserve the skeleton as a whole, but that such preservation had developed as a "more complete and more subtle ritual" out of a "ruder, older" practice concerned only with specific bones, especially the skull.

The most important question, then, is simply which of these present-day rituals is the more ancient, and therefore belongs to a culture level at all comparable to the culture of the cave-bear hunters.

At first glance it would seem that bear cult and animal interment were older, as today they are to be found only among hunting societies; and because the bear is often the principal quarry of these hunting peoples, their practices should be compared to those of the ancient cave-bear hunters. But the modern groups who sacrifice head, skull, and long bones are not exclusively hunters; they also herd and breed animals, in particular the reindeer. The Samoyedes, for instance, do not offer in sacrifice the product of the chase, but an animal from their herd. This difference in culture levels, which makes sacrifice appear to be a later development, has been stressed by Leonhard Franz. Meuli, for his part, suggests that an attempt to interpret ancient hunting rituals in terms of the sacrifices of a much later pastoral society is a flagrant contradiction of the principle that Wilhelm Schmidt so constantly (and rightly) enunciated—namely, that only data of similar cultures can be compared.

But is the culture of the reindeer herdsmen really so

much "later" than that of the hunters, and especially of the bear hunters?

Arctic reindeer herdsmen must be regarded as culturally distinct from the Central Asiatic nomad peoples who herd horses. The former retain many of the characteristics of the ancient hunting peoples, whereas the latter are in a transitional stage of culture. At the same time, the culture of the arctic and subarctic hunting communities, and particularly of the bear hunters, is undoubtedly far more advanced than that of the primitive hunters, often showing even the influence of the agricultural societies to the south. (Incidentally, Meuli entirely overlooked the fact that the skull and leg sacrifice is not confined to pastoral cultures, but occurs even among the North American Indian tribes, who are not at all in the pastoral stage.)

Gahs cites yet another proof of the greater antiquity of such sacrifice. The tribes who practice it—the Samoyedes and the central Eskimos—occupy two areas extending east and west of the Bering Straits, main route and invasion gate from Asia to America. Between them, like some dividing wedge, and extending south of them, lies the region of the bear cult and the other hunting rituals. Gahs has shown the likelihood, based on physical evidence, that the sacrifice of skull and legs, together with the veneration of a supreme being, was originally practiced in this intermediate region. The arctic hunting societies, with their bear cult and burial practices, would then seem to be later arrivals in the Bering Strait area. They destroyed the ties between the earlier hunting peoples of the area, partly by driving the Samoyedes and central

Eskimos back to the extreme west and east, partly by superimposing their own culture on those who remained.

The evidence, therefore, would seem to favor sacrifice as being of greater antiquity.

Modern primitive arctic ritual and belief has thus an all-important bearing on the religious practices of the cave-bear hunters of the last interglacial. For the inference connotes a religious survival from the ice age right into our own times, even though the actual historical link remains obscure. The rite of sacrifice was probably practiced far beyond the Alpine region, to the east, or it may have spread eastward from the foothills of the Alps during the last ice age, to survive in the high arctic in the changed form of a pastoral sacrifice and overlaid by taboo rules attributed to some "mother of animals." At all events, here for the first time we find a human group emerging from the darkness of the remote past with its specific religious beliefs and practices—the cave-bear hunters of the last interglacial, whose sacrifice of the skull and limb bones of their quarry bears witness to their faith in a divinity. And just as the modern primitive circumpolar societies profess substantially the same religious beliefs as other primitive peoples—even though their ritual forms may vary considerably—so we may infer, from the religion of the cave-bear hunters, that the rest of mankind in that period held similar beliefs, though not necessarily embodied in the same ceremonials.

The ancient cave-bear hunters of the Alps and Alpine

foothills recognized their dependence upon a supreme being—a belief whose connection with their daily lives and their hunting activities is supported by the finds. This supreme being they honored by sacrifice. Whether such sacrifice was directed to a supreme being in its capacity as dispenser of good fortune in the chase, or to a hunting god—a spirit of forest or mountain—deriving from the supreme being, we do not know. What we know is that this divinity was believed to be lord of the beasts, who replenished the hunting grounds.

It is possible that before setting out, the hunters invoked the protection of this god and promised him a particular part of their kill. The slaying of the enormous cave bear must have been a great event for those hunters. The hunt was full of risks: the hunters' skill and daring had to combine with luck to insure success. If the hunters were successful, they would render due thanks to the dispenser of their luck as soon as the spoils were brought into the dwelling cave.

The ceremonies—whose precise rubrics are, of course, unknown to us—took place by brightly flickering firelight. The matter of the sacrifice was the prized brain and the marrow, the enjoyment of which the hunters denied themselves, either wholly or in part. There has been no find in which all the marrow bones of a bear have appeared together with its skull. (In several cases the bones associated with finds indicate that the hunters often sacrificed the entire head of the bear; normally, however, they sacrificed the skull alone after the flesh had been removed. The same is true of the marrow bones, and it is even possible that the eating of the flesh on these bones constituted a sacrificial meal.) The high point of the ceremonies was undoubtedly the solemn act of the offering.

The Drachenloch finds suggest still another form of sacrifice. As we know, close by the sacrificial "chest" with the seven skulls, there was a second cist, looking much like a hearth site in which a fire could be kept permanently burning. In the 9-inch layer of charcoal and white and gray ash, there were found a number of phalanx bones and front and rear paw stumps. Did the hunters perhaps roast the tasty paws of the bear here? The position of the finds, near the cist and in the entrance to the actual cave sanctuary, implies that the burning of the paws was a further sacrificial rite.

In connection with the Salzofen cave, I have referred to the finding of a claw phalanx and a bone shaped like a penis near two of the skulls. Such an arrangement of bones could obviously not have occurred twice without a definite reason. We shall hardly go wrong if we regard the penis bone as a fertility symbol. Was it placed there as part of some magical rite, or because the hunters sought to urge the lord of beasts to replace the animals they had taken in the hunt? Kurt Ehrenberg considers these offerings evidence of magical belief and practice. In my opinion, either interpretation is plausible.

The big stone cists with their bear skulls and charred phalanx bones, the smaller deposits containing only one skull and a few bones, together with the wall niches with their exhibits and the big rock slabs or layers of stone on which up to fourteen skulls have been found—all these constitute the oldest altars of sacrifice so far known. O. Menghin, incidentally, believes that the big wall cist in the living quarters of the Drachenloch could have been used for the disposal of the remains of the offerings.

The Petershöhle was found to contain an unusually large quantity of sacrificial offerings but only very few stone tools; and there was no indication at all of any stone-tool manufacture within the cave. Moreover, the great distance of the cave from any water supply made it altogether unsuitable for habitation. Hence K. Hörmann suggests that this cave served exclusively as a sanctuary for one or more groups of hunters in the area. As to the Drachenloch, on the other hand, Emil Bächler believes that it was not only a ritual cave—the highest, doubtless, in the world—but also a dwelling cave, as evidenced by the fireplaces and great heaps of kitchen refuse found there.

Part II

THE UPPER PALEOLITHIC PERIOD

I

THE NEW MEN AND THE EMERGENCE OF ART

TREMENDOUS CHANGES took place toward the end of the last interglacial, particularly in Europe. The summers became progressively cooler, the winters more severe. In the Alps and the Scandinavian mountains, great snow masses accumulated; the ice sheets descended relentlessly into the valleys; northern glaciers invaded what is now the Baltic and once again buried large areas of northern Europe under countless millions of tons of ice.

From the two great ice caps, cold, dry air moved over Europe, completely altering the climate. As the forest zones gradually turned into open, cold steppes, the animals died, or migrated to the south and southwest; and many species became extinct. Primitive man, too, was forced to retreat before the ice and to follow the animals in their migrations. Then his own species succumbed to the change. A new fauna, including animals such as the mammoth and the woolly rhinoceros, appeared in Europe, bringing in its train a new, hardier human species, well adapted to the changed environment.

It is now accepted as fact that during the last great glaciation a new type of man appeared in Europe, incomparably superior both physically and culturally to his predecessors. The first waves of these new arrivals came from parts of western Asia. They spread over central and western Europe; another branch moved across northern Africa and into the Iberian peninsula.

Thanks to the discovery of a series of excellently preserved skeletons, we have a good idea of the physical constitution of these men. Their type was very similar to that of modern Europeans. They were already divided into a number of races.

The most important of these newcomers were the Cro-Magnon, so named after a site in southern France. They were a tall, powerfully built race, long-headed, with high foreheads and well-modeled chins. Cro-Magnon man lived, in Europe, from Moravia to southern France, from northern Italy to England. Even in Holland, whose present territory was just rising from the sea at that time, traces of Cro-Magnon people have been found. Another race, the smaller Grimaldi man, assigned its status from two skeletons found in northern Italy, had "Negroid" features, and might have originated in Africa.

The first arrivals brought with them the far richer and more developed culture known as the Aurignacian. The Aurignacian was followed by the very different Solutrean culture, succeeded in turn by the Magdalenian, which was much closer in character to the Aurignacian. These two had their North African and Iberian counterpart in what is called the Capsian culture.

These peoples lived like their predecessors—by hunting and by gathering what roots and wild fruits they could, under conditions of intense cold. It has sometimes been suggested that they domesticated the reindeer, and not only collected wild plants related to modern cereals, but also cultivated them; the facts do not support this theory, however. Yet although the Europeans of the upper paleolithic remained exclusively hunting peoples, they achieved considerable cultural advances. Their tools and weapons were superior to those of their predecessors and more varied; and to fashion them they used not only flint but horn, bone, and even ivory, all of which they manipulated with increasing skill.

The nomadic movements of these hunters had certain territorial limits. In the more densely occupied cave regions of western Europe, there existed a more or less non-nomadic population. As with the Neanderthalers, their favorite dwellings or hunting stations were caves and rock shelters. Probably they also made tents supported by poles or, in the severest winters, dome-shaped huts covered with turf and snow. In the loess fields of the eastern territories are traces of trenches that had clearly served as foundations for buildings made of brushwood and animal skins. And thanks to the traces of these more substantial dwellings, we have often been able to find deposits of a whole culture within a small area. As the dead were often buried in previously inhabited dwelling places, the burial finds are more frequent. The physical diffusion of culture groups declines somewhat as men become increasingly tied to their local habitations.

THE MOST impressive memorials of the new men are their artistic creations. The hunting art of the ice age had no precursors. It breaks through the darkness of prehistory like the dawn of a glorious spring day, flooding all things in its brilliance and giving us a wealth of insights into the daily lives of those far-off peoples. This art originated with the Aurignacians and reached its apex with the Magdalenians. In western Europe, it also extended east as far as Siberia, and south to northern Africa.

Three artistic regions may be distinguished. The most splendid is what is known as the Franco-Cantabrian province, comprising the northern Spanish and southwestern French cave regions, and sometimes extending beyond this area. Here we see the paleolithic artists developing almost every technique of representational art with astounding skill: sculpture, both large and small; engraving, executed on stone, bone, and ivory; and painting. Walls and ceilings of caves were covered with varied pictorial designs, ranging from simple color tracings on incised outlines to free painting in one or more colors. The shading and other painting effects used often appear quite modern, as, for instance, the stipple technique. By the light of smoking grease lamps or flickering torches, the artists covered the shimmering crystalline surfaces of innumerable limestone cave walls with an abundance of animal representations. Incised with flint, painted in earth colors, modeled in clay or engraved on bone, antler, and stone, the whole animal world of those times appears before us—mammoth, rhinoceros, bison, reindeer, wild horse, and the first oxen. Here is the hunting paradise of the last ice age. But it is the individual animal that dominates these designs, however crowded together the outlines may be. Groups of animals, or scenes depicting animal life or the chase, are less common. The actual representation of human beings is rare compared with that of beasts. A distinctive trait of many of these cave drawings is their astonishing fidelity to nature.

The art province of the Spanish Levant, largely of Capsian derivation, shows a related yet stylistically distinct art consisting largely of pictures painted under rock ledges. We sometimes find indications of mutual influence in the early period; later, however, each province develops along its own lines. The Capsian people, incidentally, never seem to have cultivated the "small arts," for which the usual materials were antler, bone, stone, or ivory. Their art form was the rock mural, always small in scale and characterized by the frequent use of silhouette, but revealing an extraordinary sense of movement. The pictures show men as well as animals, scenes of hunting and of fighting, of everyday life, and of ritual ceremony. This pictorial art was obviously developed by the Capsian people on European soil and cultivated there with prodigious vitality; only offshoots penetrated to the African continent, as far as South Africa.

According to a recent, probably valid theory, the rock art of the Iberian peninsula originated, from a conjunction of Franco-Cantabrian and African influences, in the paleolithic but flowered chiefly in the mesolithic.

In addition to these two western European art provinces, there is an eastern province, covering central and eastern Europe and western Siberia. Here we find almost

Fig. 7. HUNTING SCENE. ROCK PAINTING IN RED. CAVE OF LOS CABALLOS, SPANISH LEVANT. SCALE 1:5

exclusively small sculptures representing animals and, quite frequently, female figures. The complete absence of pictorial art is only partially explained by the absence of suitable caves or rock ledges. Some traces of rock painting may be found on the borders of the Franco-Cantabrian province, but these are plainly of Franco-Cantabrian inspiration. No doubt the differing art styles of the three provinces should be explained, above all, by a diversity of artistic endowments.

With the emergence of art, we see paleolithic man in a wholly new light, possessed of the power of artistic creation. We may speculate on how this power came to be developed. According to Abbé Breuil and Hugo Obermaier, the mural art of the ice age began, in all likelihood, as a kind of hand play. When the hand was dipped in clay or some mineral dye and then pressed against the wall of a cave, it would leave a colored impression. Or the three middle fingers might be drawn through the clay of the cave wall, forming "macaroni-like" designs. Here ice-age man was simply paralleling another cave dweller, the bear, which had scratched the same clay in order to sharpen its claws on the hard underlying rock. But men's fingers, guided by a superior vision, transformed the mechanical furrows into complex patterns—wavy lines, spirals, circles, and meanders, intersecting one another, overlapping and intertwining, till suddenly, as out of a maze, there would emerge the lifelike head of an animal.

The next step followed shortly after: the hunter turned artist would deliberately make pictures of the animals around him. At first these pictures were no more than outline sketches; nevertheless, the stage of groping experiment was over. Stone surfaces were covered with coats or streaks of color—single color first, then several, applied with tinting and shading effects.

The ice-age artist did not hesitate to superimpose one picture on another. In this way a real pictorial stratigraphy was created, making it possible to assess accurately and objectively the changes of style and their sequence. If we thus go back to the lowest and most ancient pictures—impressions of hands and "macaroni" tracings—we find that representative art emerged in Europe in the Aurignacian.

Perhaps it emerged even earlier. J. L. Baudet recently discovered a number of signs and symbols in caves and rock shelters in the Ile de France. The simplest of these designs, which consist of grooves, sometimes almost parallel, incised in the hard quartzite, are believed to be anterior to the Aurignacian. Even at that early stage we can recognize the intention of arranging individual signs in rhythmic order. In contrast to the great southwestern art province, with its "macaroni" designs leading to realistic portrayals of animals, art in the Ile de France, right up into the mesolithic and neolithic periods, was always characterized by convention and abstraction. Although the pictures of animals found there are related, both in content and technique, to the polychrome Magdalenian paintings of the Franco-Cantabrian province, they differ in style, being far more schematic. Thus the Ile de France appears to offer yet another element in ice-age art. Its pictures arose out of signs and symbols; they are the product of that tendency toward abstraction which, according to W. Worringer, lies at the origin of all art.

The diluvian hunting art—in particular that of the Franco-Cantabrian region—constitutes a uniquely brilliant phenomenon in human history. It is without any direct counterpart. It is the key to the religious and spiritual life of ice-age man.

II

BURIAL PRACTICES

Excavation has shown that the interment of the dead was widely practiced in the upper paleolithic. The practice did not originate with the new men; it had been current even among the Neanderthalers, and its origins should probably be sought in a much more ancient culture common to the ancestors of both peoples. But the centers of that culture must have lain outside Europe, in those parts of Asia which were the homelands of the new inhabitants of Europe. For it is on the eastern border zone of the European continent that the oldest known burials have been discovered.

The men of the last ice age buried their dead evidently believing in a physical afterlife. They, too, it seems, regarded the dead as "living corpses." As in earlier times, the dead were often buried in the dwelling caves where they had lived, so that they might remain in familiar surroundings. Grave pits were carefully dug in cave floors, and the corpse deposited either in a "sleeping position," or on its back, or crouching. A protective layer of stones was then placed around and over the grave. The dead were buried singly, or together with one or two others. In Předmost, Moravia, Czechoslovakia, a mass grave was found to contain at least fourteen skeletons, protected by a layer of stones. Apparently the dead were to keep one another company.

Frequently the corpse was laid in a hearth trough among still glowing embers; the intention was to warm the dead body, not to cremate it. A skeleton found at Solutré (Sâone-et-Loire) was lying on a layer of ashes about 8 inches thick, and covered by a thinner layer. According to Adrien Arcelin and P. Wernert, the first layer had come from the fire kindled in the trench before the burial. The second, which recalls the layer of ash of the Neanderthal burial at Spy, Belgium, must have been caused by a fire maintained over the corpse.

The dead were often interred in thick layers of ocher. With its reddish tint reminiscent of blood, its purpose would have been to provide the pallid corpse with a life-like hue. As a rule, the dead were generously provided with weapons, ornaments, and food—for their journey into the beyond.

More ornaments have been found on male skeletons than on female ones. The reason would seem to be this: owing to the development of a social structure more complex than in previous periods, men played a major part in the communal life of the group, and also were the main actors in tribal feasts and hunting ceremonies. As among modern primitive peoples, this male primacy was expressed not least by adornments and finery richer than those of women. The skulls and necks of male skeletons found in upper paleolithic graves were surrounded by pierced shells, deer's teeth, fish vertebrae, and small bone disks, which probably ornamented caps and headbands. On the skeleton's breast there frequently appears a pouch similar to the "medicine pouch" of modern primitives which is filled with amulets and other magic paraphernalia. Ornaments have also been found all over the body—around the upper arms, elbows, or wrists, about the pelvic girdle, thighs, knees, and feet. To all appearances, the dead were interred decked out as for company.

Many of the burial sites discovered were littered or surrounded with broken animal bones. It is not possible to determine whether these bones are relics of funerary or memorial feasts, or of grave offerings intended either to feed the dead or secure their help.

The theory that these bones were relics of votive gifts is most strongly supported by the discovery of animal skulls, especially of reindeer, deer, and mammoth, complete with their valuable antlers or ivory tusks, lying near the skeleton. As P. Wernert quite rightly points out, these could not have been hunting trophies, as the men of the upper paleolithic did not normally place hunting trophies near graves; moreover, unlike the ornaments and personal possessions of the dead man, such skulls are not found on or beside the corpse, but mainly around the edge of the grave. Thus, for instance, a male skeleton found at Solutré had been laid in a kind of hut surrounded by walls some 5½ feet high. At his right hand lay some finely wrought flint spear-heads, as well as rare shells from the distant Atlantic coast, all obviously personal possessions

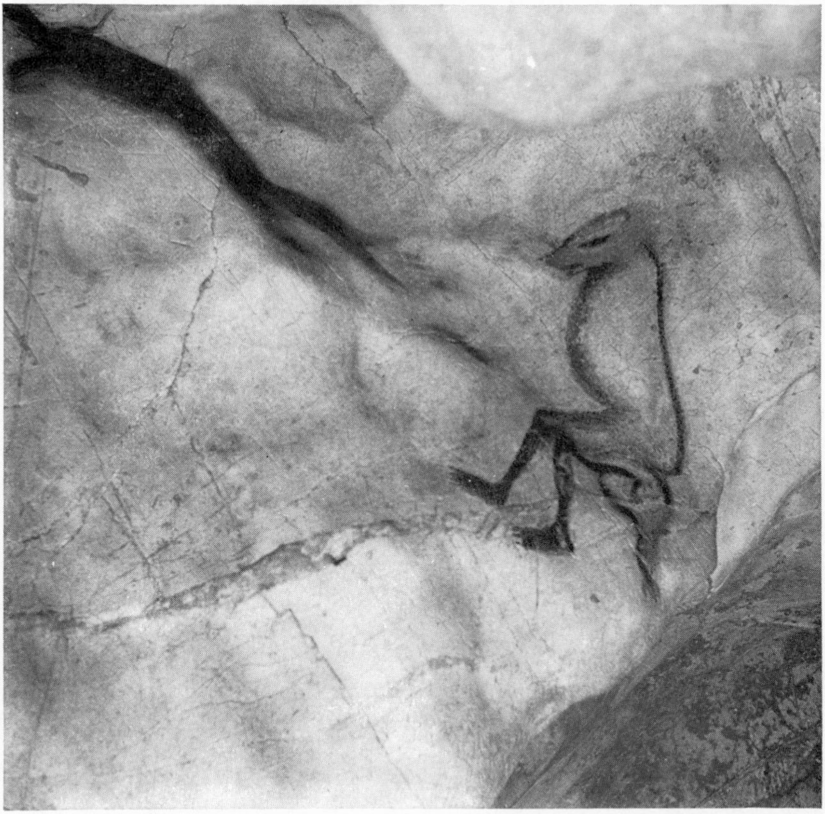

a. The "great sorcerer" of the Trois-Frères cave (Ariège), France. This famous figure, which dominates the representation of a vast assemblage of animals in the deepest part of the cave, can be reached only by means of a narrow upward spiraling passage.

b. Sketch of the "great sorcerer," 1⁄10 actual size.

PLATE IX

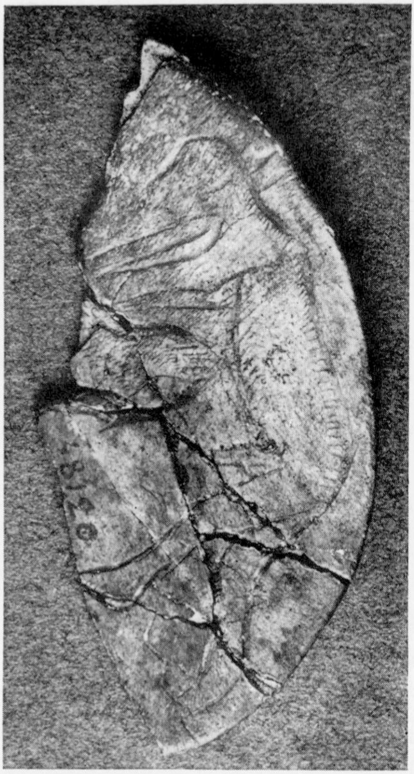

a. Figure of dancer engraved on bone. Mas d'Azil cave (Ariège), France.

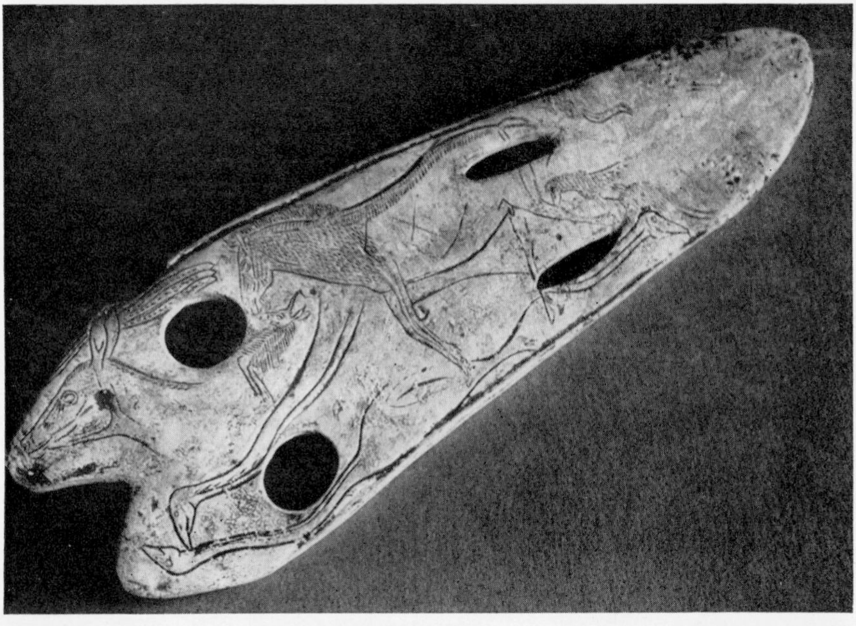

b. Perforated bone stake with engraved figures; one of these a creature half-human, half-chamois. Teyjat (Dordogne), France.

PLATE X

PLATE XI

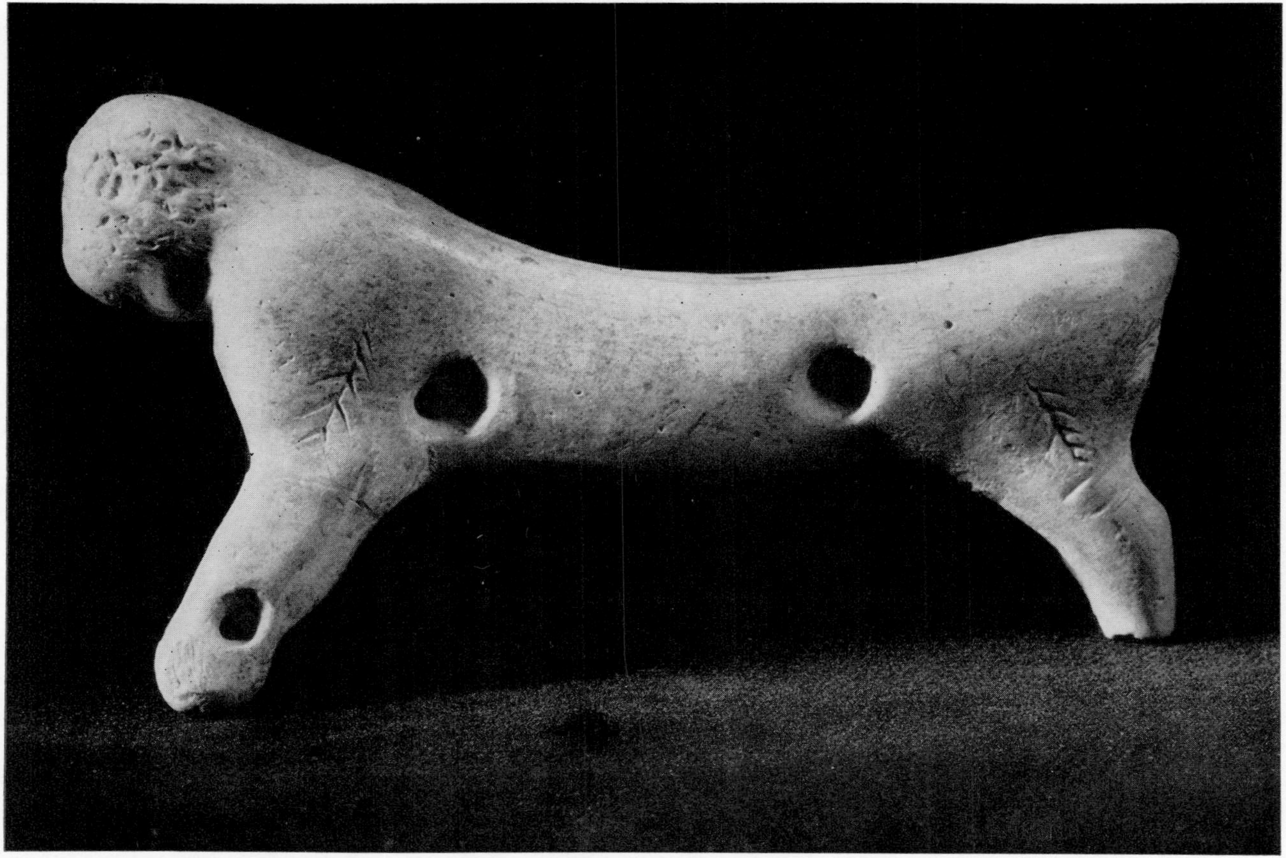

Magic feline carved out of reindeer antler. Isturitz (Basses-Pyrénées), France.

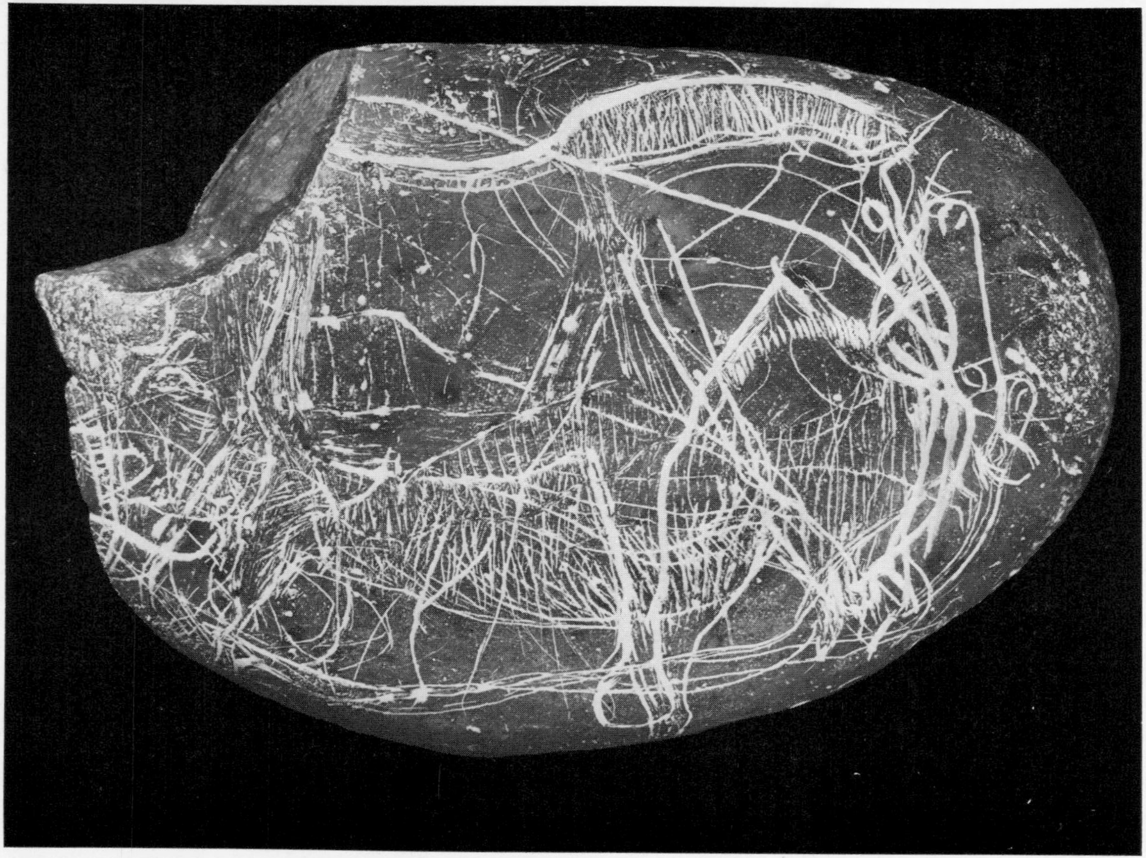

Repeatedly engraved "magic stone." La Colombière cave (Ain), France.

PLATE XII

of the dead man. Outside the actual grave, there were found a reindeer skull, about eighty reindeer antlers, and parts of a mammoth. A grave in the cave of Saint Germain la Rivière (Gironde) offers a similar picture. Here the skeleton was that of a woman, a circumstance that would seem to rule out the possibility that reindeer skull and antlers were hunting trophies. Other animal bones found at the level of the dead woman's breast must have been the remains of food offerings placed in the grave.

A striking point is the frequency with which mammoth bones occur near upper paleolithic burials, over a very wide area. Portions of mammoth skulls with tusks attached have been found in burial sites at Brno, in Moravia, at Klause, in southern Germany, and at Solutré. Jawbones and shoulder blades of the same beast surrounded the mass grave at Předmost, and on the same site a human lower jaw was covered by a mammoth shoulder blade. At Wisternitz, in Moravia, a mammoth shoulder blade covered a child's grave. Could the intention have been to place the dead under the protection of that immense beast, whose very size would frighten off the evil spirits? Wernert, for instance, suggests that the ice-age men regarded the giant mammoth as a protective spirit, rather as the pygmies of Equatorial Africa believe the elephant to be their protector, and indeed an incarnation of a supreme deity.

The finds indicate that in general ice-age man had no particular fear of the dead. Wernert, however, maintains that the offerings placed in graves were inspired by fear. To me it seems just as probable that they were motivated by a special sense of attachment to the dead and a belief in their continued relationship with the living.

However, the position of some skeletons points clearly to fear of those particular dead persons—specifically to fear lest they rise from their graves. A number have been found in a crouching position; the corpses had probably been trussed in accordance with some special ritual. Others have been found lying face down; this would seem an even more obvious measure to prevent the return of certain departed.

The Grimaldi people, on the Mediterranean coast, employed a particularly curious device to confine a corpse to the grave forever. In one of their dwelling caves, among the extinguished embers of the fire, they buried a youth fifteen to seventeen years old, placing in his arms the body of an old woman. The youth's legs were tightly flexed, with the heels under the buttocks. His left arm lay slightly curved alongside his body, while his right hand was placed under the old woman's pelvis. The woman's arms and legs were tightly pressed to her body; her face was sharply inclined downward. Both must have been buried together, probably because they had died at the same time. At any rate, the strange manner of the burial indicates that these Grimaldi people believed that the dead continued in some way to live. Here it seems to have been the old woman they feared most, and therefore secured in the arms of her grave companion. There is no reason to suppose that the young man had been sacrificed to placate the dreaded old woman; human sacrifice occurs in the latter part of the neolithic, but evidence is lacking of any such practice at an earlier period.

In addition to the many total burials found in upper paleolithic strata, excavation has revealed a large number of isolated human skeletal parts, particularly skulls, of the same period. Many of these probably are from graves that were subsequently destroyed; but the circumstances of other such finds make it obvious that these isolated skeletal parts had served some special ritual purposes.

Two types of skull finds occur, each of which holds considerable significance. In the cave of Les Hommes, near Arcy-sur-Cure (Yonne), three human skulls from the Magdalenian were found carefully arranged on a rock slab. And in the Placard cave (Charente), to the left of the entrance, a female skull intact, surrounded by a wealth of shell ornaments, was found in deposits belonging to the middle Magdalenian.

But the Placard cave revealed still another type of skeletal remain—a type that does not appear prior to the upper paleolithic. In the deposits just referred to, two fragments of skulls were found; a little deeper, in an early Magdalenian stratum, five skull fragments were found, four of which had been arranged next to one another. A humerus and a femur were discovered nearby. And deeper still, in a late Solutrean deposit, two skull fragments and one larger lower jaw were found.

A closer and much later investigation by Abbé Breuil

and Hugo Obermaier made it apparent that these skull fragments had been converted into "skull cups." Numerous traces of incisions prove that after decapitation, the scalp skin and facial musculature must have been removed with a flint knife. Then the lower portion of the skull was cut away and the edges smoothed to fashion a shallow, well-proportioned cup (fig. 8). The traces of this operation are the most reliable evidence that such cups were intentionally formed; the traces of incisions prove only that the soft parts had been removed.

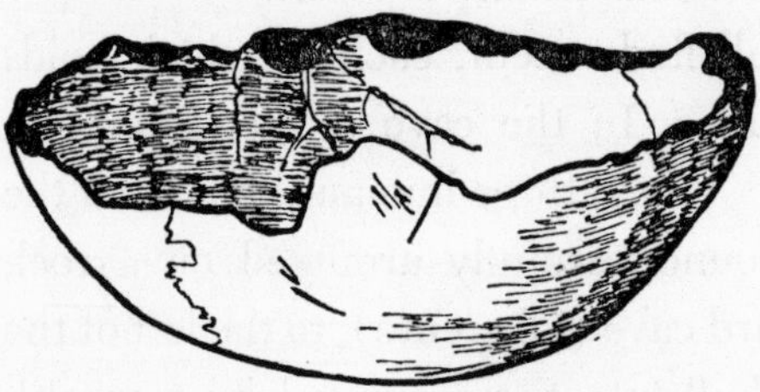

Fig. 8. SKULL CUP FOUND IN THE PLACARD CAVE (CHARENTE), FRANCE. SCALE 1:2

Skull cups of this kind have been found in upper paleolithic strata from Castillo, in northern Spain, to Unter-Wisternitz, in Moravia; the beliefs connected with them must have been widely diffused. The association of the Placard cave skull cups with an arrangement of skull fragments indicates some relation between the skull-cup cult and the veneration of skulls (which, as mentioned above, had already existed in earlier times). Most of these finds belong to the Magdalenian.

Their ritual character is obvious. Four of the skull cups in the Placard cave were discovered at the end of a little passage, arranged next to one another with unmistakable care, the hollow facing up. One of the best cups still contained traces of ocher. Two long bones were found nearby, lying close together. There can be no doubt about the use of this part of the cave as a sanctuary. The Solutrean people, and after them the Magdalenians, had practiced a skull cult there, and the ritual must have included the offering of ocher.

History and ethnology show that the use of cups fashioned out of skulls has been associated with very different and even conflicting beliefs. Herodotus claimed that the Issedones drank from the gold-mounted skulls of their ancestors to keep their memory fresh. The thirteenth-century missionary William of Ruysbroek referred to a similar practice among the Tibetans. James Rennel, in Bengal, saw finely lacquered skull cups that were used to drink to the memory of the departed. George French Angas, a nineteenth-century traveler, tells of a ten-year-old girl in southern Australia who carried upon her a piece of her mother's skull; this relic served her as a drinking cup. There are many authenticated cases of magnificently decorated saints' skulls being used, during the Christian Middle Ages, as memorial drinking cups.

At other places and times, however, cups were made from the skulls of slain foes. The Scythians turned the skulls of their enemies into such cups and proudly displayed them to visitors. According to Plutarch, the ancient Teutons drank from the skulls of those of their slain enemies who had been brave men, believing that they would thus imbibe their courage. Paul the Deacon reports that Alboin, king of Lombardy, forced his wife, Rosamund, to drink from a vessel made from her father's skull; Rosamund later took revenge by having her husband murdered. In A.D. 811 the Bulgarian prince Krum had a cup made of the skull of the Byzantine emperor Nicephorus II. In 1875 a skull was found at Pompeii; it was mounted in precious metals and bore the inscription, in Greek: "Drink and you shall live for many years."

These examples are relatively recent from the stand-

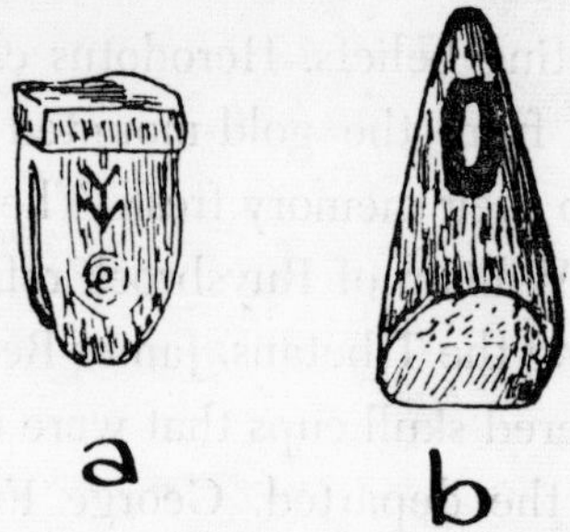

Fig. 9. HUMAN TEETH FASHIONED INTO PENDANTS. A. MOLAR WITH INCISED ARROW FOUND AT COMBE (DORDOGNE), FRANCE B. INCISOR FOUND AT THE MAMMOTH-HUNTERS' STATION AT UNTERWISTERNITZ, MORAVIA, CZECHOSLOVAKIA

point of cultural history, and therefore tell us little about the beliefs that caused men in the upper paleolithic to fashion cups of skulls. P. Wernert, however, has studied the finds in connection with certain other curious ones of the same era—for instance, a human molar found in an Aurignacian stratum in the cave of La Combe (Dordogne). The tooth was pierced, evidently to be worn as a pendant, and had an arrow incised on the surface above the hole (fig. 9). According to Wernert, this was undoubtedly a trophy.

Wernert recalls that M. de Maret, who excavated the

Placard cave during the 1880's and found human skeletal remains in the dwelling layers, concluded that the ancient occupants of the cave had practiced cannibalism. He also cites a discovery made by K. Absolon at Předmost, in 1928, not far from the communal sepulture mentioned above—fifty-four bones of one skeleton scattered, along with mammoth bones, in the ashes of an Aurignacian fire pit. Except for two teeth, nothing remained of the skull, and the left femur bore twenty-six traces of incisions. Both Absolon and Wernert consider these human bones remains of a cannibal feast, and assume that the head had served a ritual purpose. Wernert infers from the nearby communal grave that the ancient mammoth hunters of Předmost buried their own dead but ate the bodies of strangers and paid some special cult to the victims' skulls or to the cups fashioned from those skulls.

As I observed in connection with the Krapina finds, it is almost impossible to tell whether scattered human bones such as these are the result of cannibal feasts or of damaged burial sites, especially as the men of the upper paleolithic often laid their dead to rest on hearths. But we cannot rule out cannibalism and head-hunting. In my opinion, the evidence suggests rather a memorial ritual.

In the Trois Frères cave, Count H. Bégouen found a fragment of an artificially pierced lower jaw belonging to a boy between twelve and eighteen. The smooth edges of the hole indicate a constant and prolonged friction, as I was able to see for myself when I visited Bégouen in 1946. The piece had indubitably been worn on a cord for a considerable time. Similarly, the tooth found at La Combe must have served as a pendant. Absolon also found a tooth that had been artificially pierced in the mammoth hunters' station at Unter-Wisternitz (fig. 9); like Wernert, Absolon believed this tooth to have been a trophy.

What arises now is the question of whether the skulls converted into cups, and the lower jaws and teeth fashioned into pendants, were regarded and used as instruments of magic. R. Battaglia has shown that in Italy, during the upper paleolithic period, men turned human bones into all kinds of tools. The tendency, apparent in the art of the ice age, to interpret the world in terms of magic leads us to suppose that skeletal remains were regarded as possessing magic properties. Quite possibly the practice of using skulls for purposes of magic led to the fashioning of cups from skulls. Memorial cults and magic must often, in practice, have become indistinguishable from one another.

A CERTAIN ice-age hunter of Lascaux (Dordogne) was given an altogether singular memorial. He had apparently been the victim of a hunting accident. Was it some special circumstance of this event, or the hunter's special reputation that caused his fellow hunters to portray the event on the walls of their tribal sanctuary? Whatever the answer, this cave mural is unique, as far as our present knowledge goes, in Franco-Cantabrian art. Abbé Breuil suggests that the hunter's grave lies beneath the wall on which the picture appears. Unfortunately no excavations have yet been undertaken in this part of the cave, which is all but inaccessible. However, in September 1949 Breuil made some probings, and found, under the existing fill between the wall fissures, another fill consisting of stones brought from outside the cave; and in this inner fill he found stone lamps, their hollows blackened by charcoal, as well as needles and spearheads, most of them broken, a fine spearhead 18 inches long, pins of deer antler, and flint blades. One's immediate impression is that these objects, which had been placed there, together with mortuary lamps, were offerings, and that they had been deliberately broken in accordance with ritual. In that case, they must have been intended for the dead man portrayed in the picture and perhaps resting beneath it in the deep crevice of the rock.

The cave at Lascaux was only discovered in the autumn of 1940, but because of the variety, realism, and remarkable preservation of its murals, it suddenly rose to the forefront of ice-age cave art. It consists of several chambers, some nineteen feet below ground; the entrance has now been widened to permit easier access. The first chamber is oval in form, nearly 100 feet long and 33 feet wide, its shimmering crystal-encrusted walls covered with magnificent pictures of ice-age animals. In their colorfulness—a variety of reds, yellows, browns, black—these pictures are unique. A short passage leads from the first chamber into a second, smaller one, whose walls are again covered with an altogether bewildering mass of drawings of animals, many of them superimposed on earlier ones. Near the rear wall, a well-like shaft leads from an opening in the cave floor into the lower chambers, which have not yet been fully explored. The sheer descent is made by means of a rope ladder. And it is here that we find the curious portrayal of the "hunting tragedy" (plate VIIIb).

A wounded bison is shown with extraordinary realism, conveying a sense of its elemental strength. Its entrails gush from its torn belly, its tail lashes the air. Its head is turned as though to look at the injury, and the terrible horns are directed toward the dead hunter stretched out on the ground. The hunter's spear, with its great barbed hook, is shown leaning against the wound, while a similar instrument, possibly a spear thrower, is lying on the ground. On the left-hand side of the picture a rhinoceros lumbers heavily away. Breuil suggests that this rhinoceros is a part of the scene—that it was, in fact, the author of the bison's goring. And the hunter, according to this theory, was killed in the course of the struggle between the two animals.

The hunter is treated purely schematically; only the outlines of the figure are indicated—so awkwardly that one would think a child had drawn them. And yet this was the work of the same artist who painted the bison and the rhinoceros. Was he simply unable to portray a human figure, or was this spindly, naked creature with the flattened, beaklike head meant to be a caricature? Neither explanation is satisfactory. It is far more likely that the artist was trying to represent the dead man in his "deadness," as a "living corpse." And faced with the problem of translating an abstraction into picture form, his skill failed him. His realistic pictures of animals were the product of his own immediate experience in the hunt, where he could observe all their movements; hence he rarely had recourse to his imaginative faculties. But to depict "deadness," he had to call upon his imagination, which was as yet at a primitive stage of development.

Another curious feature of this group is the bird perched on a pole with a barbed hook at its base, which could be an inverted spear or possibly a spear thrower: such instruments were frequently adorned with sculptured figures of animals. In the present group it represents, perhaps, some kind of standard which might have had significance in burial ceremonies. The bird at the top may represent a bird of death. On the other hand, there is a striking resemblance between the bird and the head of the dead hunter. Possibly, therefore, the bird was the tribal totem and the mythical ancestor of the hunter's tribe, to which all the members of the tribe were assimilated after their death.

It has often been argued that the hunter artists of the ice age were totemists, who believed that men were descended from plants or animals, or bore some kinship to them. The theory is hard to prove, as T. Mainage has shown in his *Religions de la préhistoire* (Paris, 1921). Totemism is, in the first place, a sociological phenomenon, but it also has its religious aspect, expressed in the veneration of the totem and the cult of ancestors. It is quite possible that the ice-age hunters, who decorated some of their weapons and tools with animal figures, particularly animal heads—just as do totemistic hunting tribes in our own day—held beliefs of that kind.

Ancestor worship is suggested by an unusual find made

in a Magdalenian layer at La Roche (Dordogne). Here an oval object was found some 6½ inches long, made of reindeer antler richly decorated with a linear design and perforated at one end, so that a cord could be passed through the hole (fig. 10). The object shows a marked resemblance to the Australian bull-roarer, in whose humming the aborigines believe they hear the voices of their ancestors, or even, in the case of certain tribes, the voice

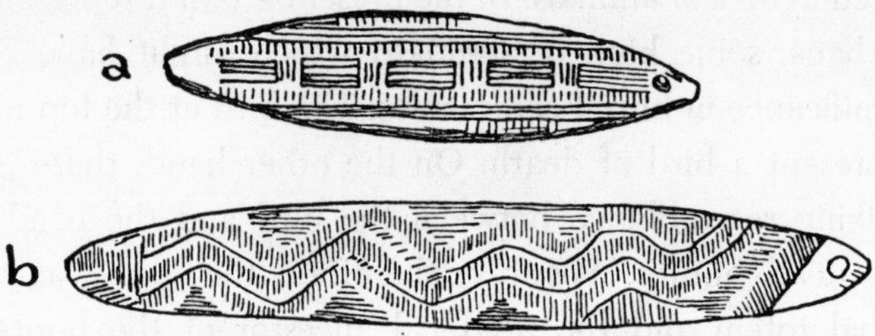

Fig. 10. BULL-ROARERS A. LA ROCHE (DORDOGNE), FRANCE B. AUSTRALIA. SCALE 1:2

of the supreme god. When the object was found, it still showed traces of the thick layer of ocher with which it had been coated. As ocher was used for various ritual purposes, its use here would indicate that the oval-shaped object had had some religious significance, and that the Magdalenian hunters used it at certain religious ceremonies to conjure the voices of their ancestors.

The "tectiform" figures of ice-age art may also be indicative of men's beliefs concerning the dead. At one time Abbé Breuil assumed that these signs represented tents and huts; then he changed his mind and maintained that they represented traps and snares. Recently, however, he reverted to his original interpretation, pointing out that the tectiform signs are almost never of the same age as the pictures of animals above or beneath them and, as a rule, occur in the most remote parts of a cave, often in very narrow niches; therefore, these signs may well have represented the homes of the spirits of the dead, homes in which the living kept them captive, far from their own dwelling places near the cave mouth.

Clearly, the dead played an important part in the lives of upper paleolithic men. Moreover, the variety of beliefs and rites practiced would seem to point to a variety of religious conceptions.

Recently H. Kirchener has offered a different explanation of the "hunting tragedy" of Lascaux. His interpretation is based on various anthropological and prehistoric analogies. He suggests that the scene is of a shamanistic conjuration; the man on the ground is a shaman, wearing a bird mask, who has fallen into a trance before the bison, the animal of sacrifice, while "his soul departs into the beyond"; the bird on the pole is his tutelary spirit. The purpose of the picture, according to this theory, was not simply to place the scene on record, but to perpetuate its efficacy; the purpose of the "séance" itself would have been to ensure success in the hunt. As we shall see, this aim was central to ice-age art. Although Kirchener's interpretation must be approached with caution, it is a fascinating one. There are, in fact, striking analogies between the scene portrayed at Lascaux and the shamanistic practices of modern circumpolar hunting peoples, whose beliefs sometimes cast a good deal of light on the religious or magical beliefs of the upper paleolithic peoples.

III

RITUAL OFFERINGS

THE PRACTICE OF SACRIFICING the head, skull, and long bones of animals survived from earlier times right up to the upper paleolithic. Nor should this occasion surprise us, as the new men, when their own culture began to evolve in the eastern territories where they originated, were at about the same stage of development as the primitive inhabitants of Europe.

Traces of this rite have been found at different places, for instance at the Reyersdorf cave in the mountainous region of Glatz, in Silesia, which early Aurignacian hunters used as a shelter. According to L. F. Zotz, several bear skulls had been discovered there lying on a natural rock bench, while another skull had been found in a crevice of the cave wall, which had been sealed with a stone slab. Unfortunately the excavation had been conducted in an altogether unmethodical fashion, so that L. F. Zotz was unable to check the accuracy of the information. In 1935, however, he himself made a find that confirmed it.

Not far from the presumed sites of the previous finds, Zotz came upon a big limestone slab placed obliquely against the cave wall. On removing it, he found a niche containing the skull of a full-grown female cave bear. Curiously enough, almost the whole of the right parietal bone was missing from the otherwise well-preserved skull.

That the skull had been deliberately placed in its niche by human hands is as little open to doubt as in the case of the finds of Drachenloch and Petershöhle. The circumstances of the finds are similar even to the protective stone coverings. It is impossible, however, to establish whether the gaping hole in the skull was caused by the blow that killed the animal, or whether the hunters made the hole after the animal's death in order to extract the brain. No other bones were associated with the skull.

This find confirms the theory that the men of the upper paleolithic continued to offer sacrifice very much as the Alpine cave-bear hunters of earlier times. The distance between them, both in time and in space, was not, after all, very great. The Silesian bear hunters belonged to the first waves of new arrivals, and may therefore still have come into contact with the earlier cave-bear hunters; it is more likely, however, that they already practiced similar rites, as had their ancestors in Asia.

The excavation of a mammoth-hunters' station on the Desna River, in the Ukraine, also suggests the survival of the old hunting rites. Here, in 1935, K. Polikarpovich discovered thirty mammoth skulls, together with ten tusks, arranged in a circle between the remains of two earth dwellings dating back to the ice age. That this was a ritual site is borne out by additional finds: an ivory statuette of a woman, and ten ivory laminae—oval in shape, between six and ten inches long, and decorated with geometrical incisions—which recall the "bull-roarer" of La Roche. The hunters of this station seem to have practiced a religion in which the very ancient animal-skull sacrifice coexisted with various later cults of the upper paleolithic.

Certain finds in France show that in western Europe, too, the new hunters retained the old cult, albeit with modifications. In 1924 A. Lemozi, in a remote part of the Pech-Merle cave near Cabrerets (Lot)—the animal bones strewn about on the floor caused him to call this part the "ossuary"—came upon what was unmistakably a man-made pit that contained four lower jaws of bears, some ribs, and some long bones, all well preserved. Some distance away, but still in the same chamber, Lemozi uncovered the skulls of these beasts lying under small earth mounds that might once have been clay figures of bears. These skulls were also well preserved, and showed no trace of damage; evidently the brain had not been extracted. The Pech-Merle finds, then, offer striking analogies to those in the Alpine caves, and, like the latter, are highly suggestive of sacrificial practices.

In Magdalenian deposits in the Raymondon cave near Chancelade (Dordogne) a bone pendant was found engraved with what appears to be a scene of ritual sacrifice (fig. 11). The head of a bison is depicted, still attached to the spine; before it lie two severed legs of the animal. On either side of the spine are human figures, schematically represented, four above and three below. One of the latter carries what appears to be a palm branch. Near this figure are objects reminiscent of bows. To regard this scene as depicting some magic rite connected with trapping, or the ritual interment of an animal, is altogether farfetched. The men facing each other from either side of the animal's spine are obviously "faithful" present at the ceremony. Moreover, the whole composition is strikingly reminiscent of the sacrificial procedure observed by the Samoyedes.

But the Raymondon pendant must have been more than merely the graphic record of a sacrificial ritual; the

Fig. 11. PENDANT FOUND AT RAYMONDON, CHANCELADE (DORDOGNE), FRANCE

hunter who wore it presumably regarded it as a charm filled with magic powers that would bring him good fortune in the hunt.

THE HUNTING rituals of the upper paleolithic were no more uniform than those of more remote prehistoric times. Among the many proofs of this diversity is a series of finds made at the Aurignacian settlement of Malta, in the Irkutsk province of Siberia.

In 1932 five reindeer skeletons were discovered on the southeastern edge of the settlement, two of them lying together, the other three separately. The bones had been arranged in anatomical order and were undamaged, but in each case the hind part of the animal was missing. In each case, too, the antlers had been removed; apparently the animals had been skinned before interment. Extensive search on the site failed to reveal the missing parts.

On the opposite, northwestern edge of the settlement, in a layer of ice-age limestone covered by a sterile culture layer of dark earth, the investigators found fourteen holes, oval and steep-sided, from 6 to 32 inches long and 2 to 7 inches deep. The holes had not been dug in any particular order. One was empty, four contained skeletons of arctic foxes with only the pads missing; the remaining holes contained either remains of a single animal, such as a mammoth foot, or of several animals—including the almost complete skeleton of an arctic fox—some rhinoceros ribs, a mammoth patella, three thoracic vertebrae, and a part of one of the front hooves of a reindeer. The holes also contained a few flint tools.

These bones could hardly be considered as kitchen refuse, or remains of meat supplies deposited in pits. But what was the purpose of carefully depositing worthless animal remains in pits deliberately dug? The present-day Siberian Yakuts wrap the foxes or wolves they have skinned in grass or hay—to replace the fur—and then set them high up in trees or bury them in the ground. They believe that this procedure will make the animals' fur grow back again, so that the following year they can get more skins. The ice-age hunters of Malta may well have believed in some magical reincarnation of this kind.

But the other finds require a different explanation.

Flint tools, for example, would have had no place in an animal burial. Furthermore, the animals whose remains have been found were a valuable source of food for the ice-age hunters. It may therefore be assumed that the hunters sometimes gave up a part of their kill, carefully concealing it in the earth to preserve it from theft or profanation. Their purpose was undoubtedly to make sacrifice to various spirits of the hunt, most probably the spirit of the earth. This sacrifice even included the offering of tools. And underlying all these offerings there must always have been one principal motive: to insure luck in the chase.

The magnificent discoveries made by Alfred Rust in 1934 and 1935 in northern Germany—at Meiendorf and Stellmoor, near Hamburg—are still more illuminating as to the diversity of prehistoric hunting rites.

Both sites had been used as hunting stations by reindeer hunters of the late Magdalenian; they were located on sandy ridges some half-mile apart. At about the present center of the valley, an old subglacial melt-water trough, Rust discovered the shore lines of two silted-up lakes or ponds. And on the site of these ponds Rust came upon a surprisingly rich legacy of the ancient hunters, including the remains of ritual offerings which have since become famous. (Stellmoor is slightly less ancient than Meiendorf; it also revealed a mesolithic layer containing no less significant deposits, which I shall discuss later.)

The diggings proved that at the height of the last ice age and during the subsequent thaw, groups of hunters penetrated the north-German lowlands, which provided little enough protection against the cold, and pursued their game right up to the borders of the inland ice cap. An abundant fauna, and especially huge herds of reindeer, were to be found in summer in the tundra belt bordering the ice fields. They would have migrated there, just like the animals in northern Asia and in the more northerly parts of North America today, to escape the insect pests that attacked them at the approach of the warm season. And the men who hunted them would likewise abandon their sheltered winter quarters in regions far from the ice cap, and move northward, following their food supply. Then, after a short summer, the autumn blizzards would begin to howl over the subarctic zone, and man and beast alike would retreat south to less inclement regions. The condition of certain bones found at Meiendorf and Stellmoor, especially the stage of growth of the reindeer antlers, makes it evident that these two settlements were inhabited only during the arctic summer.

The first remains of a ritual offering were uncovered at Meiendorf in 1934, shortly before the close of that year's diggings. Previously, Rust had found only fragments of bones; now he found the complete skeleton of a reindeer. Moreover, he found a block of gneiss weighing about eighteen pounds in the thoracic cavity of the animal (fig. 12). The marrow bones had not been split; the skull, with the antlers still attached, was intact. The skeleton was of a two-year-old doe. From the stratum in which it was resting, from its unimpaired condition, and from the presence of a heavy stone in its thoracic cavity, we may safely conclude that the animal had been submerged in the ancient lake.

The following year Rust made two finds at Stellmoor which were the exact counterpart of the one at Meiendorf. He dug up two skeletons of two-year-old does which had been submerged with stones in the thoracic or abdominal cavities. The shoulder blade of one had been pierced by a shot; it must therefore have been killed in the hunt.

The frequency with which these finds occur and the

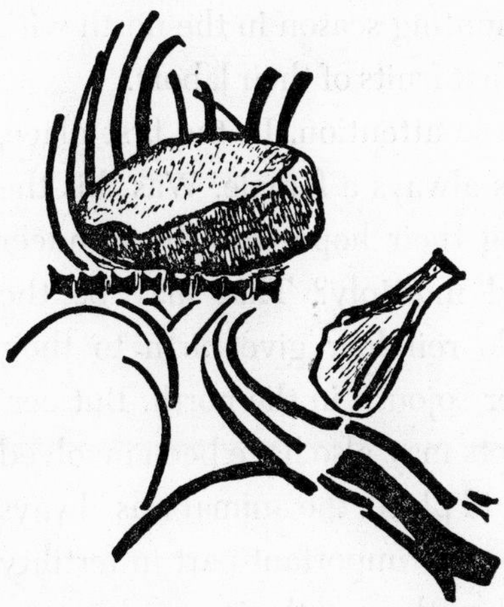

Fig. 12. ANIMAL OF SACRIFICE, WITH A HEAVY STONE IN THE THORACIC CAVITY, AT MEIENDORF, NORTHERN GERMANY

particular circumstances in which they occur leave no room for doubt that these skeletons are relics of hunting sacrifices. From the data we possess we can establish, in a general way, the manner in which such sacrifices were conducted. As soon as the hunters had killed a suitable beast—namely, a two-year-old doe—they would take it to their settlement. There a hunter, or perhaps a shaman, would slit open its chest or abdomen with a flint knife and place one or more stones in the cavity, after which he would probably sew up the incision with sinew. Then, amid ceremonies that must necessarily remain unknown to us, the hunters would submerge the animal in the lake. We can even tell at what time of the year these offerings were made. The state of the antlers of the three reindeer Rust found proves that the animals had been slain sometime in May or June—the season at which the hunters must have moved into their summer quarters at Stellmoor and Meiendorf. And this in turn would indicate that they inaugurated the summer hunting season in the north with the solemn sacrifice of the first fruits of their labors.

Two more points deserve attention. In the first place, the animal of sacrifice was always a female. Was this the hunters' way of expressing their hope that the reindeer herds would increase and multiply? That may be the explanation, as the female reindeer give birth to their young during their summer sojourn in the north. But certain special magical concepts may also have been involved in this practice. In the second place, the animal was always submerged. Water plays a very important part in fertility rites of more recent times than those of the ice-age hunters. Could it be that for these, too, water already had some special significance? At any rate, they would, by submerging the offering, protect it from possible profanation. But it may also be that those prehistoric hunters conceived of the deity to whom they directed their sacrifice as residing underground, and that they plunged their offerings into the lake so that those offerings might reach their god.

Traces of the north-German reindeer hunters have been found in Holland, in Belgium, and even in England. It is very possible that the excavation of marsh lands in those countries will provide further evidence of this sacrificial ritual. But the ice-age hunters may also, at times, have buried rather than submerged the animals they were sacrificing; and they may have had still other forms of sacrifice, of which we have no knowledge as yet.

Whatever the form of the sacrifice—and there was certainly great diversity in the rites practiced by the ice-age hunters—the underlying intention was always the same: to insure luck in the chase and an increase in the game population. Many tribes still believed in a divine dispenser of hunting luck, although the name and character of this divinity may have changed considerably since the earlier, lower paleolithic times. But the ancient religious beliefs must now have been associated with new ritual forms, by which they were gradually superseded.

IV

THE BEAR CULT

As I mentioned earlier, A. J. Hallowell placed the origins of the bear cult, which is still practiced in our own times by many primitive circumpolar hunting peoples, in the lower paleolithic. It would appear, in any event, that this cult was practiced in upper paleolithic times, as evidenced by the curious finds made by L. F. Zotz in 1936 in the Hellmichhöhle.

The Hellmichhöhle is situated seventy-six feet below the summit of the Kitzelberg, which has an altitude of 2,026 feet and belongs to the Bober-Katzbach range in Silesia. In an undisturbed bed of loam near the mouth of the cave, Zotz came upon the fossilized skull of a brown bear and some cave-bear bones. The ice-age date of this find is proved by the presence of a fragment of flint and a splinter of quartzite in the earth filling inside the skull; these were ascertainably related to the stone tools found in the early Aurignacian culture layer of the cave.

Though the bear's molars showed only slight abrasions, their cusps being still perfect, the canines and incisors were worn to the pulp. In the bear's lifetime, however, the exposed areas had been partially covered by the formation of new dentine. Now we know that bears and other predators do not wear down their incisors or great canines. In some cases teeth have been pathologically impaired, and cave-bear canines have been found partially blunted by degeneration. But the evenly spaced grooves in the tooth stumps of the Hellmich brown bear point to something quite different—a deliberate filing down of the teeth. And the incomplete regrowth of dentine leads us to believe that the interval between the filing and the animal's death cannot have been long.

No doubt ice-age men undertook this dental operation. But to what end? At first glance it would seem that it was for sport, so that they could put their hands into the beast's mouth without danger of being bitten. Or the Hellmich find might prove no more than that some men had played with a captive bear. On the other hand, ethnological research provides astonishing parallels with the case we have just described.

Zotz himself pointed out the analogy with the bear cult, particularly with the bear-slaying rites, of certain modern hunting tribes of northern Asia. But it was an ethnologist, Wilhelm Koppers, who pointed to the exact explanation, based on old descriptions of the bear cult published by Siebold in 1835 and Von Schrenk in 1881. According to these authorities, the Gilyaks on Sakhalin and the Ainus on Yeso (Hokkaido) practiced a ritual whose high point was the "bear feast," at which a bear was slain with much pageantry and elaborate ceremonial. The bear was a two- or three-year-old animal that had been captured young; and so that it would be prevented from attacking or injuring anyone at the feast, its incisors and canines were cut down by means of a sawlike instrument.

The bear whose remains were found in the Hellmichhöhle had also been a young animal, as may be seen from the slight abrasion of the molars; its incisors and canines had been filed down; and, finally, the paleolithic hunters had been at about the same stage of advancement as the Gilyaks and Ainus of our own times. Koppers concludes:

> Such singular cultural phenomena do not occur independently. In any case, the investigator who thinks and works in the context of history must necessarily favor the theory of a connection between them. A practice which existed in central Europe in the upper paleolithic survives to this day among the border peoples of northern Asia.

It is therefore possible, too, that the ice-age hunters, or at least some of them, like those at Hellmich, held beliefs similar to those that underlie the bear cult as practiced by modern primitives. The Gilyaks and the Ainus regard the captive bear as the guardian spirit of their settlement; it brings luck, and after it has been killed at the great winter feast, it becomes their ambassador to the mighty spirit of forest and mountain, presenting their wishes and especially obtaining for them a good hunting year.

The hunting artists of the upper paleolithic sometimes painted or engraved pictures of the bear on cave walls. Such pictures are rare, however, and certain peculiarities are associated with them. The bear is sometimes shown with a wolf's head or a bison's tail (fig. 13), as though the artists had feared to portray it as it really was. They may also have intended to portray men disguised as bears, and in some cases the intention is unmistakable. Sometimes they drew only the head of a bear. Such works would seem to suggest a bear cult. On that hypothesis, the ice-age

Fig. 13. BEARS WITH WOLF'S HEAD AND BISON'S TAIL. THE TROIS FRÈRES CAVE (ARIÈGE), FRANCE

hunter artists would have avoided any naturalistic portrayal of the bear because, like the bear-hunting peoples of our own day, they feared to call it by its own name; moreover, they would have dressed up in bear skins to perform ritual dances, and they would have had a special veneration for the bear's head or conducted special ceremonies in its honor.

Other art works, like those found in the Trois Frères cave, are still more strongly suggestive of a bear cult (fig. 14). Here the artist may have been portraying actual slaying scenes at bear feasts. Among the Gilyaks, for instance, it is customary to tie up the bear and then to bait and goad it into a fury, after which a selected marksman kills it with an arrow. According to Von Schrenk, boys riddle the beast with arrows so that it bleeds profusely, and only then is it given the *coup de grace*. If we compare this description with the paleolithic engraving of a bear with blood pouring from its nose while arrows and stones rain upon its body (fig. 14), we may well assume the engraving to be a ritual bear-slaying scene.

It is possible, however, to place a different construction upon pictures of this kind. As they occur in caves filled with pictures indicative of practices of sympathetic magic, they may represent nothing more than the "slaying" of a bear by magic before the men set out on their hunting foray.

At the same time, there is enough evidence in paleolithic art to suggest at least the possibility that the hunter artists of southern France revered in the bear a kind of higher being, and even observed a bear ritual that included the slaying of the beast.

In any event, it is fairly certain that the bear cult was already practiced in the last ice age. And from this we may infer that the religion of the new peoples of Europe was no longer marked by the simplicity that appears to have characterized the religion of the peoples of the lower paleolithic. The validity of this inference will become still more apparent when we come to consider the importance of magic in the lives of the upper paleolithic hunting people.

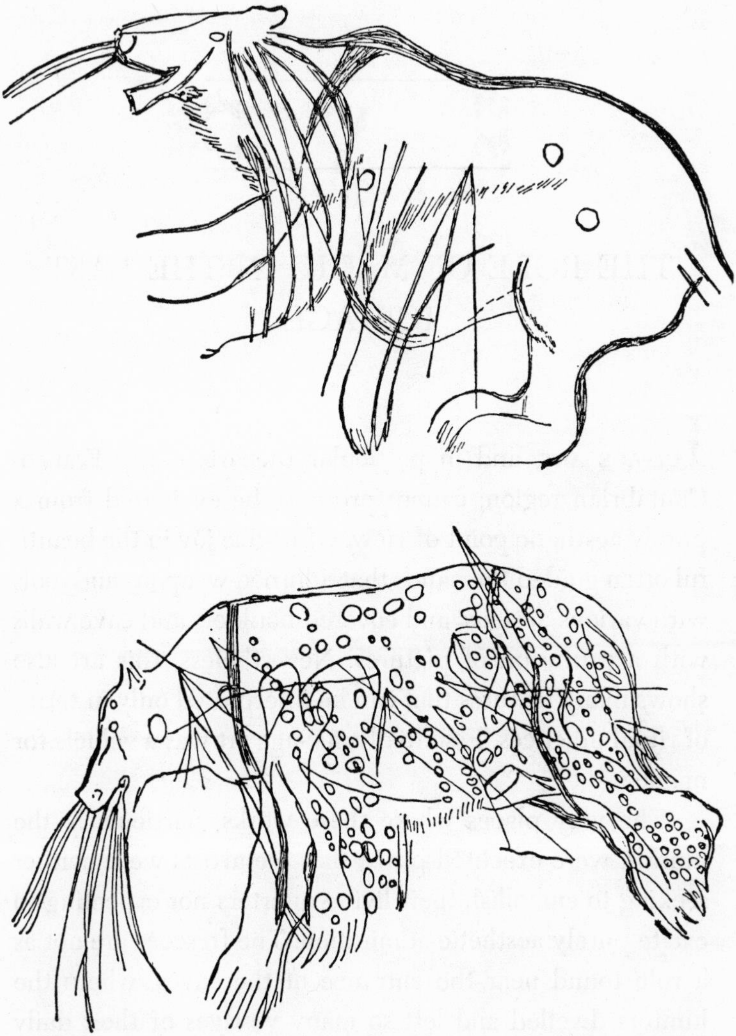

Fig. 14. BEARS WITH BLOOD POURING FROM THEIR NOSES WHILE ARROWS AND STONES RAIN UPON THEIR BODIES. PALEOLITHIC ENGRAVING. THE TROIS FRÈRES CAVE (ARIÈGE), FRANCE.

V

THE ROLE OF MAGIC IN THE LAST ICE AGE

Ice-age art, and in particular the art of the Franco-Cantabrian region, cannot properly be evaluated from a purely aesthetic point of view. Of course joy in the beautiful often guided the hands that adorned weapons and tools with various designs, and covered boulders and cave walls with a profusion of pictures. Nevertheless, this art also shows many features that can be interpreted only in terms of ritual practices. Essentially, ice-age art was a vehicle for magic.

The very places where these works, particularly the murals, were executed prove that the artists were neither seeking to embellish their living quarters nor expecting to excite purely aesthetic admiration. The frescoes are not as a rule found near the entrance of the caves, where the hunters dwelled and left so many vestiges of their daily lives, but deep in the interior, in niches and dark chambers. In fact, the greatest number of pictures, and the most important ones, are to be found in precisely the most inaccessible passages. In the Font-de-Gaume crevice cave, which is 406 feet from end to end, the first murals occur over 200 feet from the entrance. The huge Niaux cave, formed by the action of water and an ancient subterranean glacier and measuring some 4,500 feet (fig. 15), reveals its treasures only after one has ventured nearly 1,500 feet into the bowels of the earth. To reach the frescoes that adorn the walls of the Trois Frères cave, it is necessary to

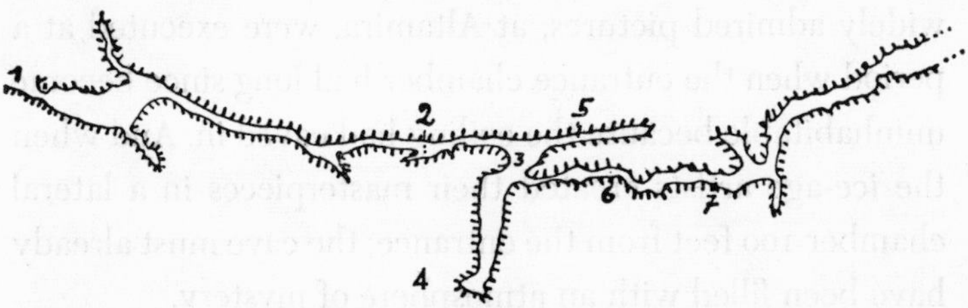

Fig. 15. PLAN OF THE NIAUX CAVE (ARIÈGE), FRANCE. 1. ENTRANCE 2. POINT WHERE FIRST SIGNS APPEAR ON CAVE WALLS 3. PAINTING OF BISON, 1,986 FEET FROM ENTRANCE 4. "SALON NOIR" CONTAINING MANY FRESCOES 5. SITE WHERE ENGRAVINGS OCCUR IN LIMESTONE FLOOR 6. AND 7. FRESCOES

walk for half an hour through a seemingly endless succession of passages and chambers. The Cabrerets cave is a real labyrinth where one has to clamber about for hours in order to find its numerous paintings and engravings.

Moreover, many of these caves were utterly uninhabitable. Take, for instance, Lascaux, the most splendid of the picture caves thus far discovered. It is quite likely that even in ice-age times it could be penetrated only through the narrow 19½-foot shaft that was its natural entrance when it was discovered. Also, the cave was both too cold in winter and too cool in summer to invite habitation; and, as a matter of fact, no traces of human occupancy have been found. It must, therefore, have been first and foremost a sanctuary.

In some caves the occupation layers demonstrably belong to other periods than the pictures. At Marsoulas, for instance, the murals date from the middle and late Magdalenian, whereas the occupation layer at the entrance belongs to the early Magdalenian. The most fabulous and widely admired pictures, at Altamira, were executed at a period when the entrance chamber had long since become uninhabitable because the ceiling had caved in. And when the ice-age artists created their masterpieces in a lateral chamber 100 feet from the entrance, the cave must already have been filled with an atmosphere of mystery.

This atmosphere characterizes practically all the sites of ice-age art. Shrouded in utter darkness, the paintings and drawings of the paleolithic artists were visible to their fellow men only by flickering torchlight or the faint illumination of a tallow lamp, the only means of lighting they possessed. Often these works of art were executed in all but inaccessible spots—on rock projections that could be reached only at great risk to life and limb; or in hidden recesses or very narrow niches. It is simply impossible that this art should have been intended, in these locations, to give pleasure to the eye of the beholder; the intention must always have been to veil it in mysterious secrecy.

Probably only the initiated were given access to the caves, or to those parts, at least, that contained the art works. In most cases the approaches to the inner sanctum

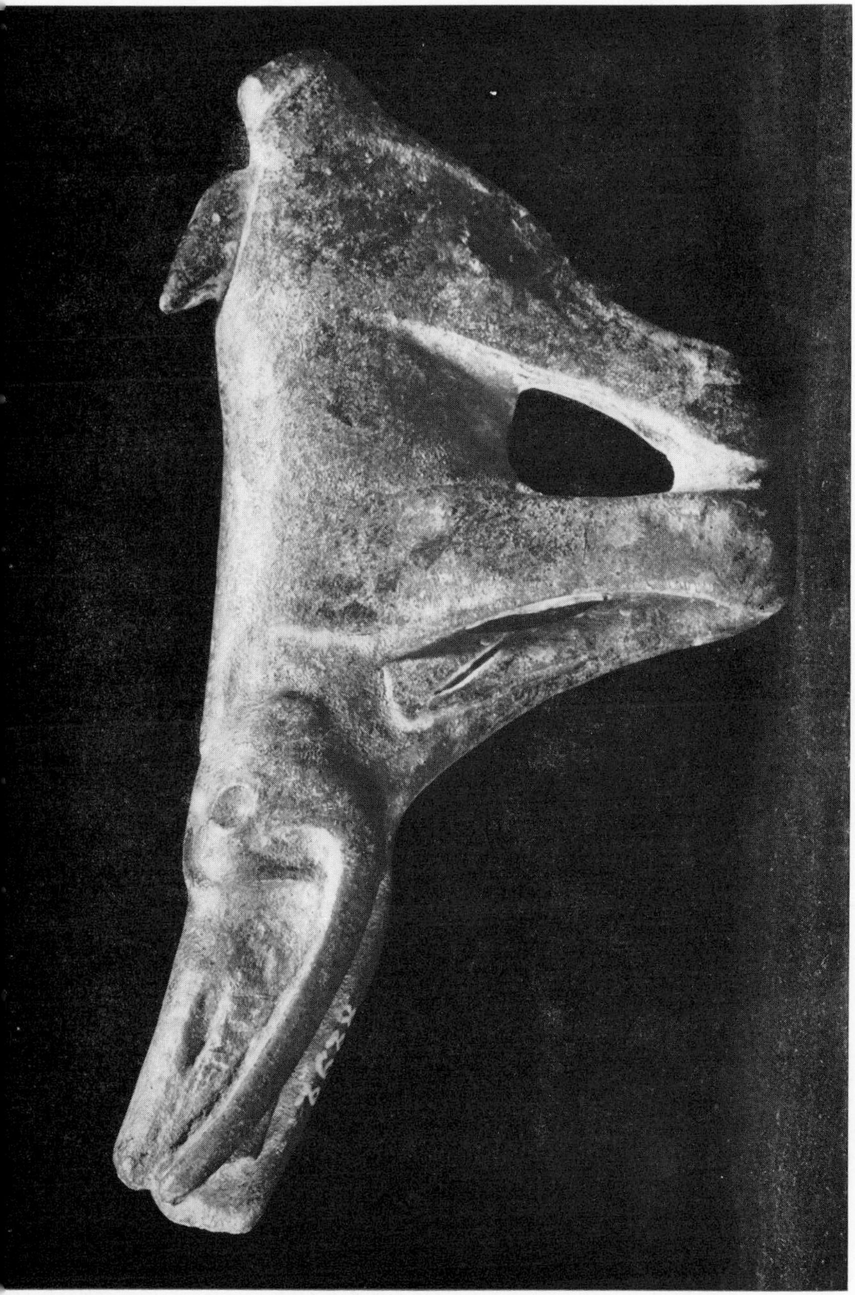

Figure of mammoth carved out of reindeer antler. Bruniquel (Tarn-et-Garonne), France.

PLATE XIII

Reindeer engraved on limestone plaque, Laugerie Basse (Dordogne), France.

PLATE XIV

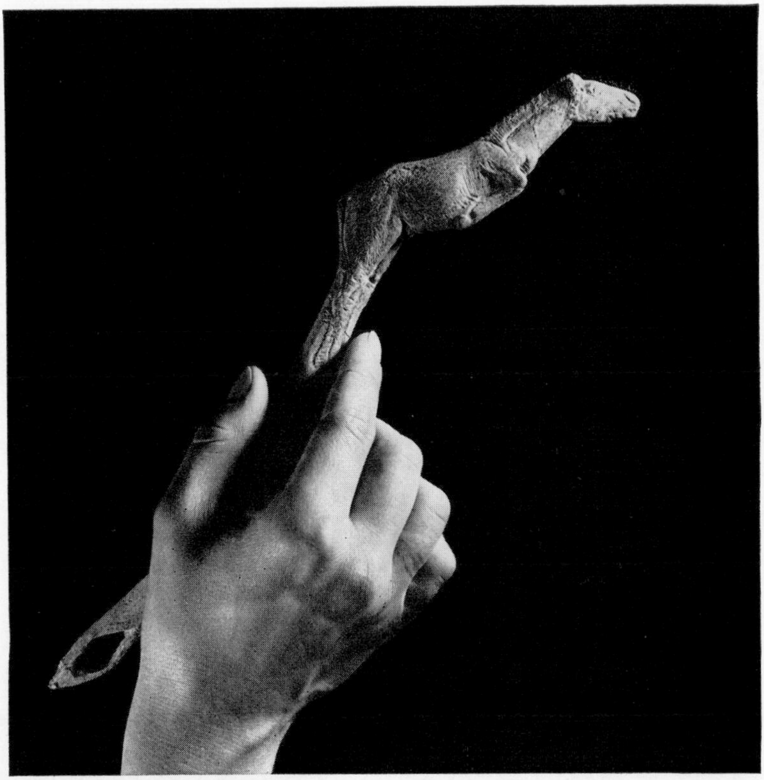

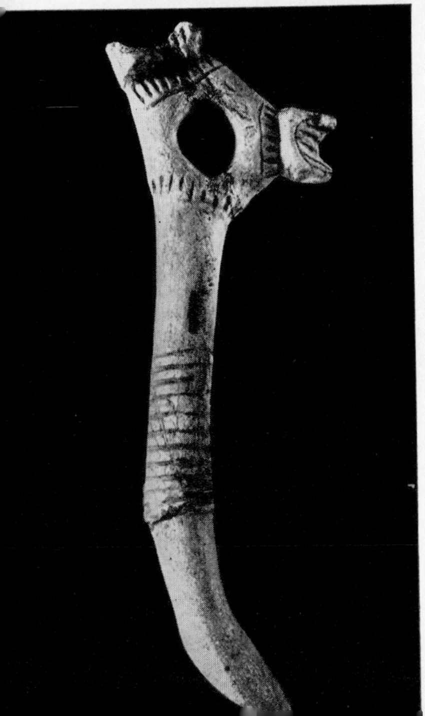

a. Perforated bone stick decorated with sculpture of horse. Bruniquel (Tarn-et-Garonne), France.

b. Perforated stick with decorations. Laugerie Basse (Dordogne), France.

Right footprint, L'Aldène cave (Herault), France.

PLATE XVI

were easy enough to seal off. The shaftlike entrance to Lascaux, for example, could have been covered at the first sign of enemies or profaners. The Pindal cave in northern Spain opens at a completely isolated point in a coastal rock high above the Atlantic. The entrance to the Tuc d'Audoubert cave is protected by a subterranean stream along which one has to travel nearly 200 feet by canoe before touching land. And even if this water barrier should not have existed in the ice age, there would have been the steep 33-foot shaft to scale in order to reach the upper level of the cave, after which it would still have been necessary to traverse a never ending series of tortuous, low-ceilinged passages before reaching the sanctuary with its extraordinary art treasures. Small wonder that the discovery and study of many of these caves constitute thrilling exploits, not without their hazards.

The ice-age artists worked on the limestone floors, on the cave walls (very low down and right up near the ceiling), and even on the ceilings themselves—clearly without the slightest regard for the convenience of the beholder. At Altamira, where some of the murals are as much as 7¼ feet high, the meager space between floor and ceiling often makes it impossible to take in the works in their entirety at a single glance. At Les Combarelles the engravings cover both sides of a passage with an average width of no more than 39 inches. In many of the caves one often has to take an extremely awkward position in order to see the pictures at all.

Another unusual feature of ice-age art is that so many

of the pictures have other pictures superimposed on them. At first sight these appear as an indistinct jumble of lines and splashes of color. Yet this confusion is not the result of mere sketching or clumsy overlapping or correction.

The key to this art and its peculiar placing can be found especially in those pictures where the animals portrayed—always game animals, incidentally—are shown with arrows and marks of wounds (figs. 16 and 17). Sometimes arrows are shown approaching the animal (fig. 18). At Montespan, in southern France, clay figures of bears and lions have been found riddled with holes; the prehistoric hunters must have shot at them, or thrown spears at them, as at real animals (fig. 19). Why had these sculptures been thus perforated, placed, as they were, in a completely secluded cave chamber? What was the purpose of depicting arrows and wounds?

There can be no doubt that upper paleolithic art is evidence of the practice of sympathetic hunting magic. The hunter artists of those days were obviously convinced, just like many primitive hunters of our own times, that the image gives power over the object represented. Hence, by making an image of the prey, pierced and overcome by deadly weapons, they thought to assure a successful hunting of the real animal.

The ice-age hunter thus held in his hands a tremendous force for compelling life or death. Did he also direct this power against his fellow humans? Here we make a surprising discovery—human representations are far fewer than those of animals. And what is more, they appear, by comparison, like the products of mere dabblers, or as grotesque distortions; the naturalness and vitality of the animal pictures are almost completely lacking. The reason is obvious: fear of becoming the victim of witchery. This fear, as we know it even today among primitive people, caused the

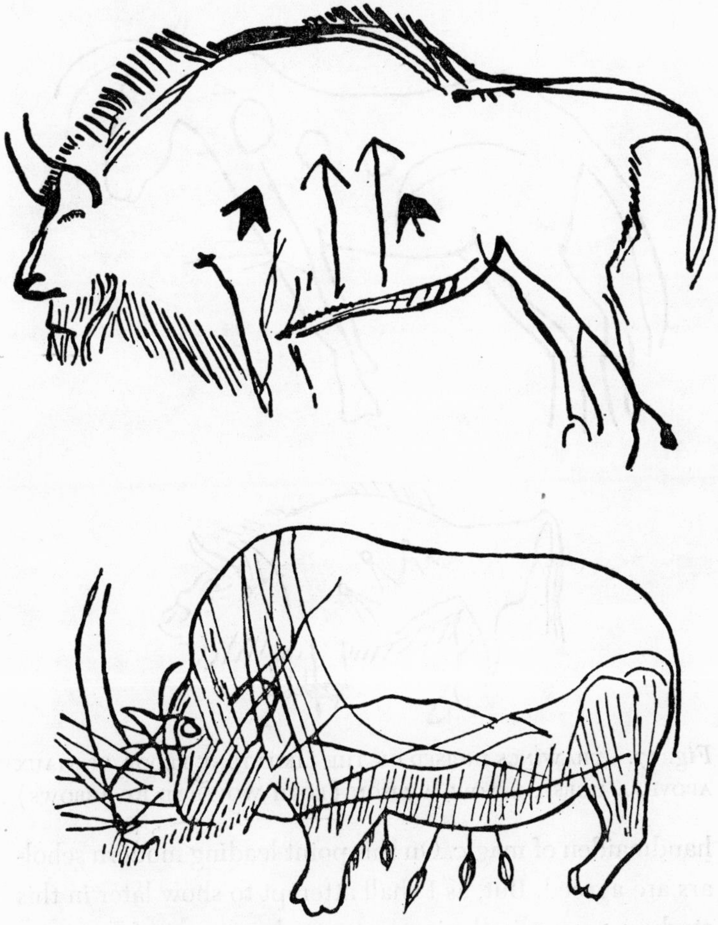

Fig. 16. ANIMALS PIERCED BY ARROWS. A. BISON, AT NIAUX, PAINTED WITH BLACK STROKES, THE ARROWHEADS IN RED B. RHINOCEROS, AT LA COLOMBIÈRE. STONE ENGRAVING.

ice-age hunter to suppress all realistic portraiture of humans. Instead, we find much caricature, disguise, and masquerade.

Ice-age art, then, was largely, though not totally, the

Fig. 17. DRAWINGS INCISED ON THE LIMESTONE FLOOR AT NIAUX ABOVE, A HORSE; BELOW, A BISON (BOTH WOUNDED BY ARROWS)

handmaiden of magic. On this point leading modern scholars are agreed. But, as I shall attempt to show later in this study, art, even in the ice age, was also a means for expression of genuine religious concepts.

First, let us see whether the art of the Eastern, or Eurasian, regions, and the art of the Spanish Levant were also inspired by magic. The evidence there is much less clear than in the case of the Franco-Cantabrian province.

The typical findings in the Eurasian province are the

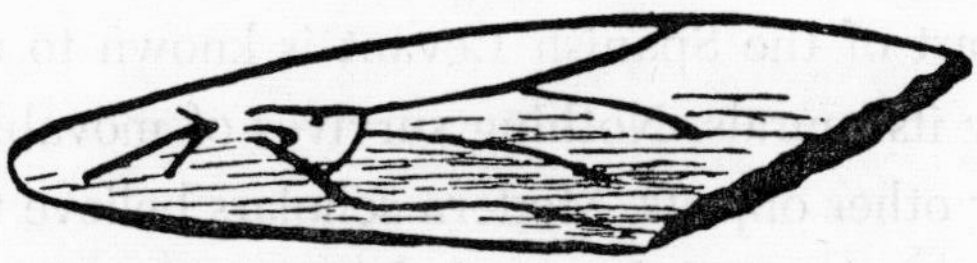

Fig. 18. FISH WITH ARROW APPROACHING IT. ENGRAVING ON A REINDEER ANTLER. FONTARNAUD (GIRONDE), FRANCE.

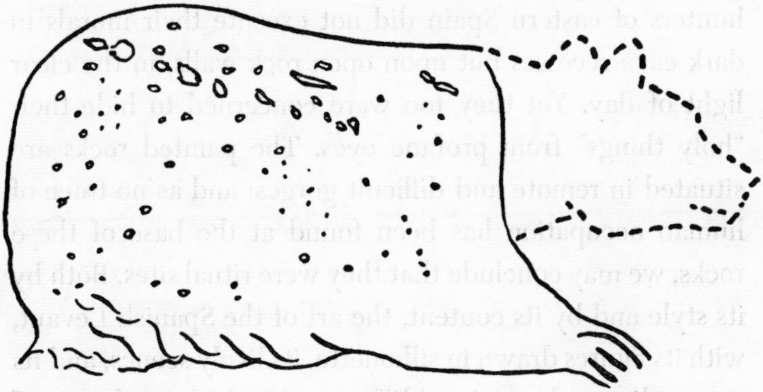

Fig. 19. BEAR, MINUS HEAD, RIDDLED WITH HOLES MADE BY ARROWS OR SPEARS. CLAY SCULPTURE. THE MONTESPAN CAVE (HAUT-GARONNE) FRANCE.

famous "small art" figures, mostly little animal sculptures and statuettes of the human female. It is possible, however, that the Eurasian hunters traced pictures, on the ground, of the animals they wished to bewitch, as there were few caves in their lands. Even in the Franco-Cantabrian province, where caves abounded, this practice existed, as we know from the incised drawings of animals which have been found on the floors of a number of caves. And as the animal sculptures of the Franco-Cantabrian province undoubtedly had a magical significance, we may assume that the same was true of those of the East.

The art of the Spanish Levant is known to us exclusively by its murals. Nothing survives of movable implements or other objects. Modern scholars believe that only the earliest phase of this art belongs to the upper paleolithic, and that its flowering should be placed in the mesolithic. Unlike their Franco-Cantabrian contemporaries, the hunters of eastern Spain did not execute their murals in dark cave recesses but upon open rock walls, in the clear light of day. Yet they too were concerned to hide their "holy things" from profane eyes. The painted rocks are situated in remote and difficult gorges; and as no trace of human occupation has been found at the base of these rocks, we may conclude that they were ritual sites. Both by its style and by its content, the art of the Spanish Levant, with its figures drawn in silhouette, its lively scenes, and its extraordinary dynamism, differs strikingly from the art of the neighboring Franco-Cantabrian province. Yet this art too must have had some religious and magical significance, as we may infer from a number of features besides the artist's obvious preference for certain rock walls despite the existence of no less suitable rocks in the vicinity: the predominance of hunting scenes showing animals pierced by spears or arrows (fig. 7); the strange practice of painting new pictures upon old ones (fig. 20); and the repeated transformation of one kind of animal into another, as, for instance, bulls into deer.

The casting of spells on animals by means of pictures was only one form of ice-age magic; many ice-age pictures reveal that early man also used mimicry and dancing for these ends. We do not know at what point art became the vehicle of magic, but it must have been quite early. In any event, art exercised a decisive influence on the devel-

Fig. 20. FIGURE OF A MAN, IN RED, OVERPAINTED WITH FIGURE OF AN IBEX, IN DARK BROWN. EL QUESO CAVE, ALPERA, SPAIN.

opment of magic beliefs among the ice-age hunters; indeed, the question arises of whether it was not substantially instrumental in the emergence of those beliefs. Studies in comparative ethnology on the origin and development of magic show that magic plays a very small part in the most primitive societies, while the belief in a supreme being is well-nigh universal. This deity is expected to provide hunting luck and, in general, everything man needs for his support; at a later stage, as we have already seen, this supreme being takes on a more specialized form and becomes the "dispenser of hunting luck." And purely primitive man expresses his dependence upon the highest being by means of prayer, sacrifice, and especially the offering of first fruits. Only among the more advanced hunters and early tillers of the soil do we find the belief in a supreme god decaying and changing, to be replaced by a steadily growing belief in magic. The hunters practice an "active magic," while the husbandmen of matriarchies practice a magic of portents. Magic achieves its maximum development with the merging of these two types of culture.

Two factors, according to Wilhelm Schmidt, stimulate magical beliefs among the more advanced hunters: first, an increasing self-confidence resulting from certain technical achievements, such as the improvement of weapons and hunting methods, with a corresponding sense of mastery over the outer world and a weakening in the belief in the efficacy of a divine being; secondly, the development of a tribal structure, in which the individual and the family are subordinated to the community, with its crippling effect on individual judgment, sentiment, and action.

These two factors were also operative in the cultures of the last ice age. Earlier cultures and social organizations, so far as one can trace them, presented a much simpler picture. As we have seen, the most primitive hunters, and in any case the cave-bear hunters, practiced a kind of offering of the first fruits. This practice, anthropology reveals, is always associated, both psychologically and historically, with a belief in a highest being who is also, pre-eminently, the dispenser of hunting luck. It is possible that some form of magic was also familiar to the hunters of the lower paleolithic, but it was not until much later, in the changed environment of upper paleolithic times, that magic became a real force in the thought and life of the new inhabitants of Europe. The emergence of art must have played a considerable part in strengthening the hunters' belief in mysterious forces; art for them was in the first place a means of exercising occult powers. These powers would have been exercised by the "grand masters"—in effect, tribal sorcerers who directed the ceremonies that took place on the sites where they painted, engraved, or chiseled their works. There is much to suggest that these ceremonies were organized tribal affairs, and we may regard most of the caves, or their decorated parts, as tribal sanctuaries.

According to figures worked out by Herbert Kühn in 1952, seventy-one decorated caves had been discovered in France, most of them in the Dordogne, Ariège, and Lot departments, and thirty-four in Spain, especially in northern Spain. In eastern Spain, or what is known as the Spanish Levant, twenty-nine rock shelters had been found with painted rocks—in some cases as many as 500 or more under a single rock shelter. Since 1952, however, new paleolithic art works have been discovered, and further finds may be expected in the future.

The Altamira cave, in northern Spain, was the first decorated cave to be discovered. Its paintings were long regarded as the finest examples of ice-age art. Only with the discovery of Lascaux in 1940 did a comparable, if not even more splendid, treasure come to light.

Altamira lies in the heart of hilly country some twenty miles west of Santander, near the little town of Santillana del Mar. This region, a veritable animal paradise in the last ice age, of course attracted human hunters; many traces of such men have been found there.

One day, in 1868, Marcelino de Sautuola, a gentleman of Santillana, was hunting in the area when his dog suddenly disappeared in a rock crevice. While trying to free the dog, he came upon the blocked-up mouth of a cave. Seven years later Sautuola began excavations there, and uncovered incontrovertible evidence that men had occupied the cave in the ice age. But it was not till 1879 that he discovered the ice-age paintings on the walls and ceilings of the cave. He had taken his little daughter with him to the site, and together they had penetrated into the interior chambers. Suddenly the child called out excitedly and pointed to a place over her head where the flickering lamp light had revealed the picture of an animal. Sautuola proceeded to examine the walls and ceilings of the cave and found a great number of paintings and engravings, most of them in a small chamber (about eighty-eight feet from the cave mouth) and at the end of the cave, which is nearly 1,000 feet long.

Since the far-off times when the ceiling of the entrance chamber collapsed, rendering the cave virtually inaccessible, no man had set foot in it until its excavation toward the end of the last century. We find evidence of human occupation of the cave as early as the Aurignacian, as well as in the Solutrean, and a part of the Magdalenian. At all these periods the ice-age hunters traced their mysterious signs and symbols in niches and dark recesses, especially along the narrow terminal passage, where they depicted the animals they hunted—bison, wild horse, stag, boar, ibex, and wild ox.

But recurring collapses of the cave roof finally made the entrance chamber uninhabitable; occupation layers come to an abrupt halt in the middle Magdalenian. Yet, remarkably enough, it was during the upper Magdalenian that the low ceiling of the small chamber, close to the entrance, was covered with a multitude of the most extraordinary paintings. The cave must already have been abandoned long before.

This "picture gallery" was the principal sanctuary of the cave. It is 57 feet long and 24 to 30 feet wide; the ceiling at the entrance is 6 feet 6 inches high, but slopes gradually to under 4 feet at the farther end. Both the walls and this very low ceiling are covered with superb polychrome paintings and engravings. Because the ceiling was so low, the paleolithic artists could easily reach it. But that was not the main reason why they painted their pictures on it. The surface of the ceiling is uneven, and marked by a number of projections. One requirement for the effectiveness of sympathetic magic was that the image should be realistically close to nature. By the skillful use of these projections, the stone-age magician or shaman was able to produce three-dimensional representations of animal forms which are thus extraordinarily true to life. We find pictures of powerful bison, either at rest, their heads lowered, their legs pressed tightly to their bellies, or galloping as they must have done in the open. We also find boars, wild cattle, and, in one place, a wild horse superimposed on a doe. Thus the ceiling alone, with its horde of animals painted in blacks, browns, reds, and yellowish white, reveals a unique animal world. However, the predominance of bison in the pictures shows that the Magdalenians of Altamira were chiefly bison hunters; great herds of those powerful beasts evidently ranged through the neighboring countryside.

Like the Altamira cave, the more recently discovered Lascaux cave must also have been a tribal sanctuary; no traces of occupation have been found. It contains hundreds of paintings and engravings, often superimposed. Again, we find representations of the animals hunted by the men of those times, especially bulls, wild horses, deer, and bison, either singly or in groups. A striking feature of the Lascaux paintings is their size: one bull, for instance, is 18 feet long. Many of the animals have missiles drawn on their bodies, or latticed patterns; there are also many pictures of gravid female beasts.

As one enters the first chamber, one perceives on the left wall an extraordinary beast that seems to lead the splendid animal procession. It is about 10 feet long, outlined in heavy black strokes, and certainly never existed in nature. A mythical beast, it combines various animal and human characteristics. The tail recalls a deer, the forequarters a wild bull, the hump a bison; the head is somewhat human, and the two straight horns belong to the realm of fantasy. The massive forelegs suggest the elephant or mammoth, while the hind legs could be equine. The mysterious beast is at an advanced stage of pregnancy, and its body is marked with patches outlined in black which look like great gaping wounds. I shall attempt later to determine the significance of this polymorphic figure.

The Niaux cave enjoys a commanding position in the heart of a region virtually swarming with caves once inhabited by ice-age men; it appears for that reason alone to have been a central ritual place. Though there are many traces of art and magic in other caves in the area, Niaux has them in such abundance as to prove that this must have been a tribal sanctuary. This underground site is immense (fig. 15), as one would expect from so important a center. Its entrance is well concealed. The way leads up over a pebble-strewn slope, but the opening that first meets the eye is only a small rock shelter. The real cave mouth is hard by, a fissure in the rock well hidden by a heap of boulders. A high and narrow passage leads into an enormous chamber. The soft limestone of the floor absorbs all sound of footsteps like a thick carpet, and the lamp's arc of light illuminates only a small space.

After walking some 1,500 feet through narrow passages and high-roofed chambers filled with magnificent stalactite formations, we come upon the first traces of ice-age art, in the shape of enigmatic symbols on the walls. Then, about 2,000 feet from the entrance, the picture of a bison catches the eye. We have reached a huge chamber from which a number of galleries branch off. Here it was that the prehistoric artist magicians created their works. In one of these lateral galleries we find animal figures incised in the limestone floor. But the sanctuary proper lies at the very end of a tremendous gallery to the right of the preceding one. An enormous rotunda, some 165 feet high, is covered with animal forms executed at eye level—bison, their humps covered with thick fleece, their heads buried in their matted beards; shaggy horses, their necks outstretched and nostrils flared as though to test the cold air of the steppes; ibex; deer—all superimposed upon one another, overlapping, their flanks often pierced by arrows or marked with red flecks, like so many bloody gashes.

I remarked earlier that the exploration of some of these underground ritual sites often involved considerable danger. The point is well illustrated by Norbert Casteret, who penetrated into the Pyrenean cave of Montespan (Haute-Garonne) in 1922–3.

The entrance to the cave is a rock fissure out of which flows a subterranean stream. It was just wide enough for Casteret to squeeze through. Inside, he found himself in a passage varying between 10 and 13 feet in width, and between 6 feet 6 inches and 10 feet in height. For about 195 feet he was able to wade through the stream; then the water deepened and the roof gradually dropped till it touched the surface of the water. This seemed to write *finis* to his reconnaissance. But Casteret felt certain that here was a water tunnel beyond which the chambers continued, and he resolved to go on. This is how he describes his bold venture:

> I placed my candle on a rock ledge, filled my lungs with air for a two-minute immersion, and dived under, one hand stretched out in front, the other feeling the roof overhead. I felt very carefully for the projections and contours of the vaulting, for I was blind and my fingers served as eyes. I had not only to advance but also to consider the return. As I was feeling my way forward, my head suddenly emerged and I was able to breathe.
>
> Where was I? I had no idea, as it was pitch black around me. Obviously I had squeezed my way through a water siphon. I immediately turned round and dived in the opposite direction, for nothing is more dangerous, in such circumstances, than to lose one's direction. Upon reaching the mouth of the siphon again, where the light of my candle was reflected in the dark water just as before, I gazed with delight at the hitherto unconquered vaulting which had just surrendered its secret to me.

The following day Casteret returned to the cave, this time equipped with candles and matches in a rubber container. Again he plunged into the stream at the mouth of the siphon and emerged at the farther end. There he lit a candle and was able to make out the flat, low ceiling stretching on before him. Cautiously he pushed on some 325 feet in the water, taking advantage of the slightest hollows in the vaulting to replenish his lungs with air, till suddenly he found himself standing at the entrance to a spacious cavern. He crossed it and entered a passage that led to yet another water siphon. Again he dived, emerged, and continued his arduous progress along a very narrow tunnel. This tunnel opened upon a still larger cavern, whose floor was covered with enormous rocks that had fallen from the vaulting. At the other end of this cavern Casteret discovered a water-logged passage along which he proceeded to wade for several hours. Then he saw a faint glimmer of daylight and soon found himself at a narrow crevice through which a meadow stream flowed into the mountain. He had traversed the mountain from end to end.

Not until the following year did further exploration of the Montespan cave yield exceptionally interesting prehistoric finds. A few yards away from the second siphon Casteret discovered a lateral passage that was not flooded; at its mouth it measured 16 feet 5 inches across and 13 feet high. It led 650 feet into the interior of the mountain; the final 100-odd feet could be traversed only on hands and knees. At one spot, where the ceiling was high enough to permit him to stand, Casteret came upon the first trace of prehistoric man: a flint implement. Thereupon he proceeded to examine the floor and walls by candlelight for other traces of prehistoric men. And sure enough, he found upon the walls, deeply incised with flint burins, sketches of the mammoth, wild horse, bison, deer, ibex, chamois, hyena, and other animals. In many cases the animal's body was marked with wounds, arrows, or unknown symbols; the outlines of a spread-out left hand were imprinted on a horse's neck.

But these animal figures were far from exhausting the

surprises in store for the explorer. At a turn of the passage, Casteret tripped over some piled-up clods of earth. His first reaction was to continue. Then he took a closer look, and found to his amazement that these clods were really broken-off pieces of three sculptures standing one behind the other against the cave wall. The first, about 67 inches long and 27½ inches high, represented a big feline, which seemed to be making its way toward the exit. This figure was vigorously modeled in very high relief, but the soft clay had partly broken away, and many of the fragments lying on the floor revealed individual portions of the animal's body. One detail—the tuft of hair at the end of the tail—unquestionably showed that the animal was a lion. The other two statues also represented lions, and the whole group faced in the same direction.

A few steps farther on, the passage broadened into a small, low chamber, which turned out to be the most fascinating place in the whole cave. Within a radius of about 33 feet Casteret found a number of clay sculptures on the cave floor; the principal one was the bear pierced by arrows, to which I referred before (fig. 19). The beast was reclining in the position of the Great Sphinx at Giseh; it was 43 inches long and 24 inches high. Like the lions, it faced the exit, but instead of being supported by the wall, it stood some three feet away from the wall on its own little base.

It was a massive work: the very strong hindquarters were well rounded, the hind legs were drawn up under the belly, the right forepaw was extended, the five digits were clearly marked, and the withers prominent, a special characteristic of the bear. The sculpture lacked a head and apparently had never had one, for the surface of the neck section was just as weathered as all the rest of the body and, unlike the neck of the lion, showed no trace of having been broken. Between the forepaws Casteret was able to make out the fossilized skull of a young bear. Evidently the skull had fallen away from the statue, to which it must have been fastened by means of a dowel rod; in the course of time the wooden dowel had rotted, but traces of it were still recognizable. Originally, therefore, the Montespan bear had been a clay statue with a real, bleeding head. The bear's body had a number of round holes, evidently made by spear or lance thrusts aimed at vital parts.

About three feet behind the bear, Casteret discovered the incised drawing of a horse in the limestone floor; the neck, adorned with curious symbols, appeared to have had a very long, fluttering mane. The entire floor of the "bear chamber" was covered with reliefs—about thirty in all, from 12 to 20 inches long and from 4 to 6 inches thick. Unfortunately, they had been largely damaged by the running water that at certain times filled this part of the cave. From the remains of most of these figures it would be impossible to tell what they had originally been intended to represent. But some of the figures happened to have been placed beyond the reach of the water, and these evidently represented a herd of horses, whose bodies, like those of various other animal figures at Montespan, were marked with obscure symbols.

The ice-age hunters' concern to celebrate their mysterious rites in hidden or remote cave chambers is especially apparent from the finds made at La Madeleine (Dordogne), whence the Magdalenian period is named. Time and again groups of paleolithic hunters had settled there, seeking the protection of the mighty rock shelter. The last occupants had cleared away the layers of refuse left by their predecessors, thereby creating an artificial chamber, which they separated from their living quarters by a walled partition. The result was a kind of "chapel" 14 feet 9 inches wide in the innermost part of the cavern. The walls of the Madeleine rock shelter were engraved with a multitude of animal forms, but the pictures belonging to the last period of settlement were to be found only on the wall of this "chapel." D. Peyrony, who discovered the site, maintained that no deeper caves existed in the area. Probably, then, this dark, man-made rear chamber served as a ritual place.

In the cold, dry climate of the late ice age, with its sparse vegetation and short arctic or subarctic summers, hunting was man's only means of subsistence. The ancient cave-bear hunters, but also certain upper paleolithic hunting groups, like the reindeer hunters of northern Germany, expected and sought to ensure good fortune in the chase by means of sacrifice, and perhaps also of prayer, to a divine dispenser of hunting fortune or lord of the beasts. The hunter artists, however, were motivated by a very different belief; they appear to have thought they could enforce success by their own means—namely, by making an image of the animal they wished to kill and by performing certain rites.

Thus we find the hunters of the Spanish Levant province seeking out wild and remote rock sites and covering the walls with hunting scenes that reflected their wishes and were intended to make these come true (fig. 7). The hunters of the Eurasian province carved animal idols out of bone, stone, or ivory, or modeled them from a kind of clay, to be used to cast a spell upon their game. The Franco-Cantabrian hunters, for their part, used murals in dark caves, as well as small sculptures. Their art gives us the clearest picture of hunting magic in its varied forms.

We have to distinguish, however, between the practice of magic rites by individual hunters or small groups of hunters, and the specifically tribal ceremonies conducted at sites that must be regarded as tribal sanctuaries. This distinction is most apparent in the case of Altamira, which became a tribal sanctuary only during the latter part of the Magdalenian. La Madeleine, on the other hand, was not a general focus of tribal ceremony, but seems to have served as a magic site only for the people who happened to be occupying the rock shelter at any one particular time.

No hunting expedition, it seems, was undertaken by the individual or the hunting group without the performance of some magic ritual. In the case of big tribal hunts, as for instance when a great herd of migrating bison was approaching the tribal grounds, a collective ceremony would take place. It is also probable that each fresh hunting season was inaugurated with special tribal ceremonies.

The first requirement for the accomplishment of any magic rite was to fashion an image of the animal to be killed. In consequence, art works of true masters are found alternating with the clumsiest approximations; not every hunter was necessarily an artist. Yet every hunter had first to prepare an image if he intended to set out on the hunt himself. It is very likely that the small models or engravings of animals which have been found were mostly idols used by hunters possessed of little artistic talent; perhaps it was enough for the hunter, before setting out, to perform certain magic procedures with his stone figure or engraving in bone, horn, or ivory.

A round pebble found by H. L. Movius at La Colombière (Ain) seems to be a particularly interesting example of a magic stone. It is covered with a series of animal engravings superimposed upon each other, a mere welter of lines to the uninformed eye. Its owner must have sketched a new animal figure on it before each hunt, just like the hunter artists who superimposed their pictures upon cave walls.

In other ways, too, the prehistoric hunters managed to avoid the task of fashioning a new image each time. We find, for instance, that they often touched up old pictures, not infrequently changing one animal into another. We shall meet a fine example of the repeated use of the same image, each time with a slight change, in the Trois Frères cave.

Certain places and parts of cave walls must have been regarded as possessing particular magic potency, for the hunter artists often executed their pictures in one relatively small area, where they intersected and overlapped, though there was plenty of room on the very next portions of the wall. At Lascaux, for instance, there is a mural of an enormous bull, about 10 feet long, done in an even black wash, under which there can be distinguished no fewer than three other layers of paintings: at the very bottom, done in yellow tones, a series of bulls' heads whose horns emerge above the great bull's back; then a bull painted in black; then two wild oxen, walking one behind the other and done in polychrome. The contours of the oxen are easily recognizable; even the heads show through the coat of black paint. Finally, between the head and the right foreleg of the great bull, we can clearly distinguish a brown horse executed in more primitive style. Count H. Bégouen has suggested that the prehistoric hunters covered the old pictures with blood or paint as a ground for new murals, but that the old pictures reappeared with time.

The hunter artists evidently believed that by making an image of their prey they had already cast a spell upon it. It remained, now, to impose their will upon the animal by a variety of practices.

As we have already seen, they marked fatal wounds on the representations of the animals they hoped to kill in the hunt; they believed they would then be able to wound and kill these animals in reality. Leo Frobenius, who led an expedition into Equatorial Africa in 1905, witnessed a striking example of this line of thought as it operates in our own day.

Four members of a pygmy tribe, three men and a woman, had accompanied him for a week. One day, when their store of meat was exhausted, he asked his little companions to kill an antelope. They shook their heads and explained that on that day it was no longer possible, as no preparations had been made. They were perfectly willing, however, to make these preparations the following morning before sunrise. The men then proceeded to survey the terrain, and finally appeared to have found a suitable place at the top of a hill.

Eager to learn what preparations the pygmies were going to make, Frobenius went to the hilltop before dawn and hid behind a bush. The four pygmies arrived at daybreak. The men squatted on the ground, cleared a small space, and rubbed it smooth. Then one of them bent over it and with his finger drew something in the sand. At the same time all four muttered some kind of ritual formula. There followed an expectant silence. As the sun rose on the horizon, one of the men took up his bow and stepped near the cleared space on the ground. A few more minutes went by, and then the rays of the sun fell upon the drawing. At this moment the woman raised her hands with lightning rapidity—as though to grasp the sun—and cried out some words that Frobenius could not understand, while one of the men shot the arrow into the drawing on the ground. Then the woman called out still louder, and the men jumped with their weapons into the bush. The woman remained standing for another few minutes and then returned to the encampment.

Frobenius now left his hiding place and found on the ground a drawing of a 3-foot-long antelope; the arrow was sticking in its neck. That afternoon the hunters came back with an antelope killed by an arrow through its jugular vein. Frobenius found out later that the morning after the kill, before sunrise, the pygmies had returned to the hilltop with some tufts of the antelope's hair and a bowl of its blood; they had smeared the picture on the ground with blood, using the hair as brushes, extracted the arrow, and then erased the picture.

Here we have a clear case of "picture magic" in modern times. If we ignore certain elements that are obviously more recent in date, we find a striking analogy between the pygmies' practices and those of the prehistoric hunters, as evidenced by the finds made in the caves they used. We need only recall the pictures of animals incised in the limestone floors at Montespan and Niaux. At Niaux the pock marks on the animals' bodies were obviously made by arrows or spear thrusts.

The Montespan finds offer even more impressive evidence of such practices. The lion reliefs and, more particularly, the bear are marked by more than sixty holes made by arrows or spears. Apparently in the course of the magic ceremonies the hunters would not only fasten a real bear's head on the clay sculpture, but would also stretch a bearskin over it. Then they would loose a hail of arrows or spears upon the mighty adversary. And where could the border between appearance and reality have been more effectively obliterated than in this deep underground cavern, with flickering torches casting their light upon the low ceiling and projecting the dark shadows of the massive beast upon the walls?

In 1926 two daring young speleologists, G. Dubuc and

F. Trombe, were exploring the Montespan cave. After a series of icy baths in the subterranean stream and a great deal of slipping and sliding and dangerous clambering over piles of rock fallen from the cave roof, they suddenly came, some half-mile from the entrance, upon a passage whose walls were incised with pictures of bison and wild horse. At what appeared to be the end of the passage they saw a hole no more than 13 inches high. This turned out to be the entrance to a 6½-foot tunnel leading into a small cave chamber.

Its floor, covered with a thin layer of calcareous sinter, showed the imprints of a great number of human feet and knees, preserved as under glass. And incised in the limestone wall at the rear they found a unique hunting scene about 10 feet long: horses riddled with "wounds" inflicted by spear or lance rear wildly against a stockade surrounded by a trench into which they are being driven. The foremost horse turns its head, with neck upstretched and nostrils flaring wide. Bégouen considers this engraving one of the masterpieces of ice-age art. The other horses are less finely executed; they are simply finger drawings, and the same is true of the stockade. All are vivid reminders of what went on, thousands upon thousands of years ago, in this secret cavern deep within the mountain, a place of terror, with its silence broken only by the gurgling of the subterranean stream. Here the ice-age hunters performed their magic rites, with miming and dancing, in preparation for the hunt of the wild horse.

The hunter artists resorted to sympathetic magic not only for success in securing food, but also for protection against the predatory beasts that threatened both man and game. It is quite possible that behind the group of the three lions at Montespan there lies the story of a struggle between man and beast for the possession of the cave. If this assumption is correct, then the reliefs were executed with a view to the magic slaying of the lions.

At the Trois Frères cave, too, there is the statue of a lion. It was obviously used on several occasions. The traces of repeated retouching, together with the "wounds" on its body, led Count Bégouen to the altogether plausible conclusion that a powerful big cat had invaded the hunting grounds of the Trois Frères people, who then resolved to track and destroy the dangerous enemy.

Such an enterprise could not have been undertaken without the customary magic rites. And now an entirely original notion appears to have occurred to these men. In a small lateral chamber within the cave, there was a vast mound of calcareous sinter, the foot of a stalagmite—and this they used to make a statue of the offending beast. The size of the cave permitted the presence of only a small group; we may imagine the hunters squatting or standing around the artist sorcerer as he was working. From under his skillful hands there emerged the head, paws, and mane of a lion. He drew a black streak to separate the belly from the hind parts; and the gratings of his flint stylus on the sinter made the lighter colors of the pelt over the belly plainly visible. Finally, the artist decorated the animal's flanks with various missiles; some he incised, others he painted black.

After the completion of their magic rites, the hunters

set out for their prey. But the first expedition must have been unsuccessful, for we see that the main features of the first lion were obliterated. The artist now proceeded to refashion the statue. The tail, previously hanging, was now furled. Both times, however, the artist sorcerer took care to add a tuft of hair to the tail, so as to make it quite clear that he was portraying a lion, not a tiger. But the second expedition also seems to have ended in failure. Here too the image is blurred and refashioned; and now, at last, the magic proved effective, as the absence of any further retouching indicates.

Certain other clearly magical symbols, whose significance, to be sure, is not immediately apparent, are often found on or near representations of animals. Consider, for instance, the significance of the human hand on an animal picture; presumably it expressed the hunter's magic power over the animal. At Lascaux, occasionally, there are on the walls certain figures that look like combs. One interpretation, favored by Abbé Breuil, is that this was a very abstract drawing of a human hand. Another possibility is that it represented an animal stockade. The hunters of the last ice age conducted the battue not only by driving animals over steep rocks, as can be seen from the great heap of horse bones at the foot of the Solutré rock, but also by herding them into strong stockades. Pictures have been found of such enclosures, which may well have been magic preparations of a hunting enterprise of this kind. The artist sketched the enclosure, then drew some animal heads or tracks inside (fig. 21). The obvious intention was to lure the animals to a particular place by means of these magic signs. This must also have been the intention behind the pictures of groups or herds of animals which we occasionally find in the Franco-Cantabrian art province.

One of the Lascaux murals depicts a herd of deer ap-

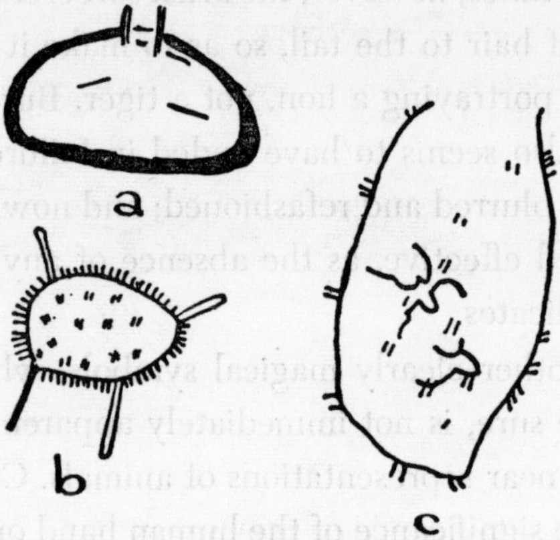

Fig. 21. GAME ENCLOSURES WITH ANIMAL HEADS, OR TRACKS, OR BOTH. A. FONT-DE-GAUME (DORDOGNE), FRANCE B. AND C. LA PILETA, SPAIN

Fig. 22. ROW OF REINDEER. ENGRAVING ON AN EAGLE RADIUS. LA MARIE CAVE (DORDOGNE), FRANCE. ACTUAL SIZE

parently swimming across a river. Most likely there was a ford in the nearby Vézère, and here the hunters hoped to take the deer. At Teyjat (Dordogne) an artist executed a brilliant engraving of a row of reindeer on an eagle radius (fig. 22); was this a magic picture used to entice migrating reindeer herds into the Teyjat hunting grounds, or simply a scene that had impressed itself on the memory of a true artist?

I have mentioned earlier the "tectiform" pictures—signs that recall, at first glance, tents or huts. Nevertheless, in their over-all context they suggest concealed traps into which the animals were to be driven (fig. 23). (Breuil

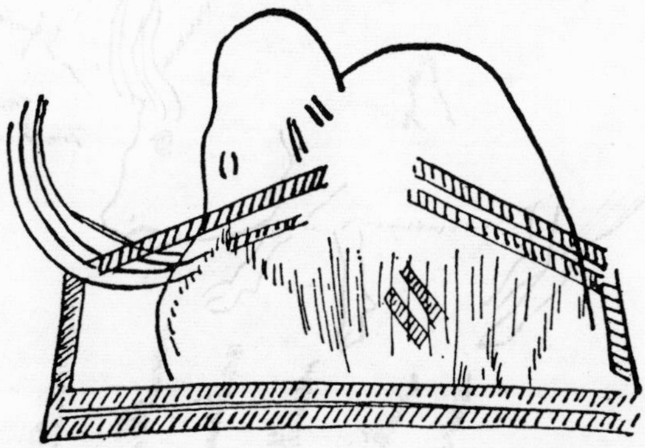

Fig. 23. MAMMOTH CAUGHT IN A CONCEALED TRAP (?) FONT-DE-GAUME (DORDOGNE) FRANCE

now favors the view that these signs represented the dwellings of the ancestors' spirits.)

At Pindal, in northern Spain, a number of clublike markings occur on a wounded bison; they may well represent the weapons with which the hunters hoped to kill that beast (fig. 24).

The paleolithic hunters were well aware, of course, that they were sorely depleting the game population, whose numbers were further thinned out by disease and other predators than man. The consequences were serious: less food, harder stalking and killing, finally severe shortage, if not long and bitter famine. Therefore it was as important to ensure increase in the herds they hunted as to kill game for supply. Here, too, the hunter artists turned to sympathetic magic as an effective remedy.

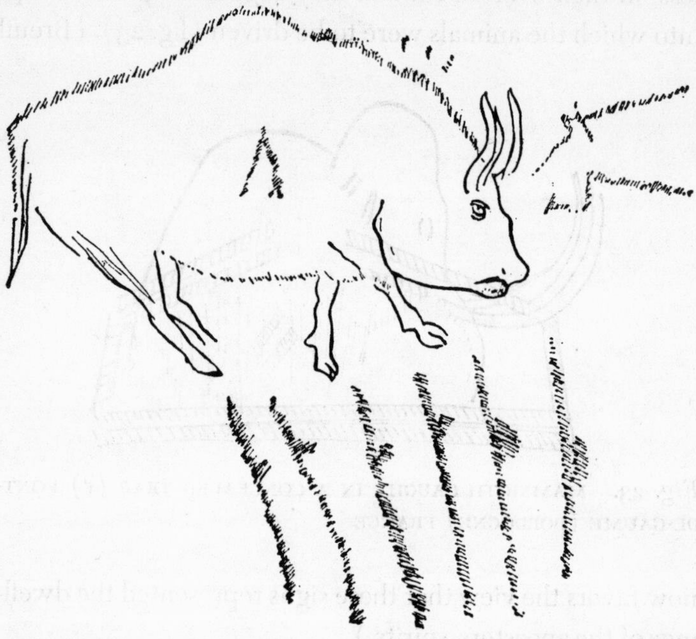

Fig. 24. WOUNDED BISON, WITH CLUBLIKE MARKINGS. PINDAL CAVE, SPAIN. AFTER H. BREUIL

Not surprisingly, therefore, we find them portraying female animals followed or covered by rutting males; great numbers of animals, moreover, appear to be pregnant females. A clay figure of a mare at Montespan has unnaturally prominent teats. The intention is not difficult to divine: the female beasts must be fertile and bear a great number of young to replace the losses caused by seasonal predations.

In 1927 H. Martin discovered a paleolithic sanctuary at Le Roc-de-Sers (Charente) where this sort of magic was assiduously practiced. Halfway up a limestone rock wall nearly 50 feet high, the explorer found a semicircular platform some 24 feet in diameter situated between two ancient dwelling caves. He proceeded to investigate the platform and found, arranged in a semicircle, a row of limestone blocks against the rock wall, with some others lying in front. On turning over the blocks, he was amazed to see that they had been cut in relief. Then he came upon similar sculptured stones on the slope below the platform. Figures of horses, bison, boars, ibex, and even human beings were plainly recognizable. A careful examination showed that the blocks must originally have been standing on the stone bank in the rear of the platform, forming a sculptured frieze. Most of the animals appear with hanging bellies, and are thus clearly pregnant. On one of the blocks a mare is represented covered by a stallion. On another block is a relief of a gravid mare, under which the remains of another animal form are still visible; the artist had apparently obliterated the old form before beginning the new one. One of the human figures appears to be masked.

The frieze stones discovered by Martin had not only been overturned and in part scattered, but several had also been broken. This would suggest that the sanctuary had been wrecked. One explanation might be that enemies of the tribe, or group of hunters living in the area, had torn the reliefs from their pedestals; if that was the case, this sacrilegious act would have aimed at destroying the game on alien hunting grounds. An equally plausible explanation would be that the hunters had decided to leave the region, and, before leaving, destroyed their idols in order to deprive them of their magic power.

Other finds, in particular those made in the Pyrenean cave of Labastide, show that the paleolithic hunters were, in fact, in the habit of destroying their magic idols before leaving a settlement. They imagined, perhaps, that this was a way of appropriating their magic powers; but they may also simply have wanted to prevent their idols from falling into the hands of strangers. At Labastide, Norbert Casteret found a stone embankment, about 1,300 feet from the cave entrance, surmounted by two great stone circles. Within the circles he found coal, charred bones, horses' teeth and jawbones, flint implements, and a number of limestone slabs engraved with horses, reindeer, bison, mammoths, and bears. Some of the slabs were broken, and all were lying with the picture-side down.

The most impressive remains of fertility magic are in the Tuc d'Audoubert cave. There, in a little chamber 2,275 feet from the cave mouth, is a clay relief of a pair of bison, the female followed by the male. Though the smallness of the reliefs—23¾ inches and 24¾ inches respectively—scarcely corresponds to reality, the characteristic features of the two are presented with extraordinary fidelity to nature. The female, whose lines are more delicate, stands with outstretched neck and raised tail: precisely the posture of a cow receiving the bull. The male, tougher and more massive, is in the act of rising on its hind legs, tail

Small ivory head of woman. Brassempouy (Landes), France.

PLATE XVII

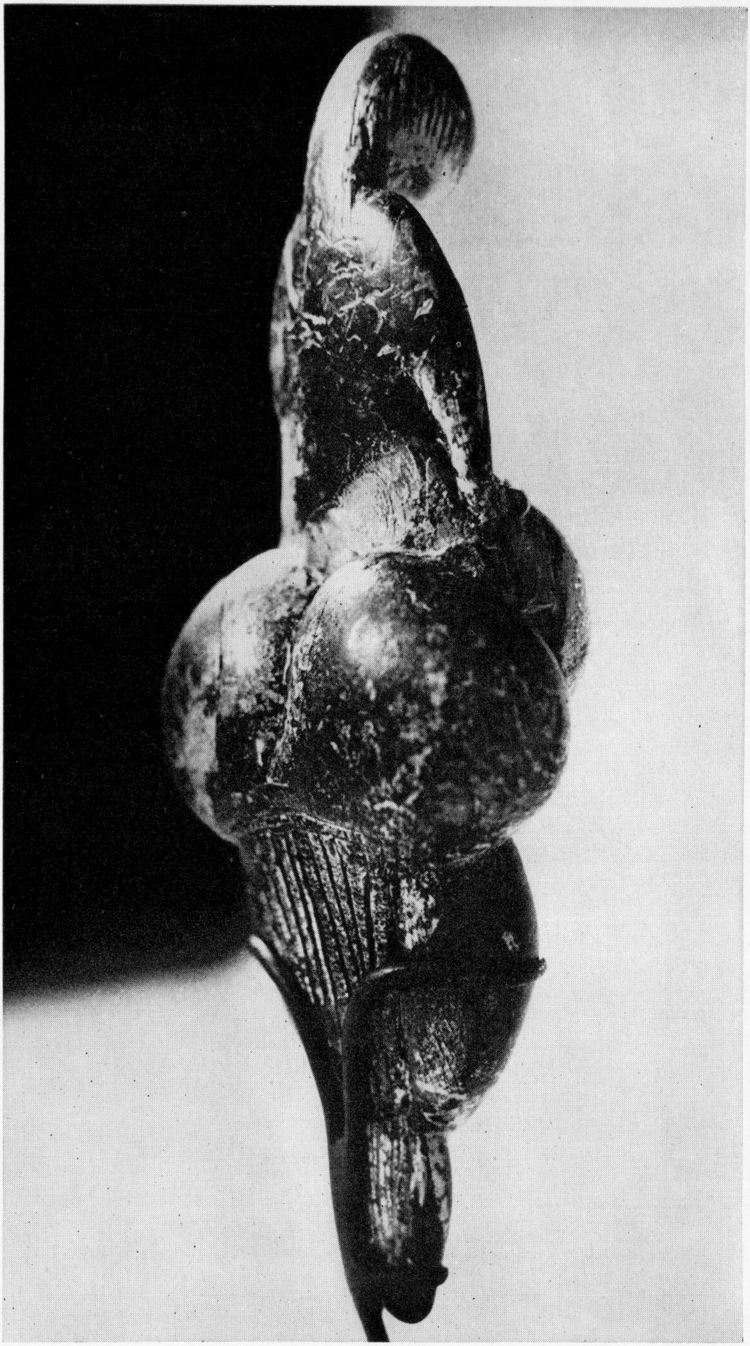

"Venus of Lespugue" (Haute-Garonne), France.

PLATE XVIII

“Venus of Willendorf,” Austria.

PLATE XIX

"The Lady of Sireuil" (Dordogne), France.

PLATE XX

pressed between buttocks in the effort. The artist placed a rock and a limestone block under this figure to give it the necessary leverage for mounting the cow.

The prehistoric hunters were obviously seeking by magic to bring about couplings among the bison of the region, so that these animals—from which they derived so large a part of their food supply—would increase and multiply and form big, strong herds. Representations of cou-

Fig. 24. BULL FOLLOWING A COW. WALL ENGRAVING, TEYJAT (DORDOGNE), FRANCE. LENGTH OF GROUP: 41⅓ INCHES.

pling animals also occur in the mural art of the period: at Teyjat (Dordogne), for instance, there is a picture of a bull following a cow (fig. 25). The phallic symbols that have been found in a number of caves may be regarded as serving the same magic purposes as these representations. This conclusion finds support especially in the discoveries made at Tuc d'Audoubert. Near the entrance of the bison chamber, small clay phallic models were found, and also—a most curious feature—the impressions of human heels, in five rows, directed toward these clay generative organs. Anthropological study has determined that these impressions were made by youngsters. A ceremonial march or some strange heel dance must thus have taken place here in front of the picture of the mating bison. Was this the occasion when the youthful members of the tribe were instructed in the great mystery of the hunters? Do the impressions in the ground bear witness to far-off initiation rites? Whatever the explanation, what took place here deep in the bosom of the earth must have been connected with fertility magic.

Further and very interesting evidence of fertility magic, and perhaps also of initiation ceremonies, was uncovered quite recently near Angles-sur-l'Anglin (Vienne). On the overhanging roof of the Bourdois rock shelter, a relief was found almost completely covered by a late paleolithic layer. Only after this had been removed was it possible to discern the subject: three nude female figures, all showing clearly the distinguishing characters of the female sex. They belonged to the Magdalenian culture level. One of them has the narrow hips of adolescence, the second is pregnant, and so may be the third. While the last two stand close together, the young girl stands somewhat apart, directly above a bison's back. The animal is obviously in heat, as its upraised tail shows. As the composition in its entirety can hardly be regarded as accidental, and as the sexual characteristics of the individual figures are so clearly indicated, there can be no doubt as to the meaning of the work.

We must assume that these rituals were actually very much more varied and dramatic than mere pictures can suggest. Invocation, dancing, singing, music, masked mime, and sorcerer's tricks—in a word, much of the paraphernalia of modern shamanism—must have existed even in ice-age magic.

Few of the relevant pictures have any adjuncts in the way of arrows, wounds, weapons, or other signs. Here the hunters' intentions with regard to the animals must have been expressed in some other way. At Tuc d'Audoubert they apparently were expressed by means of the dancing of youths. Did the cave walls also echo with the incantations of the hunters and their sorcerers? Again we find significant hints in contemporary primitive life. Before the Ojibwa Indians set out on a hunting expedition, it is customary for the sorcerer to outline on the ground or on a piece of birch bark the animal they want to kill, and to paint in the heart in red. Then he draws an arrow pointed toward the heart, chanting meanwhile:

> *I shoot you in the heart, I shoot you in the heart,*
> *Oh beast! I hit your heart!*
> . . . .
> *That is how I am, my friends, that is how I am,*
> *Every beast, my friends, I surely hit.*

Flutes and pipes made of little marrow bones have often been found in the excavated caves. If, as seems probable, these instruments were used during the magic ceremonies, then the ice-age sorcerers must have sometimes accompanied their invocations with music. In fact, one of the pictures in the Trois Frères cave (fig. 26) shows a dancer, disguised as a bison, playing on some bow-shaped instrument, possibly a kind of flute. Two curious animals are bounding away before him. The first looks like a female reindeer, yet its forelegs suggest human arms. The second animal, which is looking back at the sorcerer, as though half captivated by the music, is even more fantastic: its foreparts suggest a bison, but aft it might be a reindeer. What else can this odd scene be but a magic performance, wherein sorcerer and "animals" alike were human hunters

Fig. 25. SORCERER DISGUISED AS A BISON, DANCING, PLAYING ON A BOW-SHAPED INSTRUMENT (POSSIBLY A KIND OF FLUTE), AND PURSUING TWO ANIMALS. THE TROIS FRÈRES CAVE (ARIÈGE), FRANCE. AFTER H. BREUIL

in disguise? And what was the disguise for if not to compel animals to bow to the hunters' will?

Sometimes the artists drew pictures of animals without eyes or ears, or even without horns—indubitably deliberate omissions. We find analogous thinking in an Egyptian papyrus dealing with the art of sorcery, which prescribes a method of rendering dangerous animals harmless: they should be portrayed minus the dangerous part of their bodies—the head in the case of a snake, the tail in the case of a scorpion, etc. The ice-age hunter, quite obviously assuming the same logic of cause and effect, omitted the horns so that the bison or bull would be unable to gore him, or suppressed a beast's ears and eyes so that it would not detect him on his approach.

The conduct of the hunt itself required that the hunter imitate the game; only in this manner could he stalk the timid and fleet-footed beasts and come within shooting distance of them. But to make the camouflage fully effective, he had also to "become" the animal. Confirmed, by success in his stalking methods, in this belief in metamorphosis, the ice-age hunter may have come to consider his animal disguise no less effective a form of sympathetic magic than his images of animals. Dressed up as a beast, he mimed its movements, acted out its amorous plays, imitated its sounds, charmed, outwitted, and finally killed it. Hunting societies throughout the world believe in the magic efficacy of the mimetic dancing by which they dramatize the life and action of their quarry.

In ice-age art, there are some fifty-five known portrayals of human beings dressed in skins, often in dancing posture. One of the most perfect engraved drawings, on deer antler, found at Teyjat, is of three small masked dancers disguised as chamois bucks. There they are seen jumping in upright position, and their mighty leaps cause the skins to puff out and swirl. The legs of youthful dancers protrude from under the chamois skins.

An incision on a stone at La Madeleine shows with equal vivacity two slim young dancers, one with raised arms and wearing a musk-ox skin. We may assume that the youthful dancers at Tuc d'Audoubert were also disguised

—in this case, obviously, as bison. At Lourdes a slate slab from the Magdalenian layer shows a man, probably a sorcerer, disguised as a deer (fig. 27). The dancer is an adult, and moves with heavy gait. He is crowned with antlers, and wears a long tail. Still another drawing, at Les Combarelles, represents animal courtship and must have been used in fertility rites: a man disguised as an animal, and with a prominent phallus, bends over and pursues a woman also in animal disguise.

A great number of such masked dancers were discovered on cave walls and on smaller surfaces dating from all periods of the late paleolithic. They suggest that mimetic dancing played a vital role in the life of ice-age men.

It was mainly the hunters of the Franco-Cantabrian province who assumed animal disguises for the celebration of their magic rituals. From the evidence, it would appear that this practice was almost unknown in the Spanish Levant, which so far has yielded only very isolated works of this sort: two were found in the Gasulla gorge (fig. 28).

On the other hand, these nimble southerners loved and cultivated the dance even more than their northern neighbors, and they certainly used it for purposes of sympathetic magic (fig. 29).

The paleolithic portrayals of men disguised as beasts clearly show the role of the sorcerer in his group. As I suggested earlier, the sorcerer must have been both the artist and the master of the great rites. Two sites—Limeuil in France and Parpallo in Spain—have yielded immense numbers of engravings on stone slabs, at all stages of completion, and many of them bearing clear marks of correc-

Fig. 27. DISGUISED FIGURE WITH HORSE'S TAIL AND DEER'S ANTLERS. ENGRAVING ON A SLATE SLAB. LOURDES (HAUTES-PYRÉNÉES), FRANCE. ACTUAL SIZE

tion. These, it is believed, were the product of ice-age "art studios," or advanced schools for the training of artists; but we may with equal justification speak of schools of sorcery.

The most perfect and also the most impressive portrayal of the sorcerer of those times, in all his trappings and animation, was found in the deepest part of the Trois Frères cave. Here the walls reveal a unique animal parade, representing the most varied species. And even this extraordinary beast assemblage is eclipsed by the "great sorcerer" (plate IX, a and b) who, standing on a high rock pulpit—about twelve feet above the cave floor—dominates the animals and holds them spellbound by his dancing and his imperious gaze. Measuring about 30 inches, this famous figure, which is deeply incised upon the wall and partially delineated in black, can be reached only by means of a narrow, upward spiraling passage. Seemingly inaccessible, then, the sorcerer sports a deer's head crowned with formidable antlers. His face, however, is that of an owl, his pointed ears those of a wolf, the long beard hanging

Fig. 28. MEN IN ANIMAL DISGUISES. GASULLA GORGE, EASTERN SPAIN.

from his chin that of a chamois. The half-raised arms have bearlike paws. A horse's tail completes the costume. Only the legs are human, and the dancing gait betrays the man under the oddly assorted disguise elements. Obviously, each of these imbued the sorcerer with the special powers of the animal concerned. Who was this "great sorcerer"? It is probable that the Trois Frères engraving represented some kind of prime—or indeed divine—teacher of magic;

Fig. 29. DANCER BESIDE AN IBEX. VIEJA, ALPERA, SPAIN.

and his representative, the "current" sorcerer, would have mounted the same high pulpit under the picture to officiate, before the elders of the tribe, at ceremonies aimed at ensuring hunting luck and animal fertility.

In August 1949 an engraving about 28 inches high was discovered in the Lascaux cave, probably another representation of a magician; it was incised in the rock over some faded brown paintings. The figure is clothed from head to toe in a kind of cloak of dried grass remarkably similar to the type of disguise assumed by sorcerers today in French New Guinea. So, incidentally, are certain aspects of the picture of the deer-mask sorcerer found at Lourdes (fig. 27).

It is doubtful that these figures really represented human beings. What could have been the purpose of portraying the sorcerers at their ceremonial invocations? Were these memorial pictures, intended merely to record ceremonies that had taken place? This would appear unlikely as far as Franco-Cantabrian art is concerned. It seems far more probable, in my view, that these figures really represented spirits, beings credited by the ice-age hunters with the possession of all magic powers, or even the prime sorcerer, from whom all knowledge and skill in sorcery derived, a divine being akin to the "lord of the beasts." Breuil suggests that the "great sorcerer" of the Trois Frères was really the "god" of the hunters of that region, represented in the form of the living "current" sorcerer and adorned with all the trappings of his office.

A. C. Blanc has drawn attention to an analogous figure familiar among contemporary Melanesians: the sea spirit, whose head, feet, and hands are fish (fig. 30), guardian and lord of the sea creatures, who provides the fishermen with a good catch, but is equally capable of bringing them harm.

Could it not be, then, that these figures in late paleolithic art also represent beings of a higher order, perhaps guardian spirits of animals? Such spirits could quite possibly have been conceived of as primeval powers, a fact obscured by the luxuriant overgrowth of magic practices. Recent anthropological studies have, in fact, questioned the purely magical interpretation of ice-age art. A. E. Jenssen, for instance, observes that many practices characteristic of hunting peoples which have been regarded as "magical" are, "in fact, genuinely religious." And Hugo Obermaier suggested long ago that the ice-age engravings that were, for the most part, so inaccessible as to be barely visible were not intended at all for human eyes but for the

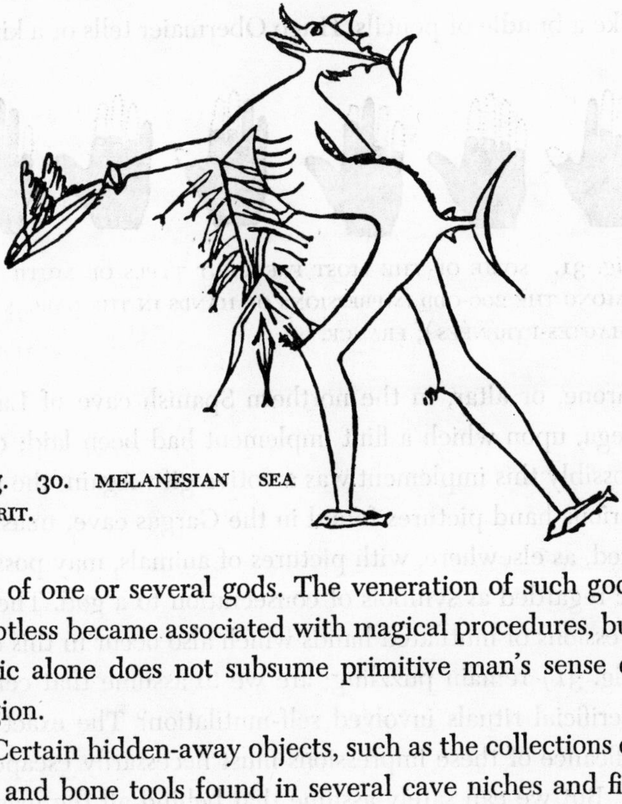

Fig. 30. MELANESIAN SEA SPIRIT.

eyes of one or several gods. The veneration of such gods doubtless became associated with magical procedures, but magic alone does not subsume primitive man's sense of religion.

Certain hidden-away objects, such as the collections of flint and bone tools found in several cave niches and fissures, may well have been votive offerings to these divinities.

At Montespan, Casteret found a number of curious

small clay objects—strips and balls stuck to the walls and bearing circular perforations, in some cases even containing tools. In the "bear chamber," Casteret discovered a slight rock projection shaped rather like a holy-water stoup; the hollow was filled with worked flints. On another rock he found a series of lines branching out like rays, and on the floor below, a number of small stalactites stacked like a bundle of pencils. Hugo Obermaier tells of a kind of

Fig. 31. SOME OF THE MOST FREQUENT TYPES OF MUTILATION AMONG THE 200-ODD IMPRESSIONS OF HANDS IN THE GARGAS CAVE (HAUTES-PYRÉNÉES), FRANCE.

throne, or altar, in the northern Spanish cave of La Pasiega, upon which a flint implement had been laid; quite possibly this implement was a votive gift. Again, the mysterious hand pictures found in the Gargas cave, unassociated, as elsewhere, with pictures of animals, may possibly be regarded as symbols of consecration to a god. The impressions of mutilated hands which also occur in this cave (fig. 31) remain puzzling; are we to assume that certain sacrificial rituals involved self-mutilation? The exact significance of these impressions must necessarily escape us.

But we can safely assume that behind all the magical beliefs and practices of the upper paleolithic hunters, there also lay a faith in higher beings, spirits or demons.

VI

CULT OF THE "MOTHER GODDESSES"

One group of art works would appear to diverge completely from the rest of the ice-age hunting art with which we have been dealing so far—and which always centered about animal forms. These are the remarkable miniatures of females, generally sculptured in the round. Excavation shows that they were diffused over an immense area, from southern France to Siberia, from northern Italy to the middle reaches of the Rhine. Curiously enough, the female figurine never crossed the Pyrenees to the Iberian peninsula.

These little statues are carved in stone, bone, or ivory, and vary in height from 2 to 10 inches. As a rule, they depict the nude female form, sometimes with traces of ornament. Almost without exception they portray the fully mature woman. All individual or personal traits seem to have been deliberately suppressed. On the other hand, the sexual characters of the female body are strongly emphasized, if not exaggerated. Among the eastern finds, clothed or draped figures are quite common.

A very perfect piece is the ivory statuette, 5¾ inches

high, that has been found at Lespugue in southern France. The figure is nude but for a kind of apron hanging down the back. The artist was obviously not interested in the head or feet of his creation. This peculiarity appears in the stylistically similar work found at Savignano in northern Italy, a serpentine statuette not quite 9 inches in height. But for realism and plastic vitality, the famous Austrian "Venus of Willendorf" eclipses all others. It is a limestone

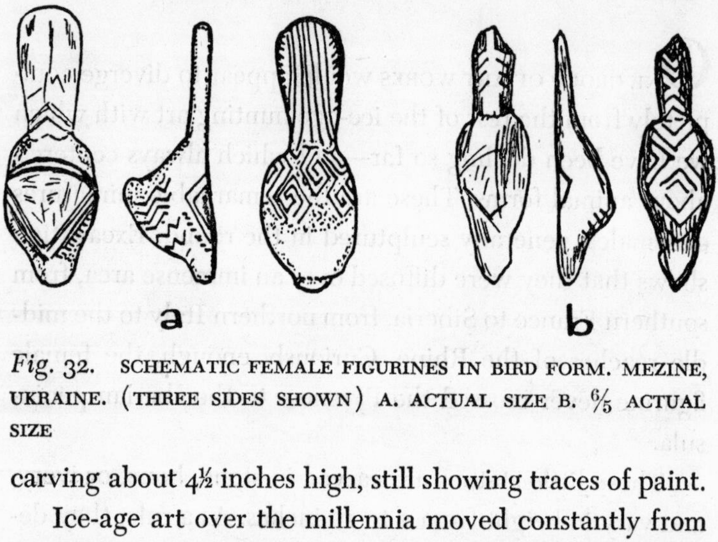

Fig. 32. SCHEMATIC FEMALE FIGURINES IN BIRD FORM. MEZINE, UKRAINE. (THREE SIDES SHOWN) A. ACTUAL SIZE B. 6/5 ACTUAL SIZE

carving about 4½ inches high, still showing traces of paint.

Ice-age art over the millennia moved constantly from realism toward stylization and abstraction. In the eastern European regions this process is most strongly marked. Thus at Mezine, in the Ukraine, it led to birdlike forms with incised geometrical patterns, but a triangle representing the female sex appears on each of them (fig. 32). The most purely geometrical treatment of the female form, and thus the furthest removed from nature, occurs in an ivory engraving found at Předmost, in Moravia (fig. 33).

Besides the small statuettes, several fairly large low reliefs are known. Six were discovered in Aurignacian deposits of the Laussel cave (Dordogne). The female figures in these reliefs strongly resemble the statuettes. One of the reliefs depicts either the act of childbirth or sexual congress. There is also a single male figure. Male figures,

Fig. 33. GEOMETRIC FEMALE FIGURE. IVORY ENGRAVING. PŘEDMOST, MORAVIA, CZECHOSLOVAKIA.

though not altogether absent in ice-age carvings, are few and far between.

The female figurines are almost entirely Aurignacian. They also occur, if more rarely, in Magdalenian deposits, and then usually show extreme stylization.

DESPITE many variations, all these art works suggest an unmistakable unity. And this external unity must surely have sprung from a substantial unity of attitude on the part of the inhabitants of Eurasia during the last ice age.

Any number of theories have been put forward to explain the meaning of these particular modelings. One of the commonest is that they represent some erotic ideal, and that they were erotic-*cum*-aesthetic creations; hence their designation as "Venuses." Yet in point of erotic emphasis these paleolithic figurines fall very far short of those of the later metal ages. Moreover, almost exclusively they depict older women, or mother figures. Most scholars, therefore, now ascribe to them a religious character, and tend to regard them as images of mother goddesses or fertility idols.

Such interpretations, however, were bound to remain merely speculative so long as the exact circumstances in which the figurines were found and the cultural environment of their origins were not sufficiently taken into account, or indeed not really well known. It is the discoveries made in Russia and western Siberia which now make it possible for us to re-examine the whole question in a new light.

It is now definitely established that the female figurines come from occupation layers. They always occur near the walls of sunken huts. At Gagarino, in the Ukraine, seven figurines were found standing on the two lateral walls of a dwelling. Sometimes it was possible to make out special niches or depressions apparently designed to hold the little figures. The feet of the statuette often taper to a point, suggesting that they might have been stuck into special bases. Many have perforations in or near the feet, as if for attachment to some other object. All this leaves little doubt that the statuettes played a special part in the domestic life of those times.

Traces of painting still appear on some of the figurines. Was this color perhaps some ritual decoration applied by the faithful on particular occasions? Even stronger indications of such practice is afforded by the small holes found in some of the statuettes, into which flowers, or other articles of adornment, might have been inserted. It is also worth noting that the artists who fashioned these figures often paid special attention to the hair arrangement.

The assumption that ice-age man practiced a cult of domestic tutelary spirits is further supported by the broken figurines found at another Russian site, that of Kostienki, on the Don. There the dwelling trenches had obviously been abandoned under duress, and the condition of the figurines could be explained only by the use of force. The intention, clearly, had been to destroy the tutelary spirits of the occupants by smashing their idols.

F. Hancar has noted that even at present the hunting tribes of northern Asia make little statues of human forms which they call Dzuli; the material they use for carving them is no longer stone or ivory, as in the ice age, but wood. According to the beliefs of one of these tribes, the idols are female and represent the human origin of the whole tribe. The Dzuli are also the tutelary spirits of the family and tribe, and their images are handed down from one generation to the next. The men confide their homes to the Dzuli's safekeeping when they go hunting, and offer them groats and fat upon return. In much the same way, the paleolithic figures appear to have served both as tutelary spirits and as symbols of the origin of family and tribe. In short, they were the "great mothers."

By what stages did the paleolithic hunters arrive at this veneration of female deities? It is indisputable that the figurines have always been found in occupation layers, which would imply that they belonged to people who lived some kind of settled life. That is certainly true of the Aurignacian hunters of Russia and western Siberia; the remains of their sunken dwelling huts have been found, and sometimes even enormous heaps of animal bones, the refuse of their meals. And the reason why such figurines are rarely found in the Magdalenian layers of western Europe is surely because the people concerned were primarily reindeer hunters who followed the migrating herds and could not settle for long in any one spot.

The transition from a nomadic to a sedentary life is dependent upon suitable economic conditions—and this for hunters means an abundant game supply. Now, Aurignacian men did not live in a hunters' paradise. However, those who lived in the vast territories of eastern Europe and western Siberia could establish themselves on a fairly permanent basis along the great water courses that were also the migration routes of the animal herds, particularly of the mammoth. Another factor contributing to a more settled life was the very harsh climate. The snow storms that raged during the long winters made hunting impossible, so that the hunters were forced to store up provisions and generally to plan ahead—activities possible only in a non-nomadic society.

One of the consequences of this new stability was a

heightening of women's importance in the economic life of the tribe. It was the women's job to ensure the most economical utilization of the meat and skins brought back by the hunters—to prepare the food, lay up meat reserves, and treat the skins that served the tribe as clothing and as coverings for their huts. The survival of the tribe during the hard winter months would have depended as much on the careful utilization of existing supplies as on the actual quantity of those supplies.

Women's social status also improved; and Hancar maintains that Aurignacian women even took part in the hunting-magic rites.

At Malta, in Siberia, two female figurines were found decorated with strange diagonal stripes that covered the entire body with the exception of the face and, in one instance, of the breasts. As V. I. Gromov has suggested—very plausibly, in my opinion—these figurines represent women clad in fur skins. Considering the proportion of the skin length to human height, and the form of the tail, which the ancient artists executed very carefully, we recognize here the skin of a big cat. Because of the diagonal, tigerlike stripings, Gromov thought it was a cave lion—whose bones, in fact, have been found under the bone heaps at Malta. It is quite possible that the skins were nothing more than ordinary garments. However, we do know other representations of fertility magic in which women partake actively, dressed as animals. By analogy, then, these skin-clad figures may well represent sorceresses, or even the "great mother" in her capacity as "prime" sorceress. The Laussel cave, one of whose curious reliefs represents the act of birth or cohabitation, may have been a sanctuary of this "prime" sorceress.

Models and drawings of the female as well as male genitalia are common throughout the Aurignacian; in the ensuing periods these drawings obviously became rarer, as did also the female statuettes. This contemporaneity is significant. In paleolithic art the sexual elements cannot be considered obscenities, the product of mere eroticism. Rather, they were symbols of the generative force that ensured the continuity of the hunting tribe; the "great," or "prime," mother appeared as the very source of that force.

It appears highly probable, then, that the female figurines were idols of a "great mother" cult practiced by the non-nomadic Aurignacian mammoth hunters who inhabited the immense Eurasian territories that extended from southern France to Lake Baikal, in Siberia.

Nor did this cult vanish entirely with the passing of the Aurignacian culture. (The group carved at Angles-sur-l'Anglin seems to indicate that the Magdalenian people still observed some form of "great mother" worship.) But when, in the Magdalenian period, a nomadic life supplanted the relatively settled existence of the Aurignacian, the role of woman began to decline, and the "great mother" statuettes lost their significance.

Thus, the "great mother" cult of the first half of the upper paleolithic appears to have been an isolated episode. Yet it can be considered a precursor of the mother cult that developed in neolithic times, when the female body reappears in various significant representations.

Part III

THE MESOLITHIC PERIOD

I

A TRANSITIONAL STAGE

WITH THE PASSING of the ice age and the withdrawal of the last great ice cap, Europe came to enjoy a climate substantially like that of the present day. Forest, steppe, heath, and moorland appeared where the ice sheets vanished or the icy breath of the glaciers ceased to blow. The cold-loving fauna died out. Isolated survivors like the reindeer migrated northward with the retreating ice cap.

The greatest transformations took place in northern Europe. After the northern ice sheet had withdrawn across the Baltic into Scandinavia, that region remained separated from the rest of the European continent by an icy sea—whose borders did not, however, coincide with those of the present Baltic, as that sea also covered large parts of what is now Finland and southern Sweden. To the south, from Finland across the Baltic countries, through northern Germany and as far as the Netherlands, there extended a belt of arctic tundra with the sparse vegetation characteristic of high latitudes. But once the ice sheet covering the Scandinavian mountains had melted, the coasts of Norway, Sweden, Denmark, and Finland rose so steeply that the Baltic became an inland sea. Only toward the end of the mesolithic, when a strait opened connecting it with the North Sea, did the Baltic acquire its present form.

As these transformations were taking place, over thousands of years, the forest was slowly gaining ground against the barren steppes. In the tundra, only the surface soil thawed a little during the short summer season, supporting mosses and lichens, occasional timid flowering plants, a few tough tundra grasses, meager patches of pasture land, and dwarf arctic birch. This was the time when reindeer and man penetrated these uninviting northern regions. Slowly the temperate fauna and flora moved northward into a belt that was at first cold and dry, then dry and warm, thus creating in the north ever more abundant means of sustenance for man and beast.

With the onset of these changes, there started all over Europe great migrations of men and beasts which were not to stop for thousands of years. The dwindling of the game population, and in particular the withdrawal of the reindeer herds, forced the hunters to abandon the cave regions in which they had been living. While at first many inhabitants of Europe tried to continue living off the diminishing game supply, supplemented by food gathered from an expanding vegetation, more and more of these bands, wandering hither and thither, tended to settle along the coast, from the Iberian peninsula into northern Asia, and on the banks of lakes and rivers, there to maintain life by fishing. Later, toward the end of the mesolithic, societies based on tillage and even some animal husbandry emerged alongside the impoverished societies of hunters and fishermen;

this development, however, was undoubtedly initiated by new groups moving into Europe from western Asia.

WE REALLY know less about the mesolithic cultures than about the cultures of the paleolithic. In western and central Europe only three mesolithic cultures have been distinguished as yet: the Azilian, the Tardenoisian, and the Campignian (though the last of these is now considered early neolithic). In northern Europe the corresponding and related cultures were the Maglemosian and the culture of the kitchen middens; further cultural phases may be distinguished, among which the Ahrensburg phase is of particular importance for this study. (Recently, however, it has been suggested that the Ahrensburg phase, owing to the environment, economy, and way of life that characterized it, should more properly be assigned to the paleolithic.)

The following table shows the relationship between the mesolithic cultures and those that preceded and followed them, as well as their approximate chronology.

Culture periods: *Western and Central Europe*	*Culture periods*: *Northern Europe*	*Approximate chronology*
Late Magdalenian	Hamburg phase	15,000 to 10,000 B.C.
Azilian Early Tardenoisian	Ahrensburg phase Maglemosian	10,000 to 5000 B.C.
Late Tardenoisian Campignian (early neolithic)	Kitchen middens	5000 to 3500 B.C.
Neolithic	Neolithic	3500 to 2000 B.C.

The mesolithic cultures, sandwiched between the rich hunting cultures of the Magdalenian and the peasant cultures of the neolithic, were both poor and unimpressive. Yet it would be altogether wrong to consider the mesolithic people poorly endowed, or the period wholly devoid of any achievement. If we consider the position of mesolithic man in the larger context of the history of civilization, and recall the problems he faced, we shall realize that his culture could necessarily be only of the simplest. His role in the postglacial transition was not to be the heir and guardian of the cultural achievement of the preceding era, but to prepare the way for a new cultural ascent. In most fields he had to acquire new skills and use his newly acquired knowledge in altogether new situations. In effect, neolithic man blazed the trail for the flowering of coming cultures, our own included.

II

RELIGIOUS PRACTICES OF THE REINDEER HUNTERS IN NORTHERN EUROPE

FROM THE BEGINNING of the postglacial age the reindeer withdrew into northern Europe, and the men who hunted them followed their trails. These mesolithic reindeer hunters lived several thousand years after the so-called Hamburg hunters, and they were certainly not directly descended from them. Yet, astonishingly enough, they practiced sacrificial rites identical with those of the earlier hunters; they too made offerings of young reindeer to their gods by submerging two-year-old does in the waters of a lake. Evidence of this, for both periods, is provided by the Stellmoor site, near Hamburg.

The lake beside which the Hamburg hunters had pitched their camp must have silted up toward the end of the ice age; there is a brownish layer of peat on the site. As the ice deep in the lake bottom began to melt—perhaps in the postglacial or, according to more recent theories, at the end of the ice age itself—the depression was again filled with water. And, as before, reindeer hunters came to settle on the lake shore. Pollen analysis has established that settlement occurred in the postglacial; Alfred Rust, who conducted the excavation, puts its archaeological age at approximately 8500 B.C. In terms of cultural history, this would mean the early mesolithic; Rust gave it the name of Ahrensburg phase.

In the muddy layer covering the brownish peat, he found no fewer than twelve whole reindeer, which the Ahrensburg hunters had sacrificed to their gods. The animals had all been submerged in the lake, weighted down by stones placed in the thoracic or abdominal cavities. A fragment of a wooden arrow, tipped with a pointed flint, was found in the thoracic cavity of one of these reindeer, indicating that here again the animals had been part of the spoils of the chase. As the same layer yielded some thirty skulls of young animals and fragments of thoracic bones in significant association with great stones, and as this layer has not yet been exhaustively excavated, we may accept Rust's conclusion that the Ahrensburg hunters had sunk about forty-five animals in the little lake. This figure need not be taken to indicate that the mesolithic Ahrensburg hunters were any more religious than their predecessors of the paleolithic Hamburg phase, but simply that they occupied the site over a period of many years. Rust has calculated that the Ahrensburg hunters must have killed, in all, some 1,000 reindeer.

The conclusion is truly astonishing: a rite of sacrifice of which we find the first traces in the paleolithic now reappears, thousands of years later, in exactly the same form. There could be no more telling example of the remarkable power of survival of religious practices. And we may also assume that the religious beliefs associated with these rites were held by successive generations of reindeer hunters over the millennia.

Rust maintains that both the Hamburg and the Ahrensburg culture phases were derived from older cultures native to eastern Europe. Hence the origin of the hunting sacrifices I have described should be looked for in the east. And this would strengthen the conclusion, supported by other evidence, that the ancient religions of the east differed strikingly from those of the west. In the east the emphasis seems always to have been on sacrifice, addressed to a divine dispenser of hunting fortune, a divinity whose nature is differently conceived of at different times. In the west, magic seems to have been the overriding force. However, scholars have concentrated so exclusively on the magnificent magical art of the ice-age hunters that they have tended to overlook the possibility that at certain periods altogether different beliefs may have been held alongside the belief in magic.

In addition to sinking animals in the lake, the Ahrensburg reindeer hunters appear to have had other sacrificial customs. Certain finds made on the Stellmoor site seem to confirm this view, bearing strong analogies to the offerings made by present-day primitive peoples of northern Asia at their sacred sites. Travelers report the finding of all kinds of objects on these modern sites, from knives to broken axes and potsherds. At Stellmoor, too, a variety of objects were found—axes made of reindeer antler, wooden arrows, and bone implements. These objects have been regarded as mere refuse, but it is quite possible that they were, in fact, votive offerings. If they were, then the small lakes where they abound must have been simply sacred or sacrificial pools. We have already drawn attention to the flint implements found at the paleolithic site of Malta, in Siberia; it is not unlikely that the Ahrensburg reindeer hunters too threw some useful object or other into the sacred pool in order to gain a hearing for their personal requests or to express their gratitude. Thousands of years later, during the bronze and iron ages, such sacrifices were to become very widespread, as is proved by countless articles recovered on moorland sites.

Quite close to the shoreline of the ancient postglacial lake of Stellmoor, Rust found a pinewood pole nearly 7 feet long and 4¾ inches in diameter. It was lying at an angle of 45 degrees to the lake; the end directed toward the shore was pointed, whereas the other end was blunt. And mounted on this blunt end was the almost complete anterior of a reindeer skull. The condition of the bones indicated that the posterior part of the skull had fallen away. The worn teeth set the animal's age at fifteen; this would make it one of the two oldest animals found on the site.

The skull, or the head and muzzle, appears to have been mounted on the pole at such an angle that the antlers, which in a reindeer sweep backward roughly parallel with the body axis, now stood upright (fig. 34). The absence of the posterior skull may be explained by the fact that after decomposition of the tissues, the weight of the antlers loosened the sutures and a storm finally tore it off. It is of course also possible that the skull broke when the pole toppled over. Rust found several complete occipitals near the pole, but he was not able to match one of them with the anterior skull on the pole.

What was the purpose of this pole? Instead of placing it at the crest of some slope above the lake where it could

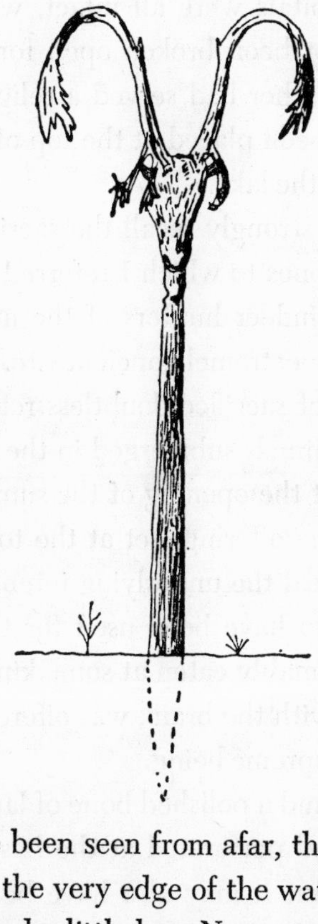

Fig. 34. RITUAL POLE OF STELLMOOR, GERMANY (RECONSTRUCTION)

have been seen from afar, the ancient hunters had placed it at the very edge of the water, at a spot where the shore formed a little bay. Now, we know that the hunters threw their sacrifices into the water from the shore. The connection with the place of sacrifice seems, therefore, to be established.

But the pole with the reindeer head must have served as something more than a mere sign—albeit a singularly impressive one—marking the sacred site; it must have been used for exhibiting the offerings. In fact, Rust discovered about a dozen big reindeer skulls close by, at the bottom of the ancient lake. Their occipitals were all intact, which shows that the skulls had not been broken open for the extraction of the brain, but rather had served a religious purpose: they had probably been placed at the top of the pole before being thrown into the lake.

All these unbroken skulls strongly recall the sacrifices of heads or skulls and long bones to which I referred earlier. Thus we see that the reindeer hunters of the mesolithic continued to practice an extremely ancient rite. The coexistence of various types of sacrifice doubtless reflects a diversity of motives. The animals submerged in the lake were offerings of first fruits at the opening of the summer hunting season. As regards the offerings set at the top of the pole, the finds do not reveal the underlying intention. Older animals seem always to have been used for these sacrifices; the flesh was presumably eaten at some kind of ritual meal, while the head, with the brain, was offered to the spirit of the hunt, or to a supreme being.

At Stellmoor, Rust also found a polished bone of laurel-leaf shape, 5¼ inches long and perforated at the base. It may have been a pendant, but it may also have been a bull-roarer. Rust discovered that it sounded a not very high-pitched note when swung on a band, and that it made that sound only when swung in a counterclockwise direction.

Aurignacian "Venus."

PLATE XXI

Hunting scene. La Vieja cave, Alpera, Spain.

PLATE XXII

a. Upper part of "ritual pole" with reindeer skull. Stellmoor, Germany.

b. Animal of sacrifice, with heavy stones in thoracic cavity. Meiendorf, Germany.

PLATE XXIII

Chalk-filled engraving of elk with numerous indications of physiological details. Vestfold, Norway.

PLATE XXIV

The same type of object was excavated from Magdalenian deposits at La Roche—a decorated bone strongly resembling the bull-roarer of the Australian aborigines. If the laurel-leaf bone found at Stellmoor was in fact a bull-roarer, then we may assume that the mesolithic reindeer hunters used it during their sacrificial rites to convey to them the voices of their gods.

The religious interpretation of the Hamburg and Ahrensburg finds has recently been disputed by H. Pohlhausen, who points to the practice among certain present-day Laplanders and Eskimos of preserving their meat supplies in the icy waters of rivers or lakes. Nevertheless, he concedes that some of the animal skeletons discovered by Rust—in particular, those of the young reindeer does—should be regarded as remains of submerged offerings.

IN 1947 Rust made an altogether novel type of find near Ahrensburg-Hopfenbach. The site, once again, was an ancient lake-side settlement. Pollen analysis has established its age at about 10,000 B.C.

In the slime in front of the camp, Rust found a crudely carved willow trunk 11 feet 5 inches long and 2 inches in diameter (fig. 35). The top end was rounded, suggesting a head; this was separated by a long "neck" from the "shoulders," below which two long grooves had been incised—evidently by a flint tool—which Rust believed to have been arms placed frontally. Some five feet below the "head" a natural curve in the wood formed the "buttocks." The top of the branch had been split to form a flat surface tapering down to the "hands"; this was the front of the "body," and may even have been painted.

At the base of the figure, which had been placed per-

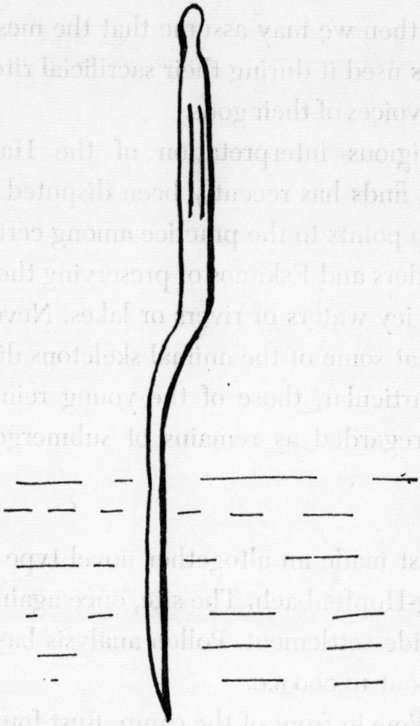

Fig. 35. WOODEN "IDOL,"
AHRENSBURG-HOPFENBACH, GERMANY.
LENGTH: 11 FEET, 5 INCHES.

pendicularly in the slime, Rust discovered a splintered wooden arrow. At a little distance, he found several other tree trunks up to 9 feet long; they had been stripped of their bark and branches, but had not been carved.

The "idol" had been set up in the waters of the ancient

lake, about fifty feet from the shore. This lake differed from those of Meiendorf and Stellmoor in that its bed yielded neither bones nor any other objects, although Rust found great quantities of such deposits in the layer of sand which had once formed the shore.

There seems little doubt that this figure represented the spirit or divinity venerated by the reindeer hunters who had camped on this site. These hunters do not seem to have practiced any rite of submerged animal sacrifice. Nevertheless, they did apparently make offerings to their god, attaching these to the poles that surrounded their idol. Indeed, neither their aspirations nor their concept of the god to whom they presented their wishes could have differed radically from those of their contemporaries in other hunting settlements.

Rust believes that the evident variety of religious practices coexisting among the early mesolithic reindeer hunters of northern Europe reflects the convergence of different cultural streams in the area. Perhaps the graven image of Ahrensburg-Hopfenbach was venerated by a group whose culture derived from that of the Magdalenian (upper paleolithic) reindeer hunters of France, Switzerland, and southern Germany.

III

THE CULT OF ANCESTORS AND SPIRITS OF THE DEAD IN WESTERN EUROPE

THE POOR COMMUNITIES of hunters and fishers who peopled most of Europe in the mesolithic left only isolated traces of their religious life. The world of hunting magic, so magnificently reflected in the art of the upper paleolithic, had almost completely vanished. Only in a few border areas of Europe, where the physical conditions had not radically changed from those of the ice age, or where fairly similar conditions had developed, was ice-age art perpetuated, nourished at least in part on the magical traditions of the past.

One of these border areas was the eastern coastal zone of the Iberian peninsula, where the climate had changed little since upper paleolithic times. This is where the "art of the Spanish Levant" had developed and reached its finest flowering—precisely in the mesolithic, as most authorities now recognize. The other border areas were those from which the glaciers retreated last—Scandinavia, Siberia, and northern Russia; nevertheless, arctic art, to which I shall refer later, developed only in the neolithic.

The peoples of the rest of Europe, living, as they were, in the midst of gradual but profound physical changes, came to adopt beliefs and attitudes altogether different from those of their predecessors. The clearest illustration of the transition is probably afforded by the rock art of southern Spain, which changed completely from naturalism to rigid geometric formalism.

The principal center of this new abstract art was the long range of the Sierra Morena, with its many niches and rock walls which the inhabitants of the region covered with pictures painted red and often superimposed on older paintings. Here we find human figures reduced to a few lines, stiff and abstract animal forms—mainly deer and ibex—and quite often, on the same walls, a great number of signs: wavy ribbons, circles, points, sun- and star-shaped patterns (fig. 36).

These are no longer pictures charged with occult power, intended to make people's wishes come true, or to cast a spell upon some distant prey; they are more in the nature of symbols or formulas. The human form predominates, in every degree of sylization.

Certain painted Azilian pebbles adorned with similarly conventionalized patterns give us a clue to the meaning of these symbols. The Azilian, named for the site of Mas d'Azil—a tunnel-like cave at the foot of the French Pyrenees—was associated with a hunting and fishing culture that spread through what is now northeastern Spain, France, Belgium, Holland, England, and Switzerland. The Azilian hunters and fishers left virtually no other specimens of their art than those flat brook pebbles, engraved or red-painted with points, circles, or lines (fig. 37). Some of them, particularly those found at Mas d'Azil, are decorated with what are unmistakable though extremely schematized human forms.

Hugo Obermaier, one of the foremost authorities on

Fig. 36. POSTGLACIAL SCHEMATIC ROCK PICTURES IN SOUTHERN SPAIN. A. SUNS, DEER, WAVY RIBBONS. GABAL, ALMERÍA. B. SUN AND MEN. CAVE OF LOS CANFOROS DE PEÑARUBIA. C. ANTHROPOMORPHIC FIGURES. LA BATANERA, FUENCALIENTE.

the paleolithic and mesolithic arts of western Europe, has shown that both historically and "ideologically" there is a definite connection between these schematized human figures and the southern Spanish rock pictures (fig. 38). In fact, the culture of the Spanish artists did penetrate into France, where we know it as the Tardenoisian. And the Tardenoisian, lacking the rock art of southern Spain but presumably maintaining the principal religious ideas associated with that art, spread, in the wake of the population movements, over western and central Europe, often intersecting the Azilian.

There exists a remarkable parallel to the painted pebbles in modern Australian and Tasmanian *churingas,* which are, to be sure, mostly made of wood; but the stone specimens, which are not rare, greatly resemble the prehistoric finds both in form and in decoration. The *churingas* are carefully preserved in caves—they are believed to

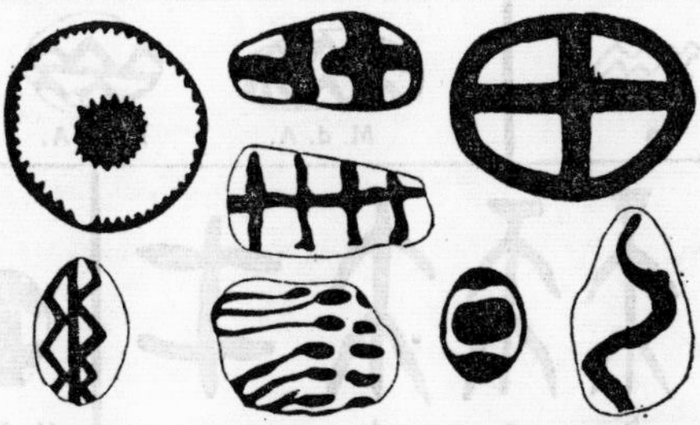

Fig. 37. PAINTED AZILIAN PEBBLES.

contain the souls of the dead. Geoffroy Smith reports that some missionaries once saw a Tasmanian woman carefully arranging a number of flat stones, variously decorated with red and black lines, next to one another. When asked about the meaning of these stones, she replied that they were her "far distant ones"—that is, deceased members of her people. Among the Arunta of central Australia, each tribe has its *churinga* storehouse—a cave where the *churingas* of all its male and female members are preserved. The *churinga,* then, is regarded as the embodiment of the dead person, whose spirit and qualities are transferred to the present possessor. In other words, the *chu-*

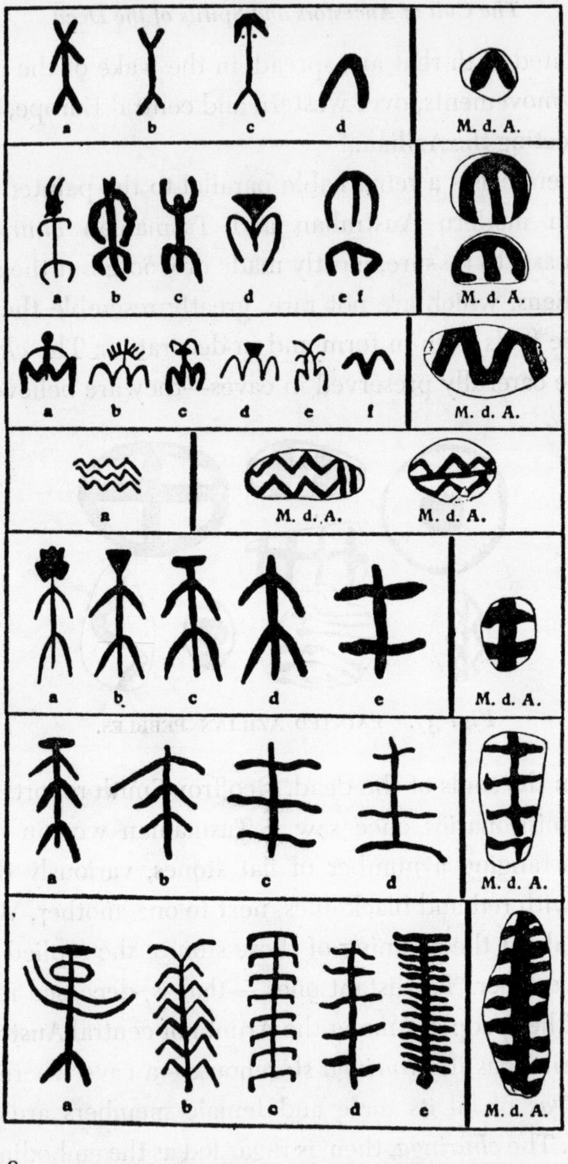

Fig. 38. COMPARATIVE TABLE OF THE SCHEMATIZED ANTHROPOMORPHIC REPRESENTATIONS CHARACTERISTIC OF POSTGLACIAL SPANISH ROCK ART (LEFT) AND THE DESIGNS ON PAINTED PEBBLES OF MAS D'AZIL.

ringa is connected with a form of ancestor worship. And we may assume that similar beliefs gave rise to the Azilian pebble paintings.

On the Azilian pebbles, as on the *churingas,* are two types of designs: stylized human figures, and symbolical or geometrical elements. Among primitives today, the use of these different signs is based on the belief that the ancestors, from whom the tribe is descended and by whom it is protected, may either be human beings or certain animals or plants. It is therefore very probable that the painted mesolithic pebbles were likewise "ancestor stones," closely related to the existence, security, and prosperity of the tribe and each of its members. This theory is far more plausible than others that interpret the Azilian pebbles variously as writing stones, phallic symbols, soothsayers' magic stones, or simply ornaments.

F. Sarasin has found in the Birseck cave, in Switzerland, 133 painted pebbles, every one of them broken. As the Azilian people surely had no special preference for broken stones, we may assume, with Sarasin, that the neolithic cave occupants destroyed the sacred relics of their predecessors whose beliefs they did not share; but what looks like an instance of iconoclasm may also have been an act of vengeance by a hostile mesolithic tribe that wanted to rob the Birseck people of their ancestors' protection.

As it is now recognized that the best art work of the Spanish Levant belongs to the mesolithic, it has been suggested that the geometrical art of southern Spain should be placed in the neolithic. But similarly conventionalized pictures occur on the mesolithic Azilian pebbles. Furthermore, as P. Wernert has shown, Maglemosian amber pendants from the north display similar schematic designs. And, finally, Tardenoisian traces have been found, according to Breuil, at the foot of the rocks adorned with stylized pictures in the Negra de Meca cave, in the Albacete province of Spain. It is therefore safe to say that the abstract art of southern Spain was the product of mesolithic peoples.

In the late neolithic, similar abstract designs occur on idols and dolmens; but these, as we shall see, were accompanied by a revival—probably to be ascribed to extra-European influences—of rock-picture art.

The form of ancestor worship which I have posited of the mesolithic peoples goes back to the upper paleolithic. Engraved and painted stones have been discovered in Magdalenian layers; and the "bull-roarer" of La Roche may similarly have been used in rites of an ancestor cult.

It would seem to follow, then, that the pictures the Iberian peoples painted upon rocks were representations of their ancestors, which they executed in the most remote and awe-inspiring places, there to venerate the spirits of their forebears and, probably, of their dead in general.

Frequently the rock tracings of stylized ancestor figures are accompanied by circular and raylike patterns; could these possibly represent the constellations? Some contemporary primitives believe that their original forebears turned into constellations and now inhabit suns and, through their astral existence, mysteriously influence the fortunes of both the tribe and its individual members.

Moreover, certain modern Australian rock paintings, which bear considerable resemblance to the mesolithic pictures of southern Spain, suggest that the latter were a kind of pictographic writing which described the myths of those creative ancestors and the spirits of the dead.

What might have been the reason for the emergence and rapid spread of the ancestor cult in the mesolithic? Might not these hunter and fishermen folk, who eked out a meager living, have preserved the memory of the game-rich ice age during which their forebears lived? Might they not have imagined the ancient hunters living on under similar conditions—conditions that these latter-day hunters embroidered with a variety of myths? By a logical sequence of thought, they would then have come to believe that their own dead went on into this world of the ancestors, to be transformed there into powerful spirits that could protect and help the living.

TRACES of a curious cult of the spirits of the dead appeared in some striking discoveries in southern Germany.

Not far from Nördlingen, in Bavaria, two limestone caves excavated in 1908—the Great and the Small Ofnet—revealed clear Aurignacian, Solutrean, and Magdalenian occupation layers. At the Great Ofnet, in a thin Azilian-Tardenoisian layer covering the earlier ones, two nests of human skulls, just over three feet apart, were discovered. The first contained twenty-seven skulls, the second, six. They were concentrically arranged in shallow trenches, with all the faces turned toward the west. The skulls in the middle were more tightly packed together than the rest, suggesting that the interments had not taken place simultaneously, but successively. Some had the cervical vertebrae attached, with the marks of forcible severence still discernible; evidently, newly severed heads had been deposited here. Of the thirty-three skulls, twenty were of children and nine of young women; only four were of men. The women's and children's skulls were richly decorated with deer teeth and snail shells; the men's were without adornments, but a few small stone implements were lying beside them. All lay in great quantities of powdered red ocher, lending force to the view that these were ceremonial burials.

It was formerly thought that these skull nests were evidence of a practice of "partial burial," that they were "tombs" in which the heads of certain members of a tribe had been piously laid to rest. More recently, however, T. Mollison has demonstrated that at least five of the skulls, and possibly sixteen others, have marks of what must have been fatal hatchet blows.

Another such nest of skulls was found in 1937 at the entrance of the Höhlenstein cave, Württemberg. This nest consisted of three skulls deep in a red ocher layer. They belonged respectively to a man of twenty-five or so, a woman of the same age, and a one- or two-year-old child. The left temples of the man and woman showed trapezoid perforations with radiating fracture lines, such as would be the result of a powerful blow from a wooden club or stone weapon. Here again, the condition of the cervical vertebrae suggests decapitation of the living. The heads had been interred facing southwest. The woman's skull bore a necklace of twelve fish teeth. The absence of other objects in the same deposits makes it difficult to date the find. Nevertheless, the stratigraphy of the Höhlenstein skulls points to the postglacial.

Another skull burial, this time of a single skull, on the Kaufert mountain, not far from Ofnet, is also of uncertain date. The skull, again without any accompanying objects, lay in a Magdalenian layer, but just beneath the line of a mesolithic-neolithic layer. Quite possibly later occupants had buried the skull in the older layer.

The skulls found at Ofnet and Höhlenstein, then, were definitely of individuals who had been murdered. Could this have been the work of head-hunters? On this theory, a whole family had been struck down at once at Höhlenstein, while at Ofnet the skulls of victims were interred at different times over a fairly long period. The absence of any other body parts would be explained by the fact that the head-hunters were not interested in the trunk and would therefore not have given it burial. Like modern head-hunters, those south-German mesolithic men presumably believed that by cutting off their victims' heads they appropriated their souls, or spirits, which would bring them luck and protection. But perhaps these mesolithic people were simply cannibals who interred their victims' heads with all solemnity in order to propitiate the outraged spirits of the slain.

In connection with both these theories, it is well to remember the uncertainty that prevails regarding the age of the skulls found at Ofnet, Höhlenstein, and Mount

Kaufert. One point against a mesolithic dating—which I have assumed thus far—and in favor of a neolithic dating is the lentiform opening in the Ofnet skulls, which could only have been inflicted by hatchets of a corresponding design; and the hatchet with a lentiform cross section did not, so far as we know, appear before the neolithic. The absence of neolithic objects in association with the skulls could be explained by the fact that the burial places were in remote tribal sanctuaries, frequented only in connection with certain religious ceremonies.

Hence, these curious south-German finds, which point strongly to head-hunting and cannibalism, are probably of neolithic date, or very close to it. This assumption is the more justified as it accords best with the anthropologically established stage of such phenomena.

Part IV

THE NEOLITHIC PERIOD

I

THE ADVENT OF AGRICULTURE

THE MESOLITHIC was a period of groping and searching for new means of sustenance. Compared with the paleolithic cultures, the necessitous hunting and fishing cultures of the mesolithic appear decadent—and this apparent regression cannot be explained solely by the physical changes that were taking place. This was not, after all, the first time a cold period had been succeeded by a warm one; the process had occurred several times before. But never before had the economic basis of men's lives suffered any radical change. The giant beasts that preferred a cold climate had simply given place, during the interglacials, to a warmth-loving fauna that could be hunted for food. But the complete extinction of the giant fauna at the close of the last, or Würm, ice age forced men to find a completely new economic basis of existence.

The solution was initiated outside Europe. It was in Asia that men first passed from a purely hunting and food-gathering economy to a food-producing economy. While continuing to gather fruits, berries, and roots, they now learned also to plant seeds in specially prepared soil, to tend and harvest the crop. And without giving up hunting, they also began to tame and eventually domesticate animals.

The precise period of this economic revolution and its precise place of origin are both matters of controversy. It is now believed that it took place earlier than was formerly thought. Some scholars go so far as to suggest that agriculture may have been practiced in Asia at a time when Europe was still in the ice age.

In Europe the first traces of a society founded on cultivation and animal breeding appear in the Campignian levels. The chief impetus reached Europe from the east, affecting the southern regions first and later moving to higher latitudes. By 3500 B.C. the new food-producing economy had penetrated most of inhabited Europe. This date marks the beginning of the neolithic proper, the preceding first 1,500 years of the neolithic having been characterized by a preponderance of mesolithic pursuits.

The division between pastoral and agricultural societies was never so clear-cut in Europe as in the boundless tracts of Asia; still, we can say that in general the later neolithic inhabitants of Europe were tillers of the soil.

The neolithic farmer's view of the world differed radically from that of the hunters and fishers who had preceded him. For the tiller of the soil, life was embraced in the twin activities of sowing and harvesting; the success of the crops was the yardstick by which all other things were measured. The factors that contributed to growth of the crops—sun, rain, wind, soil—were of prime importance to the neolithic peasant; to influence these factors favorably was the foremost aim of his offerings and his magic. His religion, while still concerned with fertility of animals and men, centered around fertility of plant life.

The economic revolution of the neolithic completely transformed men's lives. In the Near East the emergence of farming and the way of life associated with it led to a rapid flowering of culture. From the fifth millennium B.C., Mesopotamia and the Nile and Indus valleys enter the orbit of recorded history. A thousand years later the advanced cultures of the east unfold in the full light of historical evidence.

Europe, on the other hand, entered the neolithic phase very much later, despite the spread of eastern neolithic culture throughout its southeastern border areas. And even after Europe became largely neolithic, mesolithic conditions persisted long in the subarctic and eastern regions.

II

THE NORTHERN EURASIAN HUNTERS AND FISHERS

THE NORTHERN EURASIAN hunting and fishing world stretched from Scandinavia through Finland, the Baltic countries, and northern Russia as far as Siberia. Its earliest art products are in Norway, up to and beyond the Arctic Circle. Their style is magnificent. The *motifs* are fairly uniform: large animals, mainly deer, bear, seal, whale, and, above all, the elk, and in the high arctic regions the reindeer.

These depictions are generally life size, and very realistic. They cover vast granite surfaces, naturally polished, taking their size, as it were, from the dimensions of the "canvas." The outlines are chipped, rather than incised, into the rock.

Later the sphere of this art expanded, first to Sweden, then as far as Lake Onega in northern Russia, while similar portrayals of animals also occur in Siberia and central Asia. Here, however, the dimensions are smaller and the technique somewhat different: Siberian rock art consists of drawings pecked into the surface, and later also of some paintings executed in red pigment. In the course of the millennia, many of these paintings have, of course, disappeared. Those that have been preserved are to be found mainly on vertical walls beneath overhanging rocks. Only rarely are traces of such paintings found at completely unprotected sites, and in such cases the pigment is barely visible.

Still later, the range of *motifs* broadened. Human figures, ornamental signs, and boats are similar to those of present-day Eskimo art. The human figures usually show the phallus prominently; in one case the act of cohabitation is depicted. In the Solsem cave twenty human figures and a huge cross were found depicted on the interior walls, which lay in utter darkness. The humans are very simply portrayed, in part with phallic emphasis. There is no doubt about the stone-age origin of these figures.

While the earliest examples of these later pictures are still quite naturalistic, a growing tendency toward conventionalism is apparent. During the late neolithic and the bronze age, this conventionalism leads to a severely schematic style.

Altogether, the art of northern Europe and of the circumpolar regions extends over some 4,000 years, from the end of the sixth to the beginning of the second millennium B.C.

Is this hunting art of the north at all connected, in development and inspiration, with the earlier paleolithic art of western Europe? Both style and *motifs* do in fact suggest a revival of ice-age traditions. There is the same naturalism, which reaches its peak in the Leiknes engravings of animals turning their heads, and there is the same uniformity of *motif*—big-game animals. It is hard to say whether this uniformity was deliberate and based on particular religious or magical beliefs, or whether the artists' mental horizon was as yet closed to any other subjects. But as the physical environment of these artists was very similar to that of the paleolithic hunter artists, and as their art, like the earlier ice-age art, evolved from naturalism to abstraction, we may assume that circumpolar art was an independent phenomenon.

Still, we cannot altogether discount the possibility that European circumpolar art was influenced by ice-age traditions—even though there is little apparent connection between the pronounced naturalism of the earliest circumpolar art and the strongly geometrical character of late ice-age art. There is, however, some similarity between the early northern art and the naturalism of the upper Aurignacian; and this culture was not confined to western Europe but had spread across central and eastern Europe to Siberia (there to produce small art works, especially human and animal statuettes). In consequence, Eastern influences on European circumpolar art, as H. G. Bandi has pointed out in a recent study, should not be ruled out.

Most authorities assume that belief in the potency of magic was at the basis of this art. Here, too, are pictures of weapons and traps, such as signified the magical killing or capture of animals in ice-age art. Nevertheless, such pictures are decidedly less common in the north than they were in paleolithic art. At Evenhus, on the Frosta peninsula in the Trondhelm fjord, Norway, the picture of a fleeing elk closely pursued by an arrow has been discovered. But boomerangs occur far more often in these pictures. At Vingen, for instance, animals are depicted springing into a sickle-shaped boomerang. In fact, stone boomerangs of this type have been discovered in Scandinavia; like the pictures, they belong to the neolithic. Again, on rock pictures at Sletjord, at Strand, at Vingen, and at Ekeberg, there are representations of trench traps and stockades. At Ekeberg an animal is shown being driven into a trap, and at Sporanes several animals are shown on the point of entering one.

The magical character of circumpolar art is also indicated by the "life-line" on many of the animal pictures—a line traced from the animal's mouth, down its neck, and into its thorax, where it terminates in what may be either the heart or the lungs (plate XXV). I referred earlier to a practice observed among the Ojibwa Indians as late as the 1890's: their sorcerer drew exactly the same sort of "life-line" on animal pictures during a magic ritual performed to ensure success in the hunt. Many other Indians also use this symbol; Herbert Kühn saw it among the Pueblos of New Mexico and Arizona, who explained its meaning to him. The "life-line" is also found on rock pictures in North America and on Siberian engravings, as well as in Lapp art. Quite possibly this symbol passed from the

Scandinavian peoples of the stone and bronze ages to the Lapps, spread across northern Asia, and finally reached North America.

Fertility magic must also have been practiced among the circumpolar peoples, as evidenced by the number of mating scenes which occur in their rock art.

In Kühn's view, the best proof of the magical character of circumpolar art is that to this day the peoples living around the Arctic Circle, especially the Lapps, continue to make pictures before setting out on the hunt. In 1933 Frederika de Laguna found on Kodiak, off Alaska, pictures made by Eskimos which bore a striking resemblance to the late neolithic phase of Scandinavian art. Upon questioning, the local Eskimos told her that only special persons, or magicians, made these pictures, and that they did so in order to secure good fortune in the hunt. Among the men questioned was the nephew of a magician, who said that the pictures were the works of his uncle, but that some other Eskimos, members of a secret society, had collaborated. All the pictures were used in secret hunting rituals, as could also be inferred from the harpoons drawn upon some of the scenes.

Another aspect of circumpolar rock art is suggested by G. Hallström's report of 1910. On the Kola peninsula he had seen Lapps making offerings before a prehistoric rock picture.

The borderline between magic and religion, between sorcerers' spells and offerings to the divinities ruling the animal kingdom, seems to have been undefined even among the ice-age hunters. The same would appear to be true of the neolithic arctic hunters, but with the predominant emphasis on religion. The rock pictures, therefore, should reflect this emphasis. Some years ago G. Gjessing, one of the foremost authorities on circumpolar art, confirmed my opinion.

Many of the pictures were found on rocks very close to the water—beside waterfalls and rapids, around lakes, bays, and fjords—at a height that corresponds approximately to the rise in the land level since the stone age; they must therefore originally have been close to the water level. Occasionally we find bronze-age pictures lower upon the same wall, where they could have been executed only after the water level had subsided.

The fact that the pictures occur so often at water margins should have some bearing on their interpretation. Would this be perhaps a survival from an earlier tradition, that of the northern European reindeer hunters, who for thousands of years, during the mesolithic and even earlier during the paleolithic, made sacrifice by sinking their offerings in the water? Then too, the circumpolar rock pictures are often found in wild and barren places that could hardly have been actual hunting grounds, but rather the reputed abodes of the powers that ruled the beasts. To these powers, seemingly, men presented their wishes and prayers in the "language" of their pictures.

The rock-picture sites may therefore be regarded as the ritual sites of the neolithic hunters of the north. Here they gathered to assure good fortune in their expeditions. And remembering the lakes of Meiendorf and Stellmoor, we may assume that here, too, a variety of sacrifices were offered to the hunting spirit residing in the waters. Traces of such sacrifices do in fact occur.

Some yards from the edge of a marsh near Laukas, Finland, and about three feet below the surface, a patch of coarse white sand was found no more than a few square yards in area. There were also several large stones. Both stones and sand must have been brought to this spot in the midst of a marsh by human agency—a conclusion supported by the finding of a wooden spoon with a handle ending in a carved bear's head.

The marshes of Finland and Scandinavia have yielded a number of objects that can be considered ritual offerings. Laukas, in fact, may have been a kind of sanctuary. And the rites observed among certain contemporary arctic peoples help to illuminate the nature of the ancient rites. The following, for instance, has been reported of the people living in the neighborhood of Suoyarvi, Karelia, U.S.S.R. The place where these hunters celebrated their cult was situated on an isle in the middle of a peat bog, which they reached by a path of felled trees. There was a hut on that islet; it had no real floor, and a heap of stones in one corner constituted the fireplace. The hunters prepared a meat soup in a big cauldron, then dipped their wooden bowls into it and ate the soup with wooden spoons. When they had finished, they put some meat in one bowl and broth in another, and offered both to the spirit of the forest, entreating him to taste the meal and provide them with a good supply of game. It may be assumed that a wooden spoon was laid out for the spirit of the forest, together with the bowls.

Is the fact that the handle of the ancient spoon found at Laukas was shaped like a bear's head in any way related to the sacrificial rite? Or did the carved bear's head have any magic significance? Two other spoons adorned with animal heads, also found in marshlands, would seem to imply some such magic role; by and large, no other wooden objects, except snow shoes and sled runners, have been found in bogs. Wooden spoons of this kind may well have been used by the neolithic hunters to make food offerings to a forest god who was also conceived of as having dominion over the game animals.

OTHER finds suggest that the neolithic hunters and fishers of the circumpolar regions also held a variety of magical beliefs.

I have mentioned earlier the male figures, nearly always depicted with strong phallic emphasis, that so often occur in the latest period of northern rock art. Clay amulets in phallic form have been discovered on neolithic dwelling sites in Finland and southern Karelia. These objects, like the anthropomorphic figures, would indicate the existence, in those times, of magical beliefs and fertility practices.

Magical significance is also commonly ascribed to the neolithic stone weapons used by the Karelian and Finnish hunters—hatchets and hammers with perforated shafts on which handles could be fitted. The blunt ends are shaped like animal heads (fig. 39). In the same region sculptured animal heads have been found that did not belong to weapons, but likewise bore perforations through which handles could be slipped. These sculptures appear to have originated in Karelia, in the Olonek region. Similar objects have frequently turned up in Finland and occasionally also in northern Sweden. Related pieces appear as far east as the Urals.

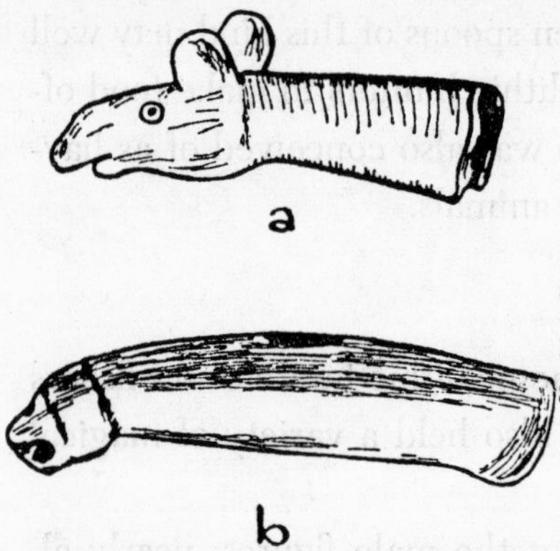

Fig. 39. KARELIAN ANIMAL-HEAD WEAPONS. A. ELK HEAD FOUND AT SÄKKIYÄRVI ½ ACTUAL SIZE B. BEAR (?) HEAD FOUND AT ANTREA ⅔ ACTUAL SIZE

Some of these carvings are strikingly naturalistic, some deliberately stylized. Sometimes their crude shape seems to be due to the resistance of a material such as gneiss. Nearly always the carvings depict the most highly prized game of the northern forests—the elk and the bear. This limitation of subject matter is a familiar phenomenon both in the neolithic circumpolar rock art and that of the preceding ice age.

The animal-head axes and hammers must have been

primarily hunting weapons; and the ornament was doubtless intended to endow the weapon with magic power over the animal represented upon it. As for the animal-head sculptures, which were not weapons but which had perforated shafts, they probably were erected on staves or sticks and used in the magical or religious ceremonies.

The Lapps today make a point of burying similarly decorated weapons in order to ensure success in the hunt. If the neolithic hunters likewise buried their carved weapons, it still would be a matter of uncertainty as to whether those weapons were intended as votive offerings to the earth god and lord of the hunting grounds, or whether the animal heads were thought to possess some magic power that would enable the hunters to bring down their prey.

There seems to be little doubt about the magical significance of the neolithic stone fish discovered mainly in Siberia, and made mostly of soft sedimentary stone. The primitive peoples who now inhabit those regions carve similar fish forms of wood and of bone. They wear them as talismans to help in the catch, and sometimes attach them to their nets, or throw them into the water.

The small neolithic art works of the circumpolar regions include many perforated sculptures representing animals and men; clearly they were worn as pendants. Those found in the Baltic are of amber, while farther east they are made of bone and various kinds of stone. It has been suggested that these objects were appurtenances of the ancient hunter magicians; and they do strongly resemble certain parts of the equipment of the Siberian shamans today. Another probable part of the ancient magicians' accouterment is the T-shaped slate object found frequently in northern Sweden and Finland, which is remarkably like the "hammer" of the modern Lapps' magic drums.

III

THE DANUBIAN FARMING PEOPLES

WHILE THE EXTREME NORTH was given over to hunting and fishing, the rest of Europe became largely agricultural in character. The earliest traces of an agricultural society come from southeastern Europe, whence it spread deep into central Europe. This type of "culture," however, based on food-raising, was by no means uniform in character in the various regions to which it spread.

Many Danubian peasant settlements consisted of sturdy huts and farm buildings, and often formed quite large villages.

The finds tell us practically nothing about the spiritual concepts of the most ancient tillers of the soil. The first clues—the Danubian idols—date from the end of the third millennium B.C.

Throughout the vast Danubian area, countless small sculptures representing human beings and animals have been unearthed. Most are of clay, some of bone, and some even of marble. As a rule, the anthropomorphic figurines represent nude females, generally standing, occasionally sitting. Their artistic merit is slight. Frequently they are little more than cylindrical forms with barely indicated head and body. Impress of thumb and forefinger mark the "features." Their eyes are mere holes or points. Secondary sex characteristics of the female are strongly emphasized. Dotted patterns represent neck ornaments, perhaps tattoo marks. Usually short, protruding stumps represent the arms; the legs are always very summarily indicated. But alongside this cylindrical, fairly slender type of statuette, there occurs another one, with prominent hips and buttocks.

In the eastern Balkans, we often find better modeling, particularly of the head, and a richer ornamentation consisting of incised or painted spirals. In regions whose art shows naturalistic tendencies, the arms of these female figurines rest on the bosom, or else one hand covers the breasts and the other the genitals. But alongside such statuettes, we regularly meet—especially in the upper, and thus more recent, deposits—stunted, stylized figurines that are barely recognizable as human.

In the Balkans, too, are flat figurines carved of bone or, more rarely, of stone. They are very schematic in style, but the head, trunk, and legs are always clearly distinguished. The neck, abdomen, and particularly the legs are often decorated with dots. The genitals are indicated by a triangle of sharply incised lines (fig. 40). One figure shows this triangle in color, probably representing a garment; we may wonder whether the triangle did not always represent a loin cloth.

Yet another type of idol found in the Danubian region is the peg idol, consisting of a wide base with two winglike

Chalk-filled engraving of coupling elks. Note "life line" within each animal. Buskerud, Norway.

PLATE XXV

Chalk-filled engravings of stylized animals. Vestfold, Norway.

PLATE XXVI

Menhir statue, Saint-Sernin (Aveyron), France.

PLATE XXVII

Stylized female figure in baked clay, Znojmo district, Moravia, Czechoslovakia. 5⅓ in. high.

PLATE XXVIII

protrusions and a conical peg fitted into the base (fig. 41). The peg represents the head, with the eyes and nose painted on, while the base represents the body, with the arms indicated by the winglike objects. But there are even more schematized idols of this kind: unpainted pegs fitted into simple cubic bases.

The extreme of schematization is to be found in some idols in the form of pyramidlike loom weights, mostly unperforated. That these objects were in fact intended as

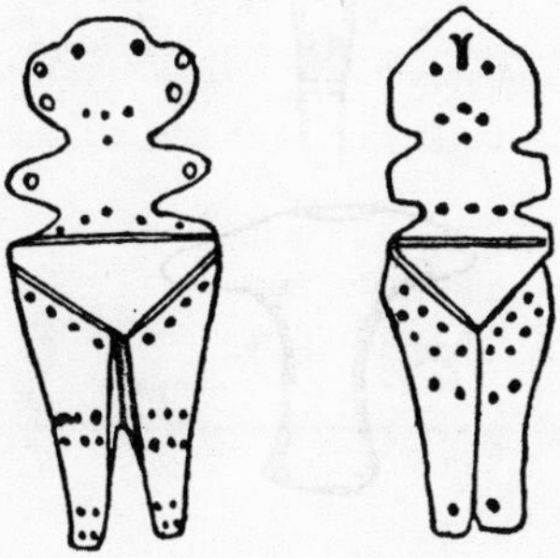

Fig. 40. FLAT BONE IDOLS. BULGARIA.

idols is sufficiently proved by their ornamentation, imitating necklaces and pendants, and also by the suggestion of a head in certain cases.

Individual sculptures of animals, animals carved upon dishes, dishes in the form of animals, and highly abstract engravings of animals on little bone tablets are also in evidence. The small clay statuettes are most common. In the north the area of their diffusion includes Poland and central Germany, and extends into Switzerland. The so-called Priests' Hill, near Brasov, Romania, has yielded a particularly rich crop of such models; its flat summit was once the site of a neolithic village. The short-legged, crudely modeled little clay figures excavated there, from the neolithic occupation layers, represent oxen, rams, goats, and pigs. In Hungary, where such animal sculptures similarly abound, they sometimes are adorned with the hooked cross (swastika). Some of the pieces of that art work found in Czechoslovakia were painted.

At first glance, this Danubian statuary does not look like a native product; the crudeness and crude schemati-

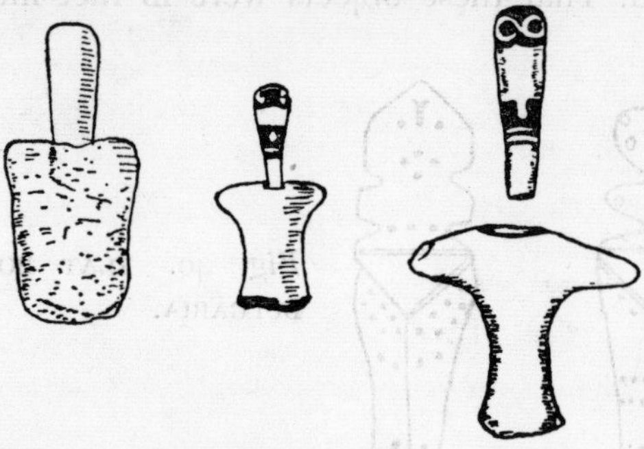

Fig. 41. PEG IDOLS.
THESSALY, GREECE.
¼ ACTUAL SIZE.

zation suggests copying, by unskilled hands, of alien models. In point of fact, the Danubian idol region is coextensive with the sphere of Eastern influence.

The neolithic statuettes of the Danubian region have never been found in graves. We therefore can discard the theory that these objects were grave offerings, miniature replicas of persons or animals the deceased would have wanted to take with him. Their technical imperfection might lead us to wonder whether these objects were not some kind of children's toy. But the subject matter alone—

female nudes with emphasis on sex characteristics—should dispose of this theory also.

Most authorities now agree in attributing a ritual significance to Danubian plastic art. Naturally we cannot say that all the statuettes were idols. But a ritual intent might be more common, even in the case of animal figures, than we are inclined to assume. In the hill settlement of Sultan, Bulgaria, some fragments of a very smooth plaster object were found showing a design of crimson spirals on a white ground; and amidst these fragments lay a quantity of animal figures. It is quite likely that here was a ceremonial site, or a niche where animal idols or votive gifts were kept.

WHEN the female statuettes of the Danube region made their appearance, the procreative principle had long been conceived of and venerated as a female deity in the East. In the Ishtar temple at Ashur a number of statuettes were discovered in deposits dating from the third millennium B.C. These artefacts can be divided into two distinctive groups: the first consists of limestone figures of clothed men, believed to represent donors or priests; the other group comprises a number of clay figurines of standing female nudes, with their hands over the bosom, or else with one hand covering one breast and the other the genitals. These figurines, which are far less naturalistic than the male statuettes found at the site, are, beyond doubt, images of the mistress of the temple—Ishtar, the goddess of fertility.

Her cult—the cult of the procreative principle—centered around a particular sanctuary where the statue of the goddess, life size or larger, must have been erected. But evidently her suppliants were also eager to own some simple image of the great goddess, whose protection was so important for the welfare of the crops, the animals, and their own offspring. The clay figures at Ashur must have been made for sale to pious visitors to the temple; in fact, they were mass-produced from molds such as have actually been discovered on the site.

This highly developed worship of the fertility goddess, as practiced by the advanced Oriental societies, cannot, of course, be posited of the primitive agricultural communities of the Danube region. Still, the character of their female statuettes as idols of a fertility cult can hardly be doubted. The poor workmanship need not surprise us—probably these figurines were made by ordinary community members rather than by craftsmen.

This does not mean that the neolithic peasantry of that region had no tribal sanctuaries with larger idols. No such sanctuaries have been discovered thus far; but in 1934, fragments of an extraordinary statue were found in three neighboring dwelling trenches at Hluboké Mašufsky, near Znojmo, Czechoslovakia. Pottery unearthed in the same deposits made it possible to date the figure in the late ice age. When the fragments were assembled and, in part, restored, this artefact turned out to be a standing female nude, with massive legs joined, and the head and members, including fingers and toes, clearly delineated. The figure was 15 inches high, and better modeled than other Danubian idols. The ears showed small perforations, presumably for earrings; a necklace and pendant had been modeled around the neck. The comparatively thin arms were flexed at the elbows and stretched forward, palms open—a position that appears to symbolize the attitude of giving, the gesture of a goddess dispensing her bounty. (Now arises the question of whether the arm stumps of other idols found were not intended to convey the same notion, and appear so shortened only because of poor workmanship.)

What is still puzzling about the statue of Hluboké Mašufsky is the fragment's distribution among three occupation layers. But its ceremonial character cannot be questioned. Probably tribal or village sanctuaries existed throughout the Danubian region, whose neolithic inhabitants sought to win the favor of the fertility goddess—conceived of as presiding over fruitfulness of earth and beast—by public worship and, perhaps, processions, as well as by domestic ritual. Many of the idols have perforations in the lobes or the head, suggesting that ear and head ornaments were used as pious tribute to this goddess.

The importance of the female fertility principle in the Danubian neolithic life appears in the exaggerated sex characteristics of the omnipresent idols. In fact, male idols are rarely found; evidently they represent the goddess's male partner. The great "earth mother" of the East had also her male partner, but his role was secondary in the cult; his image, too, appears less frequently.

The male figure played its part primarily in religious marriage ceremonies. Two idols found in Transylvania,

Romania, make the existence of such rites more than likely; the idols, a male and a female, exactly fit each other *in copula*. Quite apparently, the neolithic Danubian peasant tried to promote the fertility of field and cattle by invoking the magic of analogy. If we, then, consider certain European rural customs of our own day, as well as the wealth of evidence of special marriage rituals in prehistoric times, we may conclude that the neolithic peasants of the Danubian region carried out such rituals in public ceremony at certain seasonal festivals. Perhaps some hand-picked participants actually represented the goddess and her mate on such occasions.

While statuettes representing mother and child—human fertility—are fairly common in the Orient, they are rare in the Danube region. Numbers of such figurines have been excavated at Aegina, in the temple of Aphaia, the goddess presiding over childbirth. These must have been votive gifts offered to entreat children of Aphaia, or to thank her for blessings received.

As THE female figurines of the Danube region were undoubtedly idols, the same is probably true of the animal statuettes. The crudeness of these statuettes need not deceive us, and indeed there do exist some very well-modeled pieces. But the neolithic farmer would not have cared much about artistic quality; what he wanted was to possess an efficacious image of the power he invoked.

The animal figures were probably copies of bigger statues erected in tribal sanctuaries; this theory is supported by the discovery of a larger piece, about 13 inches high (representing a ram), at Jordansmühl, in Silesia. In any case, there can be no doubt as to the ritual character of figurines decorated with the hooked cross, a distinct religious symbol. Moreover, animal-shaped vessels appear to have been used for ritual purposes, while the flat bone plaques decorated with stylized bulls' heads (fig. 42) like those found in the cave of Bileze Zlote, Galicia, Poland, are suggestive of religious emblems or good-luck charms.

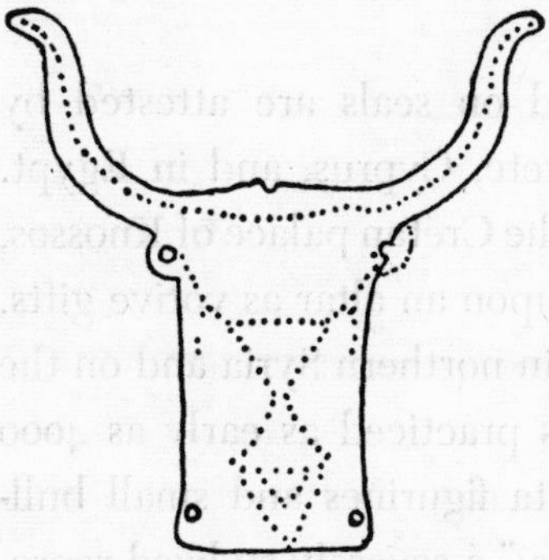

Fig. 42. SMALL BONE PLAQUE IN THE FORM OF A STYLIZED BULL'S HEAD. BILCZE ZLOTE CAVE, GALICIA, POLAND.

The statuettes, engraved plaques, and ceramics mostly represent male animals, such as bulls, boars, and rams.

The neolithic peasants of the Danube region certainly practiced a bull cult. Effigies of the bull are more widespread than those of any other animal; they take the form of statues or reliefs appearing on various vessels. The bull cult originated in the east-Aegean region, and the Danubian area where it was current merely marks the northwestern border of a vast region of its dominion stretching from the Aegean to India.

In two advanced centers of that great belt, the Indus

valley and Crete, the bull cult reached a high peak of development. Scenes from this cult often appear on seals. Three main phases are depicted: the bull fight or capture, the bull leap or play, and finally the sacrifice of the bull. Scenes of bull fighting and sacrifice are common in the early Indian culture known as Harappa (3000 to 2000 B.C.), whereas the bull leap characterizes numerous Cretan memorials. It seems that the Cretan bull play, in which men and women would leap over the backs of the huge charging beasts, belonged to a later, more secular period of development.

Bull sacrifices as depicted on seals are attested by skeletal remains found on Crete, Cyprus, and in Egypt. Bulls' horns also turned up in the Cretan palace of Knossos, where they had been placed upon an altar as votive gifts.

The bull cult is still older in northern Syria and on the Iranian plateau, where it was practiced as early as 4000 B.C., leaving behind terra-cotta figurines and small bull-head amulets. The "bucranium," a severely stylized representation of the bull's skull, appears as a common theme of ceramic ornament in this area.

No evidence of bull sacrifice has yet been found in the Danube region. Plastic or pictorial representations of such sacrifices or other ritual scenes, as we know them from Crete and the Indus valley, are lacking in the very primitive cultures. Yet we may assume some simple form of bull ritual, including the ritual slaying of the animal, even among the neolithic farmers of the Danubian area. Whatever the actual ceremony of sacrifice, the bull's head itself appears to have been the object of particular veneration, embodied in the use of the bucranium on carved vessels, amulets, and plaques.

The Orient provides us with the interpretation of the bull cult. There the bull has been depicted in association with the great goddess of fertility. The bull is the partner of the goddess, symbolizing the virile principle of generation and indomitable force. The familiar Greek legend of the goddess Europa whom Zeus, in bull form, abducts from Phoenicia to Crete is a later echo of this widespread cult.

The symbol of the bull god is the phallus, and traces of the phallic cult occur wherever the bull cult was practiced. Statuettes, dug up in Thessaly, of sitting figures shown with phallus, doubtless represent the fertility god in human form. Representations of the phallus alone are rare; however, they might easily have been overlooked by excavators, or they might have been made of perishable material such as wood, and therefore not have been preserved. In the religious rites of the neolithic tillers of the soil, this symbol must have played an important part.

Representations of boars and rams also seem to have been connected with the fertility cult. But they seem to have had a different origin from that of the bull cult. The ram points to pastoral influences. In later Germanic beliefs, the boar—to which offerings were made chiefly at lakes and springs—was particularly connected with the divine dispenser of prosperity and fertility. At the bottom of a dried-up Thuringian lake, two clay vessels were found

—one of them in the shape of a boar, with bronze eyes, the other with three boars' heads. These must at some time have been submerged in the lake as sacrificial offerings.

All this Danubian sculpture, with its zoomorphic and anthropomorphic pantheon of fertility powers, belongs to the late neolithic period. This art, like the religious conceptions that inspired it, was certainly of Eastern origin. In the ancient East these conceptions had obviously developed, under the influence of the early advanced cultures, out of older primitive beliefs connected with the sky, the earth, the sun, and the primary forces of nature.

The very earliest beliefs of these neolithic peoples could hardly have been more than a nature creed of this kind. Then, with the introduction of farming from the East, certain religious beliefs of the East were adopted likewise. Of the older, simpler belief in the forces of nature, few traces have been uncovered by excavation. Yet it is quite likely that many elements of the more primitive religious practices remain embodied in the symbols that so often adorn both the pottery and the idols of the area. Spirals and meanders are mere decorations—but circles, wheels, and hooked crosses are meaningful symbols. Originally they must have designated the sky, the sun, the earth, and other natural phenomena that played so important a part in the most ancient beliefs.

The most highly developed and best executed symbols seem to be the group of clay figures which have been described as crenated idols. These are small images with four or six prongs resembling crosses or stars, or little clay pillars that are forked at the tip and sometimes culminate in animal heads. These figures always have a perforation running through the entire body, through which some suspending cord must have been threaded.

In Lower Austria, Czechoslovakia, and Hungary, human bones have been excavated quite frequently together with animal bones in occupation layers, sometimes on the very hearthstone. In some cases such finds were made in caves, as in the south-German caves of Hohlenstein, Hohlenstein-Nördlingen, Hansele Hohl, and at Istállókö, Hungary. These finds are strongly indicative of anthropophagous practices.

At Sighisoara (Transylvania), Romania, a clay hearth was found with a covering plate 31½ inches in diameter, and greatly charred. All around, there lay a vast number of potsherds, whole pots and innumerable bones of domestic animals—and among this debris human bones. One of the pots contained the complete skeleton of a child, another a child's skull.

We can scarcely avoid connecting the vast number of skulls found in the Danubian region with these indications of cannibalism, or possibly human sacrifice. Skulls without the lower jaw often turn up in occupation sites, in completely undisturbed layers, where they could have been placed only for ritual purposes. These skulls, like the other human bones, have been found mostly in the northern parts of the Danubian region, suggesting that they were skull trophies of neolithic head-hunters rather than the skulls of ancestors. Like contemporary primitives who practice head-hunting, those neolithic peoples probably believed that the spirit residing in a skull placed in the foundations of a dwelling would be the protector of the household and guarantee prosperity and fertility to the family.

The existence of these different practices—cannibalism, human sacrifice, head-hunting—of the Danube region may be explained by the proximity of older hunting societies and their mingling with the early neolithic farmers.

IV

THE MEDITERRANEAN AREA

THE MEDITERRANEAN AREA, with its countless islands and indented coasts, was even more directly exposed to Eastern influences than was the Danube valley. This is true in particular of the eastern half of the Mediterranean area, of Crete and the Aegean islands (which, however, fall within the purview of recorded history and so cannot be considered in this study).

In the western Mediterranean, two islands arrest our attention by their unique architectural monuments dating back to neolithic times. These are Malta and the little neighboring island of Gozo.

According to the finds made so far, human settlement did not begin on Malta before the neolithic. The oldest pottery found there, in the Dalam cave, is identical with that of the earliest neolithic inhabitants of Sicily; and this would indicate that Malta was first settled by primitive farming people from Sicily late in the third millennium B.C. Around 2000 B.C. Malta came under the influence of the megalithic culture.

The most impressive memorials of the civilization of the

ancient inhabitants of Malta and Gozo—the latter island was colonized by Maltese—are the tremendous stone structures they built, which in part still stand. The authorities are generally agreed that these structures were prehistoric sanctuaries.

It used to be thought that they were Phoenician temples dating from the seventh or eighth century B.C. Pottery found there dates from a good thousand years earlier; and there can be no doubt that these structures represent an achievement led up to by centuries of work and adaptation on the part of an originally very primitive people. Many influences from Egypt and the Near East must have contributed to this development. The sanctuaries were built and used over a period of about five centuries, from somewhat before 2000 B.C. to 1500 B.C.

Most of the Maltese structures are above ground level. So far only one underground sanctuary has been discovered—the Hypogeum at Hal Saflieni.

They all show a characteristic plan. Two oval chambers lie parallel, a short passage connects them in the middle of their long axes, and facing this passage, in the front chamber, is the entrance, while a large apse extends from the center of the second chamber in line with the entrance and the connecting passage. Around this double oval, there runs a wall that forms an incurvated semicircle before the entrance. The walls of the sanctuaries are built of massive upright stone slabs capped by large horizontals that occasionally jut out. As far as one can tell, the entrance and connecting passage of each building were roofed with flat slabs, but most of the structure was roofless, the oval chambers being in the nature of open courts. The slant of the apsidial walls gives us reason to believe that the roof of the apse had been vaulted.

This plan is strikingly exemplified in the aptly named Gigantia, on the island of Gozo (fig. 43). There we find

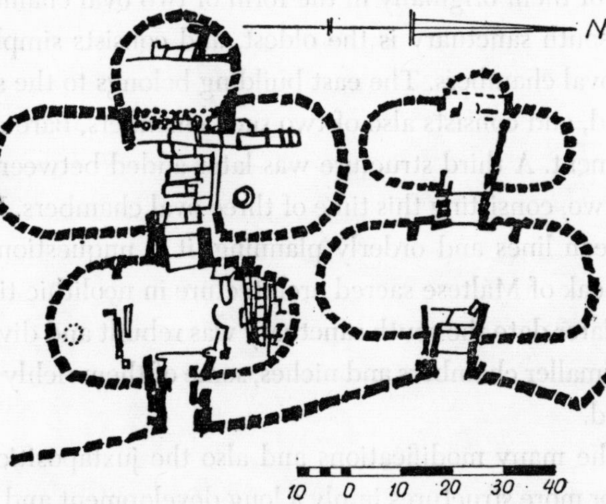

Fig. 43. GROUND PLAN OF THE TWIN SANCTUARIES OF GIGANTIA, ON THE ISLAND OF GOZO.

two buildings with double-oval chambers so close together that their façades are almost continuous. They are enclosed by a common wall. In front of the two buildings, there extends what seems to have been a large forecourt.

Buildings like the so-called Mnaidra, on the Maltese south coast, bear witness to further architectural evolution. Later modifications divided the rear chamber into a series of niches and secondary chambers. Later still, a second building was erected on the north side, and eventually a third one, with smaller chambers than those of the preceding structures.

The Tarxien group of buildings, situated on an eminence near Valetta, is an even better illustration of this evolution. Three separate structures can be distinguished, each of them originally in the form of two oval chambers. The south sanctuary is the oldest, and consists simply of two oval chambers. The east building belongs to the same period, and consists also of two such chambers, bare of all ornament. A third structure was later added between the first two, consisting this time of three oval chambers. With its clean lines and orderly planning, it is unquestionably the peak of Maltese sacred architecture in neolithic times. At a later date the south sanctuary was rebuilt and divided into smaller chambers and niches, some of them richly decorated.

The many modifications and also the juxtaposition of two or more structures imply a long development and ever more complex expression of the cult of the neolithic inhabitants. (Only one authority, C. Schuchhardt, still disputes the ritual character of these buildings; he regards them as palaces. Yet each of the buildings shows many features that can only have had a ritual significance.)

In the most ancient times the great rear apse of the sanctuary was quite obviously the holy of holies. It could be reached only through the great portal of the passage separating the two oval chambers. But the lateral apses must also have served ritual purposes. A conical pillar was found in a lateral apse of the Gigantia; it was 3 feet 4 inches high, and was near a stone structure suggestive of a table.

The small secondary chambers and recesses into which the great oval was later divided must have played an important part in the more developed cult. In a niche in the Hagiar-Kim sanctuary there stands a 6½-foot rough stone pillar behind an altar restored on what probably was its original site. In various sanctuaries the lateral chambers, with their windowlike apertures and—sometimes—carefully constructed portals, often contained great stone "tables," which must have been altars.

But there also are altars of another kind—rectangular stone blocks, in some cases ornamented with relief carvings. One of these blocks, at Tarxien, had been hollowed out, and contained animal bones and stone tools, quite obviously remnants of sacrifice. Others contained potsherds, stone tools, bones, mussel shells, or pebbles.

The stone pillars were evidently important ritual objects, as we can infer from the small models of them which have been found.

Anthropomorphic figures among the ritual objects are from a much later period. In one section of the Tarxien site, excavation revealed the lower part of a statue of a woman larger than life size. On two faces of one of the rectangular blocks ornamented with relief carvings the lower part of a seated figure can be distinguished.

In addition to these large representations, the sanctuaries of Malta and Gozo have yielded many stone and clay figurines, mostly females of exaggerated corpulence. This massive obesity and the steatopygous exaggerations are particularly in evidence in a group of seated nudes. A number of standing nudes show one arm hanging, the other—as a rule—resting on the middle of the stomach. A series of figures belonging to the latest period appear to be draped, from the hips, in curiously pleated, bell-shaped skirts.

THE ARCHAEOLOGICAL treasures unearthed on Malta and Gozo, and particularly the colossal size of the various buildings, bear witness to the astonishingly rich religious life of the neolithic inhabitants. The spacious sanctuaries were adequate for great public festivals and processions.

The ritual appears to have become most elaborate during the final period. At the same time, with the division of the great chambers into lateral rooms and small recesses, there appears to have been a falling away from the originally strict cult in favor of many different practices, perhaps more strongly individualistic in character.

The most astonishing thing about those neolithic islanders is the apparent power of their religious impulse. While they themselves no doubt lived in flimsy huts, which soon fell into ruin and left no trace, they built these enormous temples, whose cyclopean masonry endures today, after nearly 4,000 years.

What conclusions can we draw regarding their religious beliefs and the fabric of their cult?

The temples of Malta and Gozo show a certain resemblance in plan and construction to the mortuary structures of western Europe and North Africa. Some of their characteristic features, too, such as the monolithic pillars and stone tables, dating from the earliest period of Maltese neolithic culture, have strong affinities with the western megalithic remains. The neolithic Maltese, as I said before, were subjected to megalithic influences in some form or another.

This leads us to infer that their temples and ritual were dedicated primarily to the powers of the underworld. Historically, this religion is closely related to the cult of the dead; it was a more developed cult of the spirits of the dead and the godlike powers of the underworld. The monolithic pillars of the neolithic islanders, which played so important a part in the first phase of their religious development, seem to have been regarded as the thrones of souls or of gods, much like the Egyptian obelisks; and the stone tables near the monoliths served, in all probability, as altars of sacrifice. Evidently the faithful believed that some divinity or the spirits of the dead were seated on these pillars during the religious ceremonies, waiting to receive the offerings.

Is it not possible that the potsherds, stone tools, bones, and shells lying under stone slabs in the various sanctuaries represented votive gifts to the spirits or divinities residing in the earth? Moreover, the curious apertures of some of the niches and secondary chambers of the later period have led some authorities to suggest that oracles were pronounced there. If this assumption is correct, then the faithful must have come to the temples not only to offer sacrifice or prayers to the dead or the chthonian gods, but also to consult them.

In a later period, another cult emerged alongside this chthonian cult, centering around a female divinity. This new cult rapidly gained in popularity; it introduced an element of cheerfulness and artistic fantasy in what had earlier been a very dour and strict religion. And the statuary that now developed shows that the new cult must have come from the eastern Mediterranean, an extension of the cult of the fertility goddess, or "great mother," of the ancient Near East.

THE ORIGINALLY chthonian character of the neolithic Maltese religion is illustrated particularly clearly by the only underground sanctuary thus far discovered, the Hypogeum of Hal Saflieni.

This catacomblike structure is situated near the village of Tarxien. Its access, formerly, lay through a temple built above ground level, which has been only partially preserved. A passage leads down, past chambers hewn out of the limestone rock at irregular intervals, into a number of natural cave chambers. These are fitted with doors, copings, pylons, and vaulted apses.

The main part of the Hypogeum consists of two stories. The upper one includes two antechambers and a series of main chambers, to be recognized as such by their architecture or decoration. A broad flight of limestone steps leads to the lower story. At one point the steps stop abruptly and the wall drops some nine and a half feet into a large cavern. For the initiated, there was a narrow path leading off to the right of the last step into a series of smaller rooms that may have been storerooms for treasure. The noninitiated, however, risked losing their foothold in the dark and plunging into the cave below, from which there was little chance of escape.

The Hypogeum was certainly not built in accordance with any unified plan. Nevertheless, its chambers (most of them oval or round, but sometimes irregular in shape) as well as their ornamentation show that the men who built it were seeking to imitate the architecture and decoration of the other sanctuaries.

It would seem that the Hypogeum served different purposes at two different periods.

In the first period it was a sanctuary. Many of the carefully appointed inner chambers are the counterparts, as it were, of those in the sanctuaries above ground. The fact that it was constructed below ground level lends weight to the view that a cult of the chthonian powers was celebrated there.

A chamber in the upper story has acoustical effects in connection with another chamber; perhaps it was used as the sanctuary of a speaking oracle. Some curious small clay models found at Hal Saflieni, which represent women lying on a kind of couch, would seem to bear out the theory that oracles were consulted at the Hypogeum; it has been assumed that persons wishing to consult the gods took some narcotic potion, hoping to hear the answers to their questions in their dreams or in a trance. The lower chambers may also have been used for initiation into certain mysteries. In any case, the tremendous size of the Hypogeum and the other temples, as well as the variety of rites practiced there, suggest the possibility that a special priestly caste existed in the neolithic society of Malta and Gozo.

During the second period the Hypogeum undoubtedly served as a sepulcher. Some of the chambers with small side niches and cells were probably burial places; others may have been used as ossuaries, and some of the others were probably reserved for the celebration of an elaborate cult of the dead. A number of scholars believe that the Hypogeum was, from the outset, intended to serve as a communal sepulcher and a sanctuary devoted to the cult of the dead.

It certainly served as a gigantic ossuary during the last period. When it was first excavated, most of the chambers were found to be more or less filled with earth. All in all, this mass of earth, or earthlike substance, contained the remains of about 7,000 persons, as well as potsherds strewn about without any semblance of order. Rather extraordinary circumstances seem to have prevailed in the closing period of the Hypogeum's use.

The sanctuaries of Malta and Gozo are undoubtedly neolithic—late neolithic, to be sure. This singular culture, the product of a mingling of western and eastern influences, disappeared shortly after 1500 B.C., probably as a result of the conquest and settlement of the islands by a people with altogether different beliefs. The new masters had no concern for the temples they had found, and simply let them fall into decay.

Yet to this day those monumental ruins testify to the powerful religious spirit of the men who built those sanctuaries.

V

THE MEGALITHIC CULTURE OF WESTERN EUROPE

Around the third millennium B.C. important changes occurred in western Europe—first in the eastern and western coastal belts of the Iberian peninsula. These changes were certainly precipitated by cultural influences that emanated from the Mediterranean region, and were partly strengthened by the influx of fresh population elements. In any event, the Iberian peninsula now began to play a leading role: it became the focus from which cultural influences radiated far to the east.

In the course of time the neolithic peasants developed their economy, and in some places achieved a certain degree of prosperity. On the Atlantic coast, in central and northern Portugal, cyclopean stone tombs were erected—at first, doubtless, by well-to-do peasants. This development may well have been inspired by the tremendous funerary structures of the Nile valley. The most ancient of these tombs, the dolmen (from the Breton *dol,* meaning table, and *men,* meaning stone), consisted of a number of upright supports and a flat, horizontal roofing slab.

Originally the dolmen was covered by a protective mound of earth, for it was unmistakably a burial cave. Whereas in vast regions of western Europe the old forms of burial—in caves and trenches—persisted, dolmens became increasingly popular along the Atlantic littoral, and also penetrated here and there to other areas, including the Mediterranean seaboard.

From the simple dolmen, the most ancient and the most frequently found, there developed the passage grave, formed by the addition of a long stone-roofed entrance passage to the dolmen itself. This type was widely diffused in western Europe, and as far north as southern Scandinavia. The latest type was the vaulted grave, substantially confined to the Iberian peninsula and Ireland.

The megalithic tombs of all countries have certain common features, architectural and technical; they also have certain characteristics that show them to have been built by people inspired by a faith transcending cultural frontiers. Their faith spread throughout western Europe and even to other continents; we cannot help being reminded, in a way, of the spread of the world religions in later times.

Another form of the megalithic monument appears in the menhir, or "long stone" (from the Breton *men,* meaning stone, and *hir,* meaning long). These were simple uprights, sometimes of great size. Menhirlike arrangements of stones frequently occur in western Europe and beyond, but they are not always menhirs of the megalithic period. Of the 6,000 megalithic menhirs catalogued in France, more than half—about 3,500—are in the department of Morbihan, in southern Brittany. There, too, are the largest of them. The Men-er-Hroech, near Locmariaquer, for instance, which was knocked over by a storm or an earthquake and broken into five parts, originally stood 66 feet high; others measured 36 feet, 32 feet, 16 feet, and less. Miniature models of menhirs have also been discovered.

In Brittany, individual menhirs sometimes occur without any ascertainable connection with the megalithic

Fig. 44. STONEHENGE. RECONSTRUCTION OF CENTRAL STRUCTURE.

graves. Often, however, they occur together, standing in circles, semicircles, or vast ellipses. These cromlechs, as they are called (from the Breton *crom,* meaning circle, and *lech,* meaning place), have been found more frequently in England than in France. The best known and most magnificent of these cromlechs is Stonehenge, near Salisbury (fig. 44), the central portion of which at least goes back to megalithic times.

There exist even more impressive megalithic sites, most of them in Brittany—the *alignements*—consisting of menhirs standing in several parallel rows. The Carnac *alignements*, for instance, orientated approximately from east to west, cover an area 12,800 feet in length, and include 2,935 menhirs. There are three *alignements*, close to but clearly independent from one another. The most westerly site, at Ménec, is 3,793 feet long, with an average width of 325 feet. Eleven hundred and sixty-nine menhirs have been counted there, seventy of them standing in a cromlech on the west side, and 1,099 ranged in eleven rows. The biggest menhir measures a good 13 feet, the smallest about 2 feet. The position of some menhirs at the other end of the site suggests that there too a cromlech had once stood. Some 780 feet to the east of Ménec is the *alignement* of Kermario, 3,540 feet long with an average width of about 328 feet; it numbers 1,029 menhirs in ten rows. A cromlech must once have existed at its western end, where there are three menhirs standing out of line and orientated south, in the direction of a passage grave standing only a short distance away. At the eastern end, where the menhirs become smaller, but still within the rows, a high menhir stands on a grave mound; it is differently orientated from the rest. This menhir and the burial places around it appear to be older than the site as a whole. The third *alignement*, that of Kerlescan, lies 1,277 feet to the northeast of Kermario. It is 2,860 feet long and includes 555 menhirs arranged in thirteen rows; at its western end thirty-nine menhirs form a semicircular cromlech.

Parts of these megalithic sites definitely belong to the early period of the metal age.

Other important changes that took place in the neolithic were either related to or coincided with the appearance of a new culture on the Mediterranean coast of the Iberian peninsula, the Almería culture. Completely new, evidently introduced by a new population strain, this culture was characterized by an idol art similar to that of the eastern Mediterranean countries in their neolithic phase.

The Almería idols, fashioned of bone or stone, gained widespread popularity. We may distinguish two types of

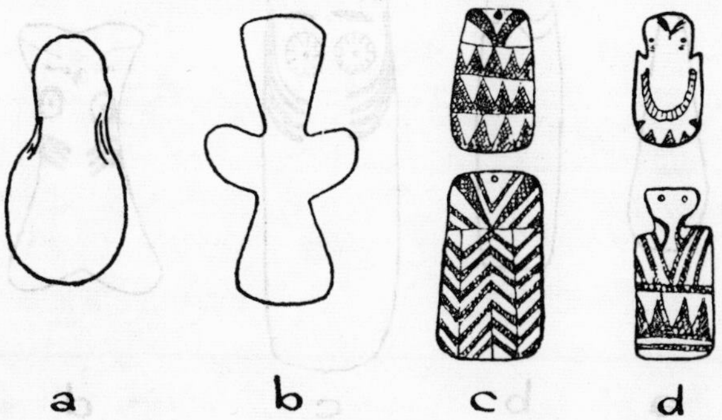

Fig. 45. FORMS OF FLAT IDOLS OF THE IBERIAN PENINSULA.

these idols, flat ones and rounded ones, each type corresponding to some degree to a different geographical diffusion.

The flat idols include fiddle-shaped pieces (fig. 45) averaging between 2 to 3½ inches in height and 1½ to 3 inches in thickness, and generally made of light stone such as marble, alabaster, limestone, or talc, but also sometimes of slate or bone. We also find similar slate and alabaster plates with projections on either side suggesting arms (fig. 45).

The finest specimens of this idol art, occurring mainly

in Portugal, are decorated slate plates, generally incised, sometimes painted. They are more distinctly anthropomorphic than the rest. The palettelike lower part is often surmounted by a "head" set on clearly defined "shoulders." For the most part, the designs are purely geometric; sometimes, however, the head shows what are obviously intended to be human features (fig. 45).

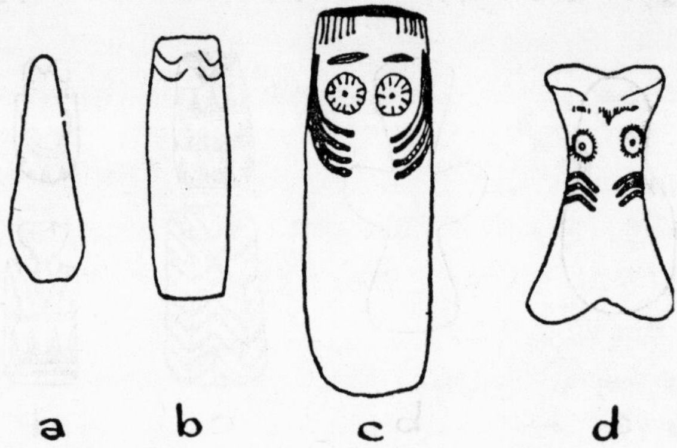

Fig. 46. FORMS OF ROUNDED IDOLS OF THE IBERIAN PENINSULA.

The rounded idols, generally of stone, are of two types. There is the unmodeled kind, in the shape of a truncated cone or cylinder (fig. 46), 1 foot high on the average, but ranging from 6 inches to somewhat less than 2 feet; then there is the modeled kind, where the head, atop a tapering neck, projects at a sharp angle from the lower part (fig. 46); on this type we sometimes find geometrical designs suggesting human features (fig. 46).

Far more common than the stone idol is the bone idol, made, as a rule, of digital bones, or phalanges, of small horses. The phalanx undoubtedly acquired ritual significance because of its natural resemblance in shape to the stone idols. From the frequency with which this type of idol occurs—mainly in the poorer inland regions—it would appear to have been the idol of the poor who could not afford the luxury of the more finely wrought stone, and especially marble, images. At the same time, it too is often adorned with fine geometrical figures.

The flat idol occurs predominantly in the interior of the Iberian peninsula, while the rounded idol is found mostly along the Atlantic and Mediterranean coasts of the peninsula.

With the influx of the newcomers who founded the Almería culture, there also began a new and flourishing period of Iberian rock painting. And the connection between this art and the idol statuary is quite apparent. This culture reached its peak in the chalcolithic, or stone-and-copper age, between 2500 and 2000 B.C., and developed principally in the mining region of southeastern Spain. The traces of copper, silver, and gold which are constantly being turned up in this area show that the Almería people were moving away from a simple farming economy toward an economy based on mining and trade.

Toward the end of the stone age and the early chalcolithic, the geometrical Iberian rock art spread into southwestern France and even farther afield. Once it was dissociated from its native rock background, it penetrated the area of the megalithic style, so that we find the inner walls and ceilings of dolmens, as well as the faces of many menhirs, adorned with similar geometrical and anthropomorphic designs. In fact, this megalithic art, derived from the Iberian rock art, is to be found throughout Brittany and as far west as Ireland.

These, then, are the main sources that can enlighten us on the religious beliefs of western Europe at the end of the stone age.

Even simple dolmens represent an expenditure of effort and resources for the sake of the dead far in excess of anything that was merely necessary. Such an expenditure is not sufficiently explained by the fact that the dolmens, passage graves, and vaulted graves were tribal sepulchers. Nor would it be true, save in a very limited number of cases, to say that they were the monuments of purse-proud families. The striking fact remains that while the megalith builders erected majestic dwellings for their dead, they erected none for themselves.

The construction of these monuments, often of colossal proportions, must have involved both enormous work and considerable technical skill. The Soto dolmen, near Seville, for instance, is just over 68 feet long, the granite block forming the front of the tomb being some 11 feet high, 10 feet wide, and 2½ feet thick, and weighing about 21 tons. It could be established that the block had been quarried some twenty-three miles away. Its transportation, presumably on wooden rollers, required the construction of an adequate roadway and the employment of many skilled hands.

Los Millares, in the Almería province, can boast of a veritable necropolis dating from the high point of the Almería culture; it consists of about 100 passage graves and domed graves. In some cases the burial chambers have a central pillar, and secondary chambers at the sides. The passages are divided into a number of sections by stone slabs forming "door frames"; sometimes circular entrance holes have been hollowed out of the slabs. The walls often show traces of paintings. Most of the graves lie under huge earth mounds surrounded by stone slabs. Natural rock gullies were also used as burial places; they were roofed with flat slabs and thus turned into passage graves. Some of the burial chambers had been hewn out of the rock by human agency. The graves, clearly tribal sepulchers, held up to 100 bodies.

Numerous megalithic tombs have also been found along the Atlantic coast, in Brittany, and as far north as the Netherlands. In Ireland the passage graves are under gigantic mounds; their funerary chambers have high vaulted roofs, and their walls are decorated with a wealth of reliefs. All these monuments bear unquestionable witness to a highly developed cult of the dead.

In Brittany, wherever a burial site is in a good state of preservation, a menhir stands at the head of the passage grave; and when the burial chamber is opened, its door points toward this menhir. What can be the meaning of this architectural arrangement?

Certain Egyptian papyri, which tell of the beliefs of those ages, offer the clue to that enigma. The Egyptians believed that the souls of the dead, transformed into birds, could leave their tombs to sit in the sun or peck in the fields. And this notion appears to have been entertained throughout the Mediterranean area and also in western Europe; the famous painted sarcophagus of Hagia Triada, in Crete, with its obelisks on which birds are perched, has been pointed out by Carl Schuchhardt as evidence of these beliefs. Like the obelisks, the menhirs must have represented thrones or seats on which the spirits of the dead could rest after leaving the graves, and landmarks by means of which they could find their way back.

Similarly, the "soul hole," usually a circular or oval opening made in the block enclosing some of the later megalithic tombs, must have originated in that belief;

Fig. 47. SCHEMATIZED ANTHROPOMORPHIC FIGURES FROM THE SOTO DOLMEN, NEAR SEVILLE, SPAIN.

those apertures were evidently intended to allow the souls to circulate freely.

Some menhirs are decorated with highly schematized figures representing men and women; occasional traces of pigment on others would indicate that they were quite frequently adorned with paintings of such figures. Most probably, therefore, the menhirs were regarded not only as "soul thrones" but also as the eternal homes of the dead.

Pictures symbolizing the tribal ancestors often occur also on the interior walls of megalithic tombs (fig. 47). On a wall of the Soto dolmen, for instance, a schematized picture was discovered representing a woman and a child (fig. 48). And excavation beneath this picture revealed the

Maltese idol.

PLATE XXIX

PLATE XXX

Pentre Ifan Burial Chamber. Pembrokeshire, England.

Stonehenge, England.

PLATE XXXI

Megalithic structure, Carnac (Morbihan), France.

PLATE XXXII

skeletons of a woman and a child. This would seem to prove that the various designs represented specific dead persons. But as the contents of most of the graves have been pillaged, the theory is hard to verify.

Probably most of the small Iberian idols, nearly all of which have been discovered in graves, were likewise images of ancestors and other souls. In one of the few megalithic tombs that had not been disturbed, such idols

Fig. 48. "MOTHER AND CHILD." SCHEMATIZED PICTURE FROM THE SOTO DOLMEN.

were found near the heads of the bodies. And in one of the dolmens at Los Millares, there was one idol to each body.

In view of their numerical correspondence to the burials, these idols may be regarded as images of the dead themselves rather than of a divinity protecting the dead. They provided, as it were, an anchorage for the homeless spirits of the departed.

On the other hand, the rounded idol, in its undifferentiated form of a truncated cone or cylinder, presents a clear analogy with the menhir. It must therefore also have been a "soul seat." In the Atlantic zone of the Iberian peninsula the cylindrical limestone idols were found inside the graves; in the Mediterranean zone, on the other hand, the truncated conical idols were found outside the graves, but within the stone enclosures of the tombs.

The separation of the image from the dead person it represents is particularly apparent in the rock-picture art.

On the rock walls are a great number of the same geometric human figures as those that adorn the faces of the dolmens and are delineated on the idols. Only very rarely are they associated with burials. The painted rocks are generally situated at some distance from the ancient settlements. The faithful probably gathered there only on special occasions—to commemorate the dead, or for some other ritual purpose. We may assume that they entreated the souls of their dead or their ancestors to send them rain, or fair weather, or a good crop, to bless man and beast, house and field. Only very few pictures of this kind have been found in dwelling caves, where they occur near the entrance.

The cult of the dead developed in even more elaborate forms outside the Iberian peninsula, especially in Brittany. The great menhir *alignements* near Carnac, for instance, must have attracted great crowds on the occasion of particular solemnities. Thousands could move in procession along the great avenues between the rows of menhirs. It is probable that the cult became equally flourishing in the British Isles, where similar menhir sites occur, though only one of them, at Ashdown in Berkshire, can be compared to the tremendous ritual avenues of Carnac. The Ashdown site comprises about 800 megaliths distributed over an irregular parallelogram whose sides measure 812 feet and 1,624 feet respectively.

We know very little, of course, as to the way the ritual was conducted on these sites. From their ground plan we may infer that the ritual consisted principally of solemn processions and some kind of sacrifice. All this would obviously presuppose considerable organization, and a priestly caste may well have existed at this time.

The cult of a female divinity was observed, alongside that of the spirits of the dead and of ancestors, at least in certain regions of France—as is apparent from small menhir models found in the south of that country, from idols in caves in the Marne basin, and perhaps, also, from certain figures on the walls of megalithic graves in Brittany. These statuettes or sculptured idols certainly did not represent the dead, for a number of persons were buried in each tomb, and there is never more than *one* such image, and it is always found at the entrance to the tomb. This cult of a goddess of the dead—their protectress—was most probably derived from the East; similar statuettes have been discovered in Liguria and Sardinia.

Yet another, completely different aspect of neolithic religion in western Europe is discernible in certain figures that appear in the rock art of the Iberian peninsula, in designs on megaliths and on pottery, and on various other objects turned up by excavation.

On the picture rocks and dolmen walls we quite often find figures of the sun in full radiance, usually in isolation, but sometimes shown with a number of little points, as, for instance, in a red rock painting at Pala Pinta de Carlâo, in Portugal (fig. 49), which obviously represents two suns in starry skies. That a ritual significance was associated with such pictures would seem to follow both from the sites where they have been found and from the schematized symbol of an ax on one of the paintings.

The ax symbol was definitely religious in character, for

Fig. 49. STARRY SKY AND RITUAL AX. RED ROCK PAINTING. PALA PINTA DE CARLÂO, PORTUGAL. 1/15 ACTUAL SIZE.

it occurs frequently on painted rocks and dolmen walls; moreover, miniature neolithic axes that were clearly amulets or votive objects have been found. In neolithic western Europe the ax was the symbol of the sky, or, more precisely, of the thunderbolt hurled by the sky god.

It is hard to say to what extent the western European sky god was regarded as personifying both sun god and weather god. At any rate, the sun god appears to have enjoyed a fairly autonomous position in the religion of the outgoing stone age.

A series of rock pictures of human figures, ax in hand (fig. 50), may represent anthropomorphic images of the sky or weather god, but they may also represent persons taking part in the ritual—in other words, scenes of religious ceremonies.

On the Iberian peninsula, the sanctuaries of the sky god would have been principally those remote sites where the rocks were adorned with the symbols of the god, or

Fig. 50. MEN CARRYING AXES, PORTRAYED ON SPANISH PICTURE ROCKS.

with figures of the divinity in human form, or possibly with figures of the faithful. Considering the frequent association of these pictures with those of ancestors, we may assume that the two types of worship merged. The fact that the sacred ax is sometimes depicted on menhirs and dolmen walls supports this assumption.

In this connection, a singular find made in the sepulcher situated within the Kermario *alignements* near Carnac is worth mentioning. The base of the giant menhir in the center is engraved with five snakes erect on their tails. When the site was excavated, in 1922, five axes were found under the engravings. The blades faced upward; obviously the axes had been deliberately placed in that position. It is most likely that even in neolithic times the serpent was a symbol of life. The serpent *motif* also occurs in rock art, significantly enough in association with symbols of ancestors (fig. 51). The five axes of Kermario, doubtless representing votive gifts and possibly coinciding in number with the bodies buried in the tomb, show that the sky god was venerated as the giver of life, and also that his

Fig. 51. SNAKE AND ANCESTOR SYMBOLS ON THE SAINT-MICAUD MENHIR (SAÔNE-ET-LOIRE), FRANCE.

cult had penetrated the worship of the dead, which played so important a part in megalithic times.

But both on picture rocks and on the walls of dolmens, representations of the radiant sun are much more frequent than those of the starry sky or the ritual ax. In the mortuary chamber of the Granja de Toninuelo dolmen, in Spain, the sun appears five times. It also occurs in pottery designs.

A remarkable scene is depicted on the fragment of a copper vessel found in Spain, dating, therefore, from the chalcolithic—the radiant sun over highly stylized deer (fig. 52). In the later Celtic, as well as in the Germanic religions, the deer was a sacred beast dedicated to the sun or fertility god; and this connection apparently existed in western Europe even in the neolithic—which would also account for the great number of deer *motifs* in Iberian rock painting.

We even find anthropomorphic representations of the sun god on Iberian rocks: figures with disproportionately large hands, the fingers spread out like rays (fig. 53). Very similar designs, incidentally, occur in Sweden in the bronze age; their significance as images of the sun god is

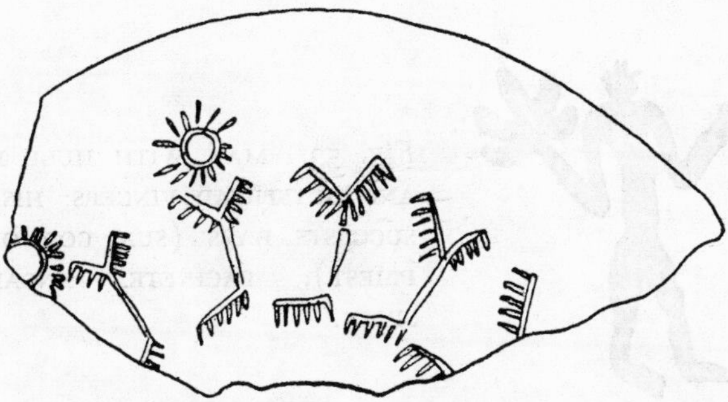

Fig. 52. SOLAR SYMBOL OVER STYLIZED DEER, ON POTTERY FRAGMENT FOUND AT LAS CAROLINAS, MADRID.

definitely established, thanks to a group of pictures (of the same place and era) showing the sun with rays formed by hands with fingers outspread.

It is not impossible that certain horned figures occurring on the painted rocks also represent the sun god. One of these figures has been discovered in the cave of Los Letreros, in Almería; the phallus is strongly emphasized, and each hand holds a sickle (fig. 54). Here the sun god seems to have been depicted in his character of a fertility or harvest god.

Among the solar symbols in western Europe in the neolithic, we may certainly also include the wheel: both the wheel with a cross in the middle and the wheel with multiple spokes. Concentric circles and spirals may likewise be regarded as symbols of the sun god. In their midst, we often find small cuplike figures. I shall discuss below the question of their religious significance.

The symbols of the solar cult were generally intermingled with those of the ancestor worship. This inter-

Fig. 53. MAN WITH HUGE HANDS AND OUTSPREAD FINGERS; HIS HAIR SUGGESTS RAYS (SUN GOD OR HIS PRIEST). BACINETE, ANDALUSIA, SPAIN.

mingling is particularly apparent in the solar symbols depicted on the walls of dolmens; and we may conclude that the megalithic monuments were more than sites of an ancestor cult. Circular sites like Stonehenge, for instance, suggest by their form alone that they were also consecrated to the cult of the sun god.

In its present form (fig. 44), Stonehenge consists of a central structure surrounded by a great circular earthwork with a ditch on the inner side. In the intervening space, there still remain traces of three concentric circles of stones. The central structure consists of an outer circle of stones nearly 100 feet in diameter, formed by thirty rectangular monoliths 13 feet high, supporting what was originally a closed architrave. Within this circle there stands another circle of smaller monoliths, which in its turn encircles, in horseshoe formation, five trilithons some 20 feet high. In the very center is the "altar stone," 16 feet long, 3½ feet wide, and 1¾ feet deep.

This imposing monument was not the product of a single period. Not only different generations, but also different civilizations took part in its construction. According to

Fig. 54. MALE FIGURE WITH PHALLUS AND HORNS, HOLDING TWO SICKLES (FERTILITY SPIRIT). CAVE OF LOS LETREROS, ALMERÍA, SPAIN.

the data furnished by the most recent excavations, three building periods may be distinguished.

The earliest cromlech (Stonehenge I) consisted of a circular ditch and an inner earth rampart, with a wide entrance to the northeast. It was about 325 feet in diameter. In front of the entrance, on the outer side, there lay a sandstone block encircled by a smaller ditch. Along the inside of the great rampart, there were fifty-six pits forming a complete circle, which had evidently served a ritual purpose. They were definitely not intended as shafts for wooden posts or stone pillars, but appear to have been used in connection with sacrificial rites, and to have been filled in deliberately with successive deposits in prehistoric times. Charred human bones have been found in these pits, as well as in other parts of Stonehenge I, including the earth rampart and the outer encircling ditch. According to Stuart Piggott, the form of Stonehenge I, the cremation pits, and the objects found there are characteristic of the cultures of the second neolithic phase in England, in the early part of the second millennium B.C. Carbon-14 analysis of some pieces of charcoal found in the stratum of Stonehenge I shows that they belong to a period between 2123 and 1573 B.C. Although Stonehenge I possessed no megalithic structures, chips of blue stone found both in the small ditch and deep in the slime of the big ditch point to the existence of some kind of stone monuments on the site, or near it, even at that remote date.

In the next period (Stonehenge II) the famous blue stone—which was brought to the site from a considerable distance—was certainly used. This period must have followed hard on the heels of the preceding one, for the "beaker folk" who built the second cromlech (that they did so is attested by pottery finds pertaining to the beaker culture) arrived in England while the older neolithic cultures were still in existence. Originating on the Iberian peninsula, the beaker culture appears to have moved first to Brittany and thence to England. Excavations undertaken in 1954 revealed the fact—previously unknown—that the beaker folk had built two concentric circles of menhirs standing only six feet apart, each composed of thirty-five stones. The entrance to Stonehenge II does not exactly face the earlier one, but lies in the axis of the present cromlech and of its avenue; the latter, incidentally, may date from this second period.

The last period (Stonehenge III) consists of three phases of construction.

In the first, the two circles of menhirs of Stonehenge II were razed, and the ring of linteled blocks of sandstone—which we can still see today—was erected; then the five trilithons were erected in horseshoe formation, in the middle of which the "altar stone" was placed.

We know least about the second phase. It seems, however, that to this phase belong fifty-nine holes dug in two irregular circles around the ring of stones; they never served as shafts, and appear to have silted up of themselves.

In the last phase sixty menhirs of blue stone were erected in a close circle within the ring of sandstone blocks. Then nineteen other blue stones were erected in a horseshoe inside the horseshoe of trilithons.

We have no means, as yet, of putting a precise date to Stonehenge III. In 1953, however, carvings were discovered on some of the sandstone blocks, among them one showing a bronze-age ax of a type very common in England in the middle of the second millennium B.C.

Like other English monuments of this kind—Woodhenge, Avebury, Arminghall, Arbor Low—the cromlech of Stonehenge lies in the midst of a field of barrows. This would indicate that the rites conducted there were in some way connected with the dead. Two finds seem to confirm this conclusion—an urn turned up in the early bronze-age barrow of Llandyssilio, Pembrokeshire, on which was depicted a cromlech of the Stonehenge type, and a similar urn found in a Coolhill barrow in Ireland.

The theory that Stonehenge was no more than a vast mausoleum is unsupported by the evidence. In general, megalithic burial places were underground; edifices erected above ground were intended for the living. And if dolmens or other megalithic graves are now found above ground, it is simply because the mounds that originally concealed them have gradually disappeared in the course of the millennia. But the numerous reconstructions of Stonehenge make it hard to imagine that it was ever concealed underground. Most authorities now agree that Stonehenge was a sanctuary, and its tremendous size would indicate that it was a tribal sanctuary.

Another factor pointing to the practice of a cult of the dead at Stonehenge is the orientation of the cromlech toward the winter solstice—not the summer solstice, as many have suggested—in other words, to the sun's death at the close of the year. It is possible that the peoples who built Stonehenge identified the sun with the common ancestor of the tribe, as do some primitive peoples today. But this interpretation could be applied only to the two earlier sites; the subsequent structure indicates at the least that the older beliefs had been overlaid by new ideas and forms of worship.

There is no basis, incidentally, for the theory that the structure was designed in accordance with strict astronomical laws and served as a kind of calender. The theory runs as follows:

There are thirty linteled sandstone blocks—that is, the number closest to the number of days in the month. Twelve times around the sandstone ring and once along the five trilithons would thus approximately equal the number of days in the year. And the avenue running through the axis of the site would—still according to this theory—have served to indicate the position of the sun at the solstice. Thus the plan of Stonehenge would prove that the men who designed and built it were influenced by the Egyptians and practiced a sun cult similar to theirs. But against this argument it has been pointed out that as the solar year comprises 365.2422 days, to ignore the fraction would have led to an erroneous calculation of the solstice and would thus have made it risky to convene great crowds of worshippers to celebrate the occasion. In any case, a much simpler structure would have served the same purpose.

That there was a connection between the sun and the rites practiced at Stonehenge is undeniable. But this connection should probably be sought in the context of a vegetation cult and peasant fertility rites.

There is little likelihood of our ever being able to find out what the exact nature of the ritual was. One thing is certain; an architectural feat like the building of Stonehenge would never have been undertaken had it not possessed some tremendous significance for those who erected it. Nothing, however, could have been of greater importance for communities dependent upon their crops and their cattle than the preservation and increase of these mainstays of their lives. And as the "farmer's year" is linked to the rhythm of the seasons, it is only natural that a solar element should have been associated with the fertility ritual practiced at Stonehenge.

An ingenious and thought-provoking theory on this subject was recently propounded by A. T. Hatto. He maintains that the group of trilithons, on the one hand, and the blue stones in horseshoe and circular formation, on the other, were intended to form one unit; the trilithons, with their openings, symbolized the female sex, while the menhirs symbolized the male sex. The concentric arrangement of the stones, Hatto continues, represented the positions of male and female dancers in a dance that was a part of the fertility ritual. Even the orientation of the opening of the horseshoe toward the point on the horizon where the sun rises at the solstice was related to this ritual; the interior of the horseshoe was a symbolic womb into which the rays of the sun penetrated. The outer linteled ring of stones represented a ritual enclosure.

A good many objections have been raised to this theory; in particular, it was advanced that the stones are too shapeless to be regarded as representing the sexes. However that may be, it is clear that the horseshoe-shaped area, with its "altar stone" and its opening directed toward the position of the sun at the solstice, must have played a central part in the ritual.

Given the form and dimensions of the Stonehenge cromlech, it is very possible that various ritual games took place there, in addition to great processions. In northern Europe, rock pictures of bronze-age date have been found depicting such games—fights, running contests, and horse and chariot races. Probably these games symbolized the movement of the sun and its contest with darkness; perhaps they also represented some form of sympathetic magic. Some of the European peasant festivals of our own day, such as the summer-solstice celebration, may well be survivals of those prehistoric customs.

MANY finds made in western Europe indicate that the neolithic inhabitants of that region practiced various kinds of magic. But the regions where magical beliefs were most prevalent seem to have been the territories bordering central Europe.

There is considerable evidence for the use of parts of the human body for purposes of magic. For instance, a number of pendants and small pipes made of human bones have been found. In Switzerland, isolated skulls have often been found in the lake-dwelling strata, some of which show marks of severe injuries, while others have perforations, which were probably suspension holes. It is most likely that these skulls of persons who had died a violent death were believed to bring their owners magic powers.

Human skulls converted into drinking cups have been found on Swiss lake-dwelling sites and in French burial places of the period, and these too seem to have been used for magical purposes. Excavation has turned up many traces of cannibalism. And as the consumption of human flesh in correspondingly primitive societies is everywhere connected with magical beliefs, we may assume the same of western European neolithic man.

Some magical significance also attaches to the trepanations, or skull borings, that frequently occur on skulls found in neolithic deposits of western Europe. Originally trepanation would have had a strictly therapeutic purpose; the emergence of the neolithic battle ax resulted in more frequent head wounds. Later, however, trepanation was also practiced on the skulls of dead people, or at least small slivers of bone were cut out of the skull. These were perforated and worn around the neck on a cord. Preferably, or perhaps even exclusively, the skulls that were cut open were those of persons who had been trepanned while alive, and where the sutures had healed. This may be inferred from the fact that the little slivers of bone sometimes show a part of the edge of old, healed scars resulting from trepanation. Evidently these slivers were worn as amulets endowed with magical properties of healing.

A similar though less common practice was that of scooping out some of the bone of the skull cap in the form of a T. But evidence of this practice has so far been found only in central France, and the skulls have been only of women (fig. 55). This operation, performed in the living flesh and bone, must have been very painful, and was presumably intended to serve some magical-therapeutic end.

Magic practices seem to have been especially prevalent in connection with the daily labors. Nevertheless, only occasional traces of such practices have been discovered. For instance, a wooden fish-net float on which a fish had been carved was found in the Swiss lake-dwelling settlement of Wauwil. It had apparently been intended, much like the fish images of the northern Siberian fishermen, to attract fish into the net.

Among the most puzzling objects found in the Swiss lake-settlement strata were some pebbles enveloped in birch bark. Recently, however, T. Ischer has suggested a clue to their meaning. The natives of New Guinea, he points out, have magic stones that they wrap in bast and bury at sowing time, leaving them in the earth till harvest.

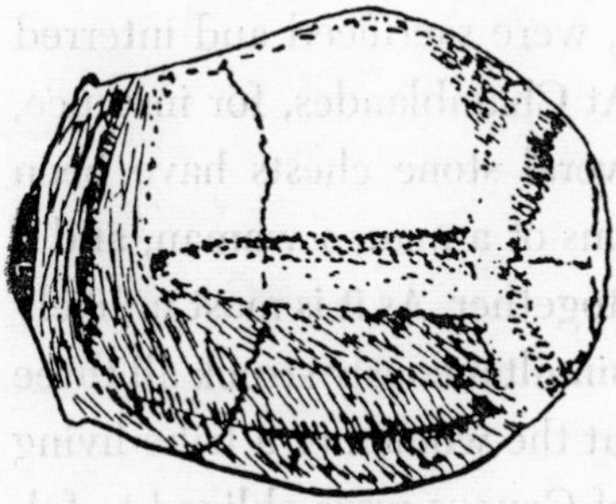

Fig. 55. FEMALE SKULL ENGRAVED WITH A "T." CONFLANS-SAINTE-HONORINE (SEINE-ET-OISE), FRANCE.

They believe that these stones contain magic power to foster the growth of the fruits of the earth. They wrap them in bast so as to preserve that power, and guard them jealously to prevent an enemy from stealing them and using them for his own ends. The neolithic lake dwellers of Switzerland, and perhaps also the agricultural societies of other parts of western Europe, appear to have practiced a kind of fertility magic similar to that of the primitives of New Guinea today.

Magical beliefs and practices must also have played an important part in the daily lives of the peoples inhabiting the regions where the great cults were dominant. Sympathetic magic seems to have been the underlying element in the sun-cult rites, and also probably in the rites of the sky cult.

Some curious finds made in graves inform us of the multiplicity of the religious ideas and related concepts current in neolithic western Europe. In northern Spain it was customary to bury dogs with the dead. But in some places, it seems, human beings, too, were sacrificed and interred with certain dead persons. At Chamblandes, for instance, on the Lake of Geneva, several stone chests have been found containing the skeletons of a man, a woman, and a child, undoubtedly interred together. As it is most unlikely that in all these cases death simultaneously struck all three persons, we must assume that the women of a tribe living on the borders of the Lake of Geneva were obliged to follow their husbands into the grave and the life beyond. When the husband died, therefore, the wife would either take her own life, or be killed together with the youngest of the children.

In the cave of Los Murcielagos, near Granada, Spain, the skeleton of a woman was found with a gold diadem about her head. The skeletons of twelve other women had been placed in a semicircle around her, each holding in her hand a little wattle basket that must at one time have contained flowers. Other objects in the tomb indicated a late neolithic dating for this burial. Evidently some noble lady—a priestess, perhaps—had been followed to her grave by all her female attendants. The altogether similar finds made in the royal tombs of Ur and also in those of Egypt, both far older than the Spanish tomb, show where this mortuary practice originated.

It seems, however, that this type of human sacrifice found few adepts in the neolithic west. At the same time, that it did occur in places as far distant from one another is indicative of the wide diffusion of the ideas underlying the practice.

VI

THE FARMING PEOPLES OF NORTHERN EUROPE

THE NEOLITHIC PEASANT cultures of northern Europe centered in Jutland and the Danish islands. Thence they spread into southern Sweden and northern Germany. The bridge between western and northern cultures was Holland, where they mingled, and influenced one another. Not until the emergence of the megalithic monuments does the picture of the northern neolithic become reasonably clear.

The influence of the megalith builders spread through most of northern Europe. Everywhere huge tribal graves were erected from massive stones the Scandinavian glaciers, in the postglacial thaw, had strewn over the countryside. Only the central and western parts of the Jutland peninsula remained aloof to the new beliefs and practices; their inhabitants continued to bury their dead as before, in simple, individual graves. In the more southerly regions of the northern European cultural province, where there were no great stone blocks deposited by glaciers, tombs were erected of heavy stone slabs. But again, the distinctive external feature of this culture was the enormous expenditure of effort and resources on behalf of the dead.

Central Germany, at this time, was a crossroads for the cultures of the Danubian lands, the west and the north, and the resulting mingling led to the emergence of a number of mixed cultures.

The older, native form of burial was undoubtedly the individual burial, which, as a rule, did not reflect any particular attempt to honor the dead more highly than the living. The later, megalithic grave was clearly the product of quite different thinking. But not all the important features of western European megalithic culture penetrated into northern Europe. Menhirs, stone avenues, and stone circles are virtually unknown in the north. In particular, the northern graves are innocent of pictorial decoration. Almost the only kinds of decoration thus far discovered are cuplike depressions and a few symbolic signs. We may conclude that the external forms of religion were less elaborate than in the west. Probably they also included certain older, indigenous customs.

The northern megalithic graves often yield traces of "fires of the dead," and no doubt of burnt offerings. There is also evidence of certain ceremonies conducted outside the grave. For instance, just under the surface of the mound covering a grave at Ziesendorf, in Mecklenburg, a kind of well was discovered made of stones somewhat larger than a man's fist. It was 18¾ inches in internal diameter, and 29½ inches deep. Near the opening lay a stone slab that fitted like a lid. Presumably this was a well of sacrifice; and as no objects were found, only liquid sacrifices could have been offered there—perhaps the blood of slaughtered animals.

The northern megalithic graves were often built in the immediate vicinity of massive stone blocks, which to this day are popularly known as "altar stones." Small cuplike markings carved into some of these altar stones prove that they enjoyed some special significance. In one instance, near Gross Ziethen, a flint hatchet was found in a man-made hollow of this kind; and another hatchet, a flint chisel, two clay vessels, and several animal bones were discovered under the four-foot-thick stone.

Artificial cuplike hollows are quite frequently found on megalithic graves, but more often on the stones forming the roof than on the lateral wall stones. In some cases it is indisputable that the markings were made in prehistoric times—even though the practice continued right up into historical times. In the middle of a megalithic grave near Beldorf, in Schleswig-Holstein, there was found an upright stone ornamented with flutings reminiscent of designs on western European idols; and in front of this "statue" lay a stone with cup markings which looked very much like an altar or sacrificial stone (fig. 56).

In the north, just as in the west, the megalithic cult of the dead seems to have merged with the sky or solar worship. The surface of the slab covering a grave at Bunsch, in Ditmarschen, reveals not only a number of cuplike hollows, but also incised drawings of a four-spoked wheel, several pairs of hands, and a foot—in other words, symbols of the sky or solar cult.

The frequent location of graves near small lakes or

pools, many of which have since silted up, is another peculiarity of northern megalithic building. As objects that may be identified as sacrificial offerings have quite often been found at the bottom of marshes, the choice of location for those graves was hardly fortuitous; the lakes or pools were, in all likelihood, ritual sites.

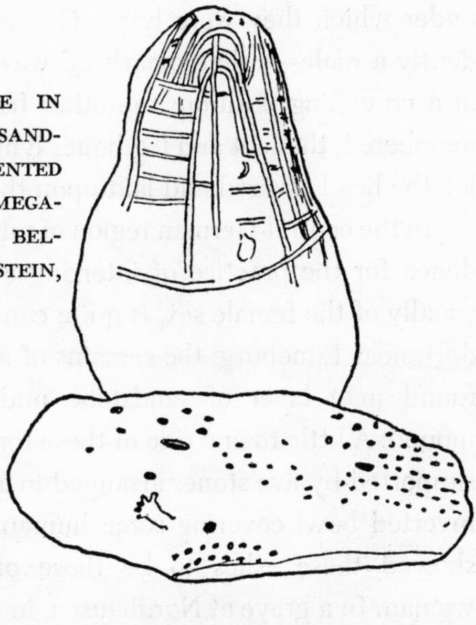

Fig. 56. CUP STONE IN FRONT OF AN UPRIGHT SANDSTONE BLOCK ORNAMENTED WITH FLUTINGS, IN A MEGALITHIC GRAVE NEAR BELDORF, SCHLESWIG-HOLSTEIN, GERMANY.

The megalithic graves, in which the bodies were deposited in a procumbent position, are in striking contrast to the individual graves of the preceding and following periods, in which the dead were buried in a squatting position. From the remains that have been turned up, it is not clear whether the corpse had been bound—whether the burial proceedings in general were governed by fear of the dead. In the mixed cultures of central Germany, however, finds have been made in certain graves which show clearly that the neolithic inhabitants of those regions feared at least some of the dead. Some of the individual graves of these cultures contained ritually dismembered corpses. At Ziesendorf two skeletons were discovered under a thick layer of stones, their legs turned toward each other. Simultaneous burial may be inferred from the great heap of stones under which they were lying. One of the skeletons, evidently a male—a flint spearhead was found near it—was in a crouching position; the other had been ritually dismembered, the foot and leg bones lying unnaturally parallel, the head severed and laid upon the chest.

In the central-German region of mixed cultures, the evidence for the practice of interring a human companion, usually of the female sex, is quite considerable. At Bavendorf, near Lüneburg, the remains of a male skeleton were found in a layer of sandstone under a massive earth mound. A little to one side of these remains, on a flat stone supported by five stones arranged in a circle, there was an inverted bowl covering some human ashes; and analysis showed these ashes to be those of a twenty-year-old woman. In a grave at Nordhausen, in the Harz mountains, a woman's skeleton, with its skull showing traces of two ax blows, was found lying directly alongside that of a man.

As I have previously noted, the megalithic structures of the north, as those in other regions, are sometimes decorated with drawings of hands and feet, alongside the four-spoked wheel (fig. 57). Research in comparative religions has shown that these pictures are, as a rule, symbols of the sun god, especially the hand with fingers spread out; we are reminded here of the "rosy-fingered dawn" of the Greeks.

Sometimes the simple cuplike depressions occur together with those symbols on one stone—not only on megalithic tombs, but also on the massive blocks that are deposited by glaciers and that are occasionally found in close

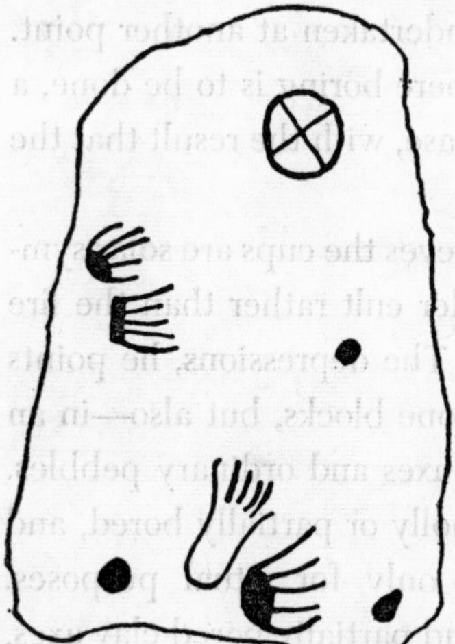

Fig. 57. CUP STONE DECORATED WITH WHEEL, HANDS, AND FEET. KLEIN MEINSDORF, SCHLESWIG-HOLSTEIN, GERMANY.

proximity to these tombs; and now and then those symbols appear even on isolated stone slabs. While the neolithic dating of the "cups" is indisputable in most instances, the purpose they served is still a matter of controversy. They cannot have been intended merely as receptacles for votive gifts—blood, food, or implements—for they occur on the side and the underside of the rocks, as well as on top.

Sophus Müller suggests that the cups signified the kindling of fire, then fire in general, and, finally, the great fiery day star and life giver, the sun. He bases his theory on the fact that the cups are arranged in rows on certain stones. Then he draws attention to the means used by certain primitive peoples today to generate fire. With a pointed wooden stake, they bore a hole in a wooden wedge. In the process, a part of the wood is pulverized and, through the heat generated by the boring, begins to smolder. Once the hole has reached a certain depth, it becomes useless, and boring is undertaken at another point. In order to mark the places where boring is to be done, a groove is usually made in the base, with the result that the holes gradually appear in rows.

G. Schwantes, who also believes the cups are solar symbols, prefers to take the thunder cult rather than the fire cult as the point of departure. The depressions, he points out, occur not only on great stone blocks, but also—in an initial stage—on broken stone axes and ordinary pebbles. Many of the stone axes are wholly or partially bored, and could therefore have served only for ritual purposes. Among them are amber axes and partially bored clay axes, as well as very small ones, precluded by their diminutive size from serving any practical purpose, yet obviously far too well made to have been mere toys. All these were probably objects the neolithic people consecrated to the sun god hurling his thunderbolts. The diminutive ax, his symbol, must have been worn about the neck as an amulet, just as in later times the Germans, especially the women, wore Thor's hammer as a silver ornament on a chain.

The holes in the axes must have had some special religious significance; this accounts for the borings begun but not completed in certain axes, which clearly served no practical purpose. Schwantes believes that in order to avoid the troublesome task of grinding axes for the sole purpose of piercing holes in them, people began boring holes in objects naturally shaped like axes. Then, attributing greater importance to the perforation than to the ax itself, they began to bore holes in pebbles, and finally in great stones to which they paid some kind of religious veneration.

The cup stones may well have been altars on which offerings were laid, but it is significant that no traces of burnt offerings have been found in their immediate neighborhood.

The interpretations suggested by Müller and Schwantes both lead, in effect, to the conclusion that the people of the northern megalithic area venerated a sky god, chiefly conceived of as a sun or weather god. Because of the absence of pictorial art in that region, only the simplest symbols of this god—without any anthropomorphic representations—have come down to us. Only in one of the mixed cultures in Moravia is there what appears to have been a crude representation of the sky god, doubtless a result of the influence of the neighboring Danubian idol art.

In excavating a megalithic settlement at Troldebjerg, on Langeland, J. Winther uncovered a number of huts with fireplaces and the usual refuse. One hut, however, differed from the rest in that it contained several fireplaces. And while traces of coal were found over and around these fireplaces, there was not the slightest trace of any refuse. Moreover, the fireplaces were not built directly on the floor (as in the other huts) but above it, separated from it by a layer of gravel. On removing the deposits around one of these fireplaces, Winther discovered a lighter patch of earth just underneath it, indicating that digging had taken place at that spot. Winther proceeded to dig in his turn, and soon came upon a ground flint ax that had been placed blade up in a trenchlike hollow, and secured by small stones around the base. Near the ax, Winther found the lower part of a clay vessel; he was unable to discover any other fragment, either there or nearby. Recalling the offerings made to the Sacred Ax in Crete in the second millennium B.C. (depicted on the famous sarcophagus of Hagia Triada), Winther declared that the vessel of Troldebjerg had been the receptacle for an offering to the ax which he had unearthed.

The analogy seems to provide the clue to the meaning of the fireplaces in the Troldebjerg hut: they were simply ritual hearths on which the sacred fire was kindled, and which were, by a layer of gravel, protected from pollution by the unclean earthen floor.

No doubt the ritual observed at Troldebjerg centered around the ax in association with the kindled fire. Both must have been symbols of the sky god who held sway over lightning and fire. It was the same god to whom the peasant made offerings by placing them in the soil of his field, burying them in the earth, or hiding them under a stone. In many cases finds of this kind may, in fact, be merely objects hidden away for some reason. But others, from their deliberate arrangement, betray their religious character.

At Ryssvitz, in southern Sweden, fifteen large and well-ground flint axes were found, arranged in a semicircle, with the blades facing east. Near Lottorf, in Schleswig, two unground, thin-necked flint axes standing upright in the ground next to a big stone block were unearthed. And at Norgaardhols, in Schleswig, four such axes were discovered, also upright, arranged in a rectangle. At Freltofte, in the Odense district of Denmark, a whole set of flint sickle blades was discovered, the blunt edges slightly rounded and carefully worked. The blades were worn smooth, presumably from use. They are believed to have been votive gifts of a peasant to the god of fertility after the harvest.

Animal sacrifice was also practiced in the northern megalithic region—as evidenced, for instance, by the skull of a young horse found in the mud of the Ullstorp stream in Scania, Sweden, with the fragment of a flint dagger piercing the frontal bone. This find is the more significant in that the horse was later the favorite sacrificial animal of the Germans, and symbolized the sky god.

On the Troldebjerg site, in a furrow in which a hut wall had been built, Winther also found a crudely fashioned flint ax. As flint axes were fashioned with the greatest care, it must be assumed that a piece so crudely shaped could not have been intended to be ground and used. Winther therefore describes the object as a "thunder ax" to be placed under the foundations of the hut in order to obtain the protection of the sky god. This interpretation points to the prehistoric origin of the superstitious practice, still to be encountered in some places in rural Europe, of keeping an old stone ax in the house as a protection against lightning.

Part V

THE RELIGIONS OF PREHISTORY

Our knowledge of prehistoric religious beliefs and practices is still very incomplete. To be sure, a considerable number of telling finds have been made. But these finds are not equally revealing of all periods and all forms of religion. Nor, as I have indicated throughout this study, can they always be interpreted with absolute certainty.

Still, we can distinguish two main categories of religion in prehistoric Europe—that of the hunters, and that of the tillers of the soil.

The religion of pastoral people—an important third category in other parts of the prehistoric world—played only a minor role in Europe. It appeared during the transition from the stone to the metal age, at the time of the Indo-European migrations; and the period of its spreading influence can be regarded as the threshold of recorded history.

I

THE RELIGION OF THE HUNTERS

THE MOST ANCIENT prehistoric hunters left a great many traces of their everyday lives in deposits dating back to the early ice age. But thus far virtually no traces have been discovered that could enlighten us on their religious ideas and practices.

That the primitive hunters were men of fully developed mental faculties is sufficiently attested by their skill in making tools, their communal undertakings (such as big-game hunting), and the faculty of speech, which is a concomitant of such activities. In other words, like modern man, they must have been capable of reasoning, of using their imagination constructively, of forming careful plans, and of pursuing autonomous action. Consequently, like the generality of men, they would most likely have had spiritual needs, which they sought to satisfy. And certain elements in our fragmentary picture of primitive life in fact point in this direction.

While not numerous in Europe, the skeletal remains that have been unearthed are all of one kind—namely, skulls—and probably come from ancient settlements, which would indicate the existence, in those remote times, of some ritual centering around the human skull. Viewed in the light of practices observed among modern primitive tribes of a similar level of advancement, these finds show that the prehistoric hunters treated their dead with great reverence. Like their modern counterparts, they probably preserved certain parts of the skeleton, mostly the skull or lower jaw, in special places, perhaps adorning them with ornaments or painting them with ocher. When the tribe moved, the skulls were probably taken along. At a very early stage they also must have begun to believe that the possession of the skulls assured them the protection and help of the dead. In any case, reverence toward those who have passed beyond human society and the world of sensory perception comes close to being a religious attitude, particularly if higher powers are ascribed to the dead.

On the strength of finds from later periods, we may assume that even the earliest prehistoric hunters, like certain modern primitive hunters, believed in a higher, divine being. However, practices of modern primitives lead us to believe that that worship must have been so spiritual a thing that it could leave no material traces in the ground. If we consider, moreover, the enormous span of time that separates us from those hunters, and the tremendous geological changes that have taken place, the complete absence of finds of a ritual character is doubly understandable.

The first to leave specific traces of their religion were the hunters who lived during the last great interglacial, and this was due to exceptionally favorable conditions of conservation. These men inhabited wide stretches of land skirting the Alps, and, during the summer hunting season, pushed far into the mountains and even into the highest regions in pursuit of their quarry, particularly the cave bear—an enterprise fraught with danger but rich in reward. That these ancient hunters were a tenacious, capable, and intelligent breed of men is clear not only from their proven skill in capturing and killing the powerful cave bear, but also from their choice of hunting stations in caves over 8,000 feet up in the mountains, which they made habitable by placing stone slabs in the entrance, building gutters for draining the water, and making fireplaces in stone chests with lids.

They were poor in material goods, these sons of a munificent nature, but they believed in a great being, a deity who governed both their own lives and those of the animal kingdom.

When a cave bear was slain, it was dismembered on the spot and brought in pieces to the hunting station. Probably from the start the beast's head, with fur and limbs attached, was treated with special honors. We know nothing about the ceremonies conducted in front of or inside the cave. The finds do tell us, however, that the undamaged head—that is, with brain intact—was sometimes carefully deposited in the dark interior of the cave, behind the hunters' living quarters, in a covered, altarlike stone chest. More often the undamaged skull, together with one or several equally undamaged long bones, was deposited in the most hidden recesses of the cave, in secret niches or clefts of the rock, or inside artificial stone formations designed to protect the skull from destruction. We do not know whether the flesh was disposed of as a result of exposure in the open or in the course of a sacrificial feast. But it is quite clear from the finds that the center of the ritual was not the head or skull or long bones in themselves, but those most prized delicacies of all hunters—the brain and marrow. These precious parts of the animal were offered to the divine dispenser of hunting fortune in token of thanks for benefits received and to entreat success in future expeditions. The frequent orientation of the remains toward the exit may well mean that this deity was believed to abide somewhere in the universe beyond the cave.

These finds as a whole are unmistakable evidence of religious beliefs. The closest ethnological parallel is in the sacrifices of head or skull and long bones practiced by circumpolar peoples today. Psychologically and historically, such sacrifices are always connected with the concept and the veneration of a supreme being, specifically in the capacity of a god who dispenses fortune in the hunt.

The dark recesses of the caves which were the prehistoric hunters' habitations, the hidden niches and clefts in the rock walls, are thus the most ancient sanctuaries known to us, and the artificial arrangements of stones and stone chests which sometimes occur there are the most ancient shrines.

Finds of this kind have not been made outside the Alpine and sub-Alpine regions. It should be recalled, however, that the hunters of the last interglacial normally camped in the open. When they were hunting in areas where caves existed, and used these as temporary dwellings, they probably piled up ritual deposits there; but these would have been destroyed in the course of repeated occupation of the caves during the subsequent—and last—period of glaciation. In other words, we owe the unique deposits found in the Alpine caves to the circumstance that the Alps at that time were enclosed by an impenetrable ice wall, so that during the millennia preceding the final retreat of the ice a huge layer of earth could form over the deposits and thus preserve them. We may therefore assume that the other hunters of the last interglacial shared the religious beliefs of the Alpine cave-bear hunters, and practiced the same or similar sacrificial rites.

We may also assume that the hunting ritual, the only kind attested by excavation, represented only one facet of the ancient hunters' religion. Their faith must have influenced other areas of their lives, too, by its practices and prescriptions. But evidence of this may never be forthcoming, as it would appertain to a largely intangible sphere of human conduct.

THE HUNTERS of the upper paleolithic, on the other hand, and particularly the hunter artists, have left us a rich and variegated picture of their religious life and related practices.

By their time, the ancient belief in a divine dispenser of hunting fortune had survived—considerably modified, to be sure—chiefly in the eastern regions of Europe and northern Asia. Thus we find groups of reindeer hunters from the east following their game to the very edge of the ice cap in northern Germany, and opening the annual summer hunting season by submerging young does in lakes or pools. These offerings, as well as buried offerings like those found in Siberia, point strongly to a belief in a god who dispensed good fortune in the hunt, and who dwelled somewhere in the bowels of the earth.

This is the period, too, when other hunters appear to have developed a cult of their principal prey, the bear, seeing in it a being akin to man but superior to him, which they approached with religious awe and which they killed with special ceremonies. This was probably the origin of the bear cult that is still practiced today by certain peoples of the subarctic belt of northern Asia. Even the bear festivals of these peoples, at which a bear is ceremonially slain and sent forth as an envoy to the divine lord of the game, had their counterpart, it would seem, in the last part of the ice age.

But most of the hunters who moved into Europe at this time appear to have been adepts of a quite different set of beliefs, which they brought with them from their former homelands and which may be summed up under the heading of magic. These beliefs were quite possibly rooted in still more ancient prehistoric cultures, but it was in western Europe of the upper paleolithic that they came to their full flowering.

The external cause of the growth of magical beliefs and practices may be that the hunters who inhabited those parts of Europe which lay in the more or less immediate vicinity of the ice sheets were for the first time living in a true ice-age environment, in which hunting was the determining element of man's existence. The icy steppes, with their short summers and sparse vegetation, afforded them far fewer opportunities than their predecessors had enjoyed of supplementing the product of the chase by gathering wild plants. The hunters of the upper paleolithic were forced to improve their weapons and methods, to band together more closely, to undertake joint expeditions more often, and not least to resort to magic.

We may say, then, that magical beliefs and practices became widespread in western Europe in the upper paleolithic because man's principal problem was game. Animals were both the staff of life and the chief adversaries of man, ever prepared to escape their would-be captors by fight or flight: hence the feeling that hunters and hunted belonged, as it were, together. The mimes and dances in which hunters had doubtless engaged since time immemorial now began to acquire a wholly new significance. For in imitating the animal, the hunter of the upper paleolithic believed he was assuming the nature and the life of the animal. Because he was often able to lure and kill his prey by imitating it, he must have come to believe that he could turn himself into an animal and thus have power over other animals. In other words, likeness must have seemed to him the key to mysterious powers whereby he could control other creatures.

Art, the most effective instrument for creating likenesses, was utilized in the service of magic almost as soon as men discovered they could draw. Magic did not engender art, but it gave art its greatest scope and impetus. Magic was responsible for art's magnificent upsurge. The connection between art and magic has provided us with the wealth of evidence we have concerning hunting-magic practices in the upper paleolithic. And this, in turn, has led only too often to the view that the religion of the period was altogether dominated by magic.

It is quite true that magical beliefs were held by a great number of hunting tribes scattered over vast territories. These beliefs caused the hunter artists to adorn their weapons and tools with engraved or sculptured representations of their game animals. These beliefs also prompted the hunter artists to descend into the most hidden and often perilous recesses of their caves, there to cover the walls with pictures—engravings or paintings—chiefly of their game, or to fashion sculptured models of these animals. Gathered before these representations of beasts, they performed their mock fights and invocatory dances to the accompaniment, perhaps, of singing and the clang of crude musical instruments. No hunting expedition was embarked upon without prior magical preparation.

Magical concepts and practices must have influenced many other areas of daily living besides hunting. It would seem that the maturity and initiation rites of the tribe's youthful members were conducted in some of those decorated mountain caverns. The frequent occurrence of works of a sexual character leads us to believe that magic must have played a particularly important part in the sphere of procreation; these works of art were no mere product of eroticism, but rather the expression of a far more fundamental aspiration—human fertility. Often, too, by ritual performance of the act of copulation, or by its portrayal, or simply by the portrayal of the organs of generation, the hunters would seek to insure the increase of the game population, which their own hunting, predatory beasts, pestilence, and inclement weather had depleted.

The evidence of the art works notwithstanding, magic was not the sole determinant of ice-age man's outlook. True, a clear distinction must be made between the religion of the earlier cave-bear hunters and that of the upper paleolithic hunters; the latter, relying on their own powers, seem to have believed that by certain rites, by some occult projection of their wishes, they could achieve what their predecessors had sought (and some of their isolated contemporaries still did seek) to obtain by offering sacrifices to a divine dispenser of hunting fortune. Yet even in the very centers of ice-age art, some finds have been made that bear the unmistakable stamp of sacrificial practices. The pictures of the so-called magicians—for instance, the "great sorcerer" of the Trois-Frères cave—constitute the principal evidence for the existence of a belief in spirits *personifying* the magic power.

Most probably that belief was but another form of the ancient belief in a hunting god; and the tribal magicians most likely considered themselves only the representatives of the prime magician, the agents of his power. Scenes such as I described on p. 59 afford us an insight into the religious beliefs that must always have been in the background of the magic of the hunter artists. It is quite possible that most of the late ice-age hunters' ritual practices that are referred to as "magical" were in fact—like most of those of primitive hunting peoples of today—genuinely religious.

The religious practices of the upper paleolithic peoples were far from uniform. We might recall that the cult centered around small female figures, which is characteristic especially of the hunters of the Aurignacian; traces of this cult have been discovered from the Pyrenees to Siberia.

THE TYPE of hunting life characteristic of the upper paleolithic survived in the mesolithic only among the reindeer hunters of northern Europe. These hunters, like their predecessors thousands of years earlier, inaugurated their annual hunting season by submerging a young doe in a lake or pond, in sacrifice to their god. In their everyday needs they would have had recourse to the same deity, and again by means of sacrifice—this time by casting various personal possessions into the water as votive gifts. On special occasions, perhaps at seasonal tribal festivals, the hunters killed an older, stronger reindeer, ate its flesh, and then set up the skull, complete with its magnificent antlers, on a ritual pole on the bank of the pool of sacrifice. Some groups of reindeer hunters erected an image of their god in the middle of the pool, in the form of a pole rising high up out of the water, its upper part crudely fashioned as a human figure. Around this "idol" they placed other poles, with notches, and on these they would hang their votive gifts.

In the rest of Europe, after the extinction or migration

of the ice-age fauna, people were reduced to living as best they could by hunting or fishing; however, the game and fish were becoming increasingly scarce. Their religion, characteristically, centered around the spirits of the dead and their ancestors. They traced schematic designs representing their ancestors on rocks, as in southern Spain, or painted them on pebbles, as at the Mas d'Azil; they believed, apparently, that in this way they could enter into communication with their dead and obtain their protection and assistance in all the affairs of their daily lives. The same belief may have prompted the mesolithic hunters of southern Germany to resort to head-hunting; they must have thought that the possession of the skull would secure them the services of their victim's spirit.

In the next period, the neolithic, the ancient religion of the hunters survived only in the extreme north. There the hunters selected remote, deserted places, in the vicinity of rivers, lakes, or fjords, as sites for the worship of their deity, or of the spirit that ruled the beasts. They engraved or painted pictures of their game animals, especially the reindeer and the elk, on great granite surfaces polished by the action of the ice. These tremendous rock pictures, larger than life size, do not appear to have had any magical significance, but rather to have been a kind of picture language. The hunters used them to entreat the god who abode in the waters to give them good hunting, and they probably accompanied their prayers by offerings. In some cases the place of sacrifice was located in the middle of marshland to which access was very difficult. There the hunters gathered to dispose the game spirit in their favor by offering him food.

The evidence of certain rock pictures and small sculptured pieces of the period would indicate, however, that various magical practices existed concurrently with the belief in a hunting god or spirit. Weapons and tools decorated with animal heads are suggestive of instruments used in magic rites, and various perforated sculptures may even have served as part of the equipment of shamans.

The culture and religion of the prehistoric arctic hunters survived well into the era of recorded history; in part they still exist today in certain arctic territories of Europe and Asia.

II

THE RELIGION OF THE FARMING PEOPLES

We have little information about the beliefs of the earliest neolithic peasant communities. But many and varied traces exist, in different parts of Europe, of the religious life of farming man in the middle and late neolithic. These traces are largely signs, symbols, and stylized figures, all of them connected with a widespread cult of the sky and the sun. Earth, sky, sun, rain, and wind were of course the most important things for the tiller of the soil.

At some stage in the neolithic, representations of this kind began to be used as merely decorative *motifs* on pottery. In earlier times, however, their religious significance must have been generally understood. We may in any case infer that the symbolism characteristic of the prehistoric peasantry of Europe dates back to the beginnings of the neolithic, and therefore that those earliest farmers, like their successors, worshipped the sky, probably already personified in a sky god who was also the god of the sun and of thunder.

It is even more likely that the early neolithic farmers also practiced a cult of ancestors and of spirits of the dead. This cult had been widely observed in the mesolithic, and became even more popular toward the end of the neolithic. The continuity of the cult is evidenced by the schematized rock paintings of southern Spain.

The religious practices of the middle and late neolithic varied considerably with the different parts of Europe where they occurred.

In southeastern Europe, for instance, in what is known as the Danubian region, the religious views and practices of the farming population were strongly influenced by the East. Thus the Danubian cult of a fertility goddess was derived from the Middle Eastern cult of the earth goddess, or great-mother goddess. Every Danubian peasant hut must have had its little image of the goddess—for the most part, of the peasant's own crude workmanship—which the family would piously adorn, and before which it would place offerings of food. Alongside these little idols, there probably existed big statues in regional or tribal sanctuaries.

The Danubian farmers also venerated the goddess's male partner, whom they, like their Eastern contemporaries, conceived of in the form of a bull. This cult, however, was secondary to that of the great goddess; various phallic rites, religious orgies, and ritual nuptials were associated with it. Some of these rites have survived to this day in the rural customs of certain European countries.

The cult of the great goddess also spread to the Mediterranean area, where her effigies are to be found in the great stone temples of Malta and Gozo.

In western Europe the neolithic farmers developed new and splendid forms of the ancient cult of spirits of the dead and of ancestors, as evidenced by the great megalithic structures. The focus from which this cult spread to other regions was the Iberian peninsula, whence it was borne with all the impetus of a world religion far into northern Europe and southward to the Mediterranean. At the same time, there was a reflorescence of the Spanish rock art, with its schematic ancestor figures.

The tremendous efforts these people expended on their dead cannot be explained solely in terms of their concern with life beyond the grave; the explanation lies at least equally in their belief that the dead exercised some kind of power over the living and over the forces of nature.

The megalith builders erected magnificent stone structures for the dead which were far superior to the dwelling places occupied by the living. They were, above all, anxious to tie down the souls or spirits of the dead by means of symbols traced either on remote rock walls or on the graves themselves, and also by means of "soul seats" in the form of menhirs, steles, or idols. The picture rocks, like the dolmens, were sanctuaries to which the devotees came to entreat the help and protection of the dead with prayers and votive gifts. In Brittany and England the farming peoples erected even more splendid sanctuaries, especially the huge *alignements* of menhirs along whose avenues great masses of people could move in solemn proces-

Chronological Table

GEOLOGICAL TIME	GLACIAL CHRONOLOGY	CULTURE AGE	B.C.	ASSOCIATED HUMAN FORM	CULTURE TYPE
Recent or Holocene	Postglacial or Fourth Interglacial	Neolithic	3,000		Neolithic
		Mesolithic	5,000		Azilian-Tardenoisian
			10,000	Chancelade	Magdalenian
				Cro-Magnon	Solutrean Gravettian
			20,000		Aurignacian
PLEISTOCENE: Upper	Würm Glaciation	PALEOLITHIC: Upper			Chatelperronian Acheulean-Levalloisian-Mousterian
			50,000		BLENDED CULTURES
	Third Interglacial		100,000	Neanderthal Fontéchevade Ehringsdorf	Mousterian ACHEULEAN: Upper LEVALLOISIAN Tayacian
	Riss Glaciation	Middle	200,000		ACHEULEAN: Middle
Middle	Second		300,000	Steinheim Swanscombe Galley Hill	

Lower	Interglacial	I C Lower	400,000	Heidelberg	A N Abbevillian — Lower — A N Clactonian
	Mindel Glaciation				
	First Interglacial	Eolithic?	500,000		Cromerian Eolithic?

sion. On Malta and Gozo the cult of the dead developed into a cult of chthonian powers. The islanders built veritable temples to which they flocked; they offered various gifts and consulted oracles. The emergence of the cult of the great goddess gave their religion new impetus. The great goddess was also the protectress and goddess of the dead, and therefore in some way related to the chthonian powers; this was the form in which her cult eventually penetrated to western Europe.

In western and northern Europe, the farming peoples worshipped the god of the sky, sun, and thunder, alongside—and often in close connection with—their ancestors and the spirits of the dead. The symbol, or symbols, of this divinity—for a distinction was often made between the sky god and the god of the sun and of thunder—frequently occurs together with symbols of ancestors on the Iberian picture rocks and on a great many megalithic tombs. It is probable that the great menhir sites in Brittany, and the circular sites in England, such as Stonehenge, were dedicated not only to the cult of the dead but also to that of the sky and sun god.

The burden of the farmers' entreaties to the heavenly powers was the welfare of their crops, favorable weather, and a rich harvest. On the Iberian picture rocks, the sky or sun god is occasionally represented as a spirit of fertility or a harvest god, and the peasants probably gathered before the pictures or symbols of this deity to offer their prayers or their thanks.

In northern Europe the peasants expressed their thanksgiving for the harvest by burying used sickle blades or stone axes in their fields. Probably they already observed seasonal festivals with ritual dances and games.

The discussion of neolithic religion has taken me more than once across the frontiers of the outgoing stone age into the metal age. Where prehistory and history overlap, we more and more often find ritual forms closely resembling those of the earliest recorded times. To be sure, the divinities around which these cults center cannot yet be named. But the peoples who are later known as Celts or Germans or Illyrians already exist, and so apparently do their gods.

SELECTED BIBLIOGRAPHY

Almgren, O.: *Hällristningar och kultbruck.* Göteborg, 1927.

——: *Nordische Felszeichnungen als religiöse Urkunden.* Frankfurt am Main, 1934.

Atkinson, R. J. C.: *Stonehenge.* London, 1956.

Bächler, E.: *Das alpine Paläolithikum der Schweiz.* Basel, 1940.

Barandiarán, J. M. de: *Huellas de artes y religiones antiguas del Pireneo Vasco.* Vitoria, 1935.

Barocelli, P.: *"Le Manifestazioni Religiose nella Preistoria." Le Religioni del Mondo,* edited by N. Turchi, Rome, pp. 49–71.

Bégouen, H.: *"La Mentalité spiritualiste des premiers hommes."* Paris, 1945.

——: *"Les Bases magiques de l'art préhistorien." Scientia,* 1939, pp. 202–16.

——: *"Pierres gravées." Quartär,* 1954, pp. 136–8.

——: *"The Magic Origin of Prehistoric Art." Antiquity,* 1929, pp. 5–19.

Beninger, E.: *"Die Leichenzerstückelung als vor-und frühgeschichtliche Bestattungssitte." Anthropos,* 1931, pp. 769–81.

Blanc, A. C.: *"I Paleantropi di Saccopastore e del Circeo." Quartär,* 1942, pp. 1–37.

——: *Il Sacro Presso i Primitivi.* Rome, 1945.

Bouyssonie, A.: *"La Religion des temps préhistoriques." Manual d'histoire des religions,* edited by J. Huby, Paris, 1944, pp. 48–75.

Bouyssonie, J.: *"Les Sépultures moustériennes." Quaternaria,* 1954, pp. 107–16.

Breuil, H.: *Four Hundred Centuries of Cave Art.* Montignac, 1952.

——: *Les Peintures rupestres schématiques de la péninsule Ibérique.* Lagny, 1933–5.

——: *"Pratiques religieuses chez les humanités quaternaires." Scienza e Civilta,* 1951, pp. 45–75.

——: *Sociologie préhistorique: Les Origines de la société.* Paris, 1931.

Breuil, H., M. C. Burkitt, and M. Pollock: *Rock Paintings of Southern Andalusia.* Oxford, 1929.

Breuil, H., and R. Lantier: *Les Hommes de la pierre ancienne.* Second edition. Paris, 1959.
Breuil, H., and H. Obermaier: *The Cave of Altamira.* Madrid, 1935.
Brøgger, A. W.: *"Die arktischen Felsenzeichnungen und Malereien in Norwegen." Ipek,* 1931, pp. 11–24.
Brønsted, J.: *Danmarks Oldtid.* 2 vols. Copenhagen, 1939.
Bursch, F. C.: *De Westerse mens ontdekt zijn wereld.* Leiden, 1951.
Carvallo, J.: *"Caverne de 'las Monedas' au Monte-Castillo (Puente Viesgo)." Bulletin, Société Préhistorique de L'Ariège,* 1953, pp. 69–74.
Casteret, N.: *Dix Ans sous terre.* Paris, 1934.
Chalus, P.: *L'Homo religiosus: A La Recherche de la mentalité préhistorique.* Paris, 1953.
Childe, V. G.: *The Dawn of European Civilisation.* Sixth edition. London, 1957.
——: *The Prehistory of European Society.* London, 1958.
Clark, J. G. D.: *Excavations at Star Carr.* Cambridge, 1954.
——: *The Mesolithic Settlements of Northern Europe.* Cambridge, 1936.
Clemen, C.: *Urgeschichtliche Religion: Die Religion der Stein, Bronze, und Eisenzeit.* Bonn, 1932–3.
Closs, A.: *"Das Versenkopfer." Wiener Beiträge zur Kulturgeschichte und Linguistik,* 1952, pp. 68–70.
Cogni, G.: *Il Cannibalismo.* Turin, 1949.
Cook, A. B.: *"Les Galets peints du Mas d'Azil." L'Anthropologie,* 1903, pp. 655–60.
Crawford, O. G. S.: *The Eye Goddess.* London, 1957.
Daniel, G.: *The Megalithic Builders of Western Europe.* London, 1958.
Dumitrescu, V.: *L'Art préhistorique en Roumanie.* Bucharest, 1937.
Ebert, M.: *"Die Anfänge des europäischen Totenkultes." Prähistorische Zeitschrift,* 1921, pp. 1–19.
Ehrenberg, K.: *"Die paläontologische, prähistorische und paläoethnologische Bedeutung der Salzofenhöhle im Lichte der letzten Forschungen." Quartär,* 1954, pp. 19–58.
——: *"Dreissig Jahre paläobiologischer Forschung in österreichischen Höhlen." Quartär,* 1951, pp. 93–108.
Eliade, M.: *Images et symboles.* Paris, 1952.
Engelstad, E. S.: *Østnorske ristninger og malinger av den arktiske gruppe.* Oslo, 1934.

Franz, L.: *Religion und Kunst der Vorzeit.* Prague, 1937.

Gahs, A.: *"Kopf,- Schädel,- und Langknochenopfer bei Rentiervölkern." Festschrift P. W. Schmidt,* Vienna, 1928, pp. 231–68.

Gehlen, A.: *Urmensch und Spätkultur.* Bonn, 1956.

Gimbutas, M.: The Prehistory of Eastern Europe. American School of Prehistoric Research, Bulletin No. 20, 1956.

Gjessing, G.: *Arktis og nørskandinavisk i Nord-Norges yngre steinalder.* Viking, 1941.

——: *Nordenfjelske ristninger og malinger av arktiske gruppe.* Oslo, 1936.

Glory, A., and R. Robert: *"Le Culte des crânes humains aux époques préhistoriques." Bulletin of Social Anthropology of Paris,* 1948, pp. 114–33.

Golomshtok, E. A.: *The Old Stone Age in European Russia.* Philadelphia, 1938.

Hallowell, A. J.: "Bear Ceremonialism in the Northern Hemisphere." *American Anthropologist,* 1926, pp. 1–175.

Hallstrom, G.: *Monumental Art in Northern Europe.* Volume I. Stockholm, 1938.

——: *"Nordeuropäische Felskunst und Entwicklungsprobleme." Ipek,* 1936, pp. 50–61.

Hancar, F.: *"Zum Problem der Venusstatuetten im eurasischen Jungpaläolithikum." Prähistorische Zeitschrift,* 1939–40, pp. 85–156.

Hörmann, K.: *Die Petershöhle bei Velden in Mittelfranken: Eine altpaläolithische Station.* Nuremberg, 1933.

Hultén, E.: *"Magiska ornament i Mesoliticum?" Fornvännen,* 1939, pp. 193–225.

Huth, O.: *"Märchen und Megalithreligion." Paideuma,* 1950, pp. 12–22.

James, E. O.: *Prehistoric Religion.* London: New York, 1957.

Kern, F.: *Der Beginn der Weltgeschichte.* Bern, 1953.

——: *"Die Weltanschauung der eiszeitlichen Europäer." Archiv für Kulturgeschichte,* 1926, pp. 273–99.

Kirchner, H.: *Die Menhire in Mitteleuropa und der Menhirgedanke.* Mainz, 1955.

——: *"Ein archäologischer Beitrag zur Urgeschichte des Schamanismus." Anthropos,* 1952, pp. 244–86.

Klingender, F. D.: *"Palaeolithic Religion and the Principle of Social Evolution." The British Journal of Sociology,* 1954, pp. 138–53.

König, M.: *Das Weltbild des eiszeitlichen Menschen.* Marburg, 1954.

Koppers, W.: "*Der Bärenkult in ethnologischer und prähistorischer Beleuchtung.*" *Palaeobiologica,* 1933, pp. 47–64.

——: "*Künstlicher Zahnschliff am Bären im Altpaläolithikum und bei den Ainu auf Sachalin.*" *Quartär,* 1938, pp. 97–103.

——: *Primitive Man and His World Picture.* London: New York, 1952.

Kraft, G.: *Der Urmensch als Schöpfer.* Second edition. Tübingen, 1948.

Krenn, K.: *Schädelbecher. Sudeta,* 1929, pp. 73–122.

Kühn, H.: *Das Erwachen der Menschheit.* Frankfurt am Main: Hamburg, 1954.

——: *Das Problem des Urmonotheismus.* Wiesbaden, 1952.

——: *Die Felsbilder Europas.* Stuttgart, 1952.

——: *Kunst und Kultur der Vorzeit Europas: Das Paläolithikum.* Berlin, 1929.

Lehmann, F. R.: "*Die Religionsgeschichte des Paläolithikums und die Völkerkunde.*" *Archiv für Religionswissenschaft,* 1938, pp. 288–306.

Leisner, G. and V.: *Die Megalithgräber der Iberischen Halbinsel.* Berlin, 1956.

Lemozi, A.: *La Grotte-temple du Pech-Merle.* Paris, 1929.

Leroi-Gourhan, A.: "*La Caverne des Furtins.*" *Préhistoire,* 1950, pp. 17–142.

Luquet, G. H.: *The Art and Religion of Fossil Man.* Oxford, 1930.

Mainage, T.: *Les Religions de la préhistoire: L'Age paléolithique.* Paris, 1921.

Maringer, J.: "*Menschenopfer im Bestattungsbrauch Alteuropas.*" *Anthropos,* 1942–3, pp. 1–112.

Maringer, J., and H. G. Bandi: *Art in the Ice Age—Spanish Levant Art—Arctic Art.* London: New York, 1953.

Marquez, M. F.: *El Sentimiento Religioso en el Arte Prehistórico.* La Plata, 1930.

Martin, H.: *La Frise sculptée et l'atelier solutréen du roc (Charente).* Paris, 1928.

Menghin, O.: "*Der Nachweis des Opfers im Altpaläolithikum.*" *Wiener Prähistorische Zeitschrift,* 1926, pp. 14–19.

——: *Weltgeschichte der Steinzeit.* Vienna, 1940.

Meuli, K.: *"Griechische Opferbräuche." Festschrift P. von der Mühll,* Basel, 1945, pp. 185–288.

Mollison, T.: *"Zeichen gewaltsamer Verletzungen an den Offnet-Schädeln." Anthropologischer Anzeiger,* 1936, pp. 79–88.

Movius, H. L., Jr.: *"El Arte Mobiliar de Perigordiense Superior de La Colombière (Ain)." Ampurias,* 1952, pp. 1–36.

——: "The Mousterian Cave of Teshik-Tash, Southeastern Uzbekistan, Central Asia." American School of Prehistoric Research, Bulletin No. 17, 1953, pp. 11–71.

——: "The Rock-Shelter of La Colombière." American School of Prehistoric Research, Bulletin No. 19, 1956.

Narr, K. J.: *"Menschwerdung und älteste Kultur." La Nouvelle Clio,* 1953, pp. 341–55.

——: *"Nordasiatisch-europäische Urzeit in archäologischer und völkerkundlicher Sicht." Studium Generale,* 1954, pp. 193–201.

——: *"Streiflichter ins Geistesleben des jungpaläolithischen Europa."* La Nouvelle Clio, 1952, pp. 1–36.

Nordman, C. A.: *"Die steinzeitlichen Tierskulpturen Finnlands." Ipek,* 1936–7, pp. 36–49.

Nougier, L. R., and R. Robert: *The Cave of Rouffignac.* London, 1958.

Obermaier, H.: *Fossil Man in Spain.* New Haven, 1924.

——: *Urgeschichte der Menschheit.* Freiberg, 1931.

Octobon, M.: *"Statues-menhirs, stèles gravées, dalles sculptées." Revue Anthropologique,* 1931, pp. 299–579.

Péquart, M. and S. J.: *Hoëdic, deuxième station-nécropole du mésolithique cotier Armorican.* Antwerp, 1954.

Péquart, M. and S. J., M. Boule, and H. V. Vallois: *Téviec, station nécropole mèsolithique du Morbihan.* Paris, 1937.

Pericot, G. L.: *La Cueva del Parpallo (Gandia).* Madrid, 1942.

Pittioni, R.: *Vom geistigen Menschenbild der Urzeit.* Vienna, 1952.

Pohlhausen, H.: *"Zum Motiv der Rentierversenkung der Hamburger und Ahrensburger Stufe des niederdeutschen Flachlandmagdalénien." Anthropos,* 1953, pp. 987–90.

Porcar, J. B., H. Obermaier, and H. Breuil: *Las Pinturas rupestres de la cueva Remigia (Castellón).* Madrid, 1936.

Randonikas, W. I.: *Les Gravures rupestres des bords du lac Onega et de la mer Blanche.* Paris: Moscow, 1936–8.

Richthofen, B. von: *"Zur religionsgeschichtlichen Auswertung vorgeschichtlicher Altertümer." Mitteilungen Anthropologische Gesellschaft in Vienna,* 1932, pp. 110–44.

Ripoll Perello, E.: "*Las Representationes Antropomorfas en el Arte Paleolitico Español." Ampurias,* 1957–8, pp. 167–92.

Roder, J.: *Pfahl und Menhir.* Neuwied, 1949.

Rust, A.: *Das altsteinzeitliche Rentierjägerlager Meiendorf.* Neumünster, 1937.

——: *Die alt-und mittelsteinzeitlichen Funde von Stellmoor.* Neumünster, 1943.

Saccasyn-Della Santa, E.: *Les Figures humaines du paléolithique supérieur Eurasiatique.* Antwerp, 1947.

Santasin, F.: *Magiska skifferredskap från Norrlands stenålder.* Stockholm, 1941.

Schmidt, R. R.: *Vom Geist der Vorzeit.* Berlin, 1934.

Schmidt, W.: "*Das Primitialopfer in der Urkultur." Festschrift E. Bächler,"* St. Gallen, 1948, pp. 81–92.

——: "*Die älteste Opferstelle des altpaläolithischen Menschen in den Schweizer Alpen." Acta della Pontificia Academia Scientiarum,* 1942, pp. 269–72.

——: *Völkerkunde und Urgeschichte in gemeinsamer Arbeit an der Aufhellung ältester Menschheitsgeschichte.* Bern, 1942.

Shetelig, H., and H. Falk: *Scandinavian Archaeology.* Oxford, 1937.

Talve, I.: "*Votivfisk och fiskellycka: Ett bidrag till nordeuropeisk Votivforskning." Svio-Estonica* (Lund), 1951, pp. 3–49.

Trauwitz-Hellwig, J. von: *Urmensch und Totenglaube.* München, 1929.

Trombe, F.: "*Une Scène de chasse inédite de la grotte de Ganties, Montespan* (*Haute-Garonne*)." *La Nature,* 1927, pp. 306–7.

Trombe, F., and G. Dubuc: *Le Centre préhistorique de Ganties-Montespan.* Paris, 1947.

Wernert, P.: "*Culte des crânes: Représentation des esprits des défunts et des ancêtres." L'Histoire générale des religions,* edited by M. Gorce and R. Mortier, Paris, 1948, pp. 51–102.

——: "*L'Anthropophagie rituelle et la chasse aux têtes aux époques actuelle et paléolithique." L'Anthropologie,* 1936, pp. 33–43.

——: "*Les Religions de la préhistoire: Histoire des religions,"* edited by H. Brilland and A. Aigrain, Paris, 1953, pp. 137–62.

Windels, F.: *The Lascaux Cave Paintings.* London, 1949.

Wölfel, J. D.: "*Die Religionen des vorindogermanischen Europa:*

Christus und die Religionen der Erde," edited by F. König, Vienna, 1952, I, pp. 161–537.
Zammit, T.: *Prehistoric Malta.* Oxford, 1930.
——: *The Hal Saflieni Prehistoric Hypogeum.* Malta, 1927.
——: *The Neolithic Temples at Hajar Kin and Mnaidra.* Valetta, 1927.
Zotz, L. F.: *"Altsteinzeitlicher Bärenkult in den Sudeten." Altschlesische Blätter,* 1937, pp. 4–7.
——: *Die Altsteinzeit in Niederschlesien.* Leipzig, 1939.

INDEX

A NOTE ABOUT THE AUTHOR

BORN in Cologne in 1902, Johannes Maringer studied philosophy, theology, geology, anthropology, and prehistoric archaeology at the universities of Münster, Breslau, Vienna, Fribourg, and Paris, and received his Ph.D. at the University of Fribourg, Switzerland. From 1942 to 1952 he was a member of the editorial staff of the journal Anthropos, *Fribourg. From 1952 to 1959 he worked as the director of the Archaeological Institute, Ichikawa, Japan, at the same time holding the chair for Prehistoric Archaeology at the Nanzan University, Nagoya. Dr. Maringer is a Catholic priest and a member of the Society of the Divine Word (S.V.D.) which is well-known for its anthropological studies. He has done field work in western and northern Europe, and was engaged in the study and final publication of the prehistoric collections of the Sven Hedin expedition to Mongolia (1927–35). He has traveled extensively in southeastern Asia, Japan, Hawaii, Mexico; has directed a number of archaeological excavations in central and northern Japan; and has participated in research in southeastern Asia and Hawaii. A regular contributor to learned magazines, he also has published several books on prehistoric archaeology, among them* ART AND THE ICE AGE, *published in this country in 1953.*

A NOTE ON THE TYPE

THE Text of this book is set in Caledonia, a Linotype face designed by W. A. Dwiggins (1880–1956), who was responsible for so much that is good in contemporary book design. Caledonia belongs to the family of printing types called "modern face" by printers—a term used to mark the change in style of typeletters that occurred at the end of the eighteenth century. It is best evidenced in the letter shapes designed by Baskerville, Martin, Bodoni, and the Didots.

This book was composed, printed, and bound by Kingsport Press, Inc., Kingsport, Tennessee. Typography and binding based on designs by W. A. Dwiggins.